"After-sales excellence, precision and pricing are crucial to sustaining brand prestige and profitability. This book offers a strategic approach to after-sales pricing, ensuring that brands can maximize value while maintaining the excellence their customers expect."

Stephan Winkelmann, *President and CEO,*
Automobili Lamborghini

"A game-changer for the industry. Danilo Zatta distills complex parts pricing strategies into clear, actionable insights. This book is essential for anyone serious about unlocking hidden profits in aftersales."

Markus Schrick, *Managing Director at*
XPeng Motors Germany

"Especially in the premium segments, individualization plays a key role. Consequently the pricing should be well differentiated in line with the value for the client. Applying this to the whole customer journey for products and services means that a comprehensive pricing strategy has to include the after sales business accordingly.

Thankfully Danilo Zatta offers in his new book valuable guidance for exactly this topic."

Henning Jens, *Executive Director & Chief Financial*
Officer at Ducati Motor Holding

"This book delivers great insights and inspiration for unlocking your untapped potential in the world of Aftersales and Spare Parts Pricing. It clearly shows how a well-defined pricing strategy and smart price differentiation can drive customer loyalty, boost competitiveness, and fuel profitable sales growth. A big thank you to Danilo for this long-overdue and incredibly valuable contribution to the field!"

Andrea Seyfang, *Head of Global Pricing MT, Trumpf*

"This is a book needed to be written! Aftermarket pricing requires a very specific approach and this book is a solid roadmap towards your spare parts pricing excellence. Warmly recommended."

Pol Vanaerde, *Chair EPP European Pricing Platform*

"Aftermarket sales and parts pricing are often the best way for manufacturers to improve their monetization and profitability. Danilo Zatta is a world-renowned expert in 'price setting' and 'price getting.' This book will give you and your company a great plan with instructions on how to achieve higher margins."

Kevin Mitchell, *President – Professional Pricing Society*

"This book is a must read: *Smart Parts Pricing* extends Danilo's series of mandatory readings for business leaders and pricing professionals. Danilo, whom I have the honor to know personally as a pricing thought leader and pricing enthusiast, has created another piece of inspiration, which is – by the way – also entertaining to read."

Johannes Lehr, *Director Marketing Services, Fendt,*
part of AGCO Corporation

"Spare parts pricing is often overlooked in terms of pricing focus as it's considered a given that this is a better than average contributor to profitability; and in many companies this leads to money being left on the table. This book offers an excellent approach to both price setting and price getting for aftermarket and spare part pricing, and is highly recommended."

Karl Holm, *Director & Head of Pricing at*
ASSA ABLOY Global Solutions

"This book will help to take a significant step forward in aligning parts pricing with customer value and market dynamics, making your spare parts pricing more strategic and consistent."

Gabor Kapus, *Vice President Pricing and*
Quotation Transformation Deployment, Schneider Electric

"*Smart Parts Pricing* is a must-read for executives who understand that aftersales is no longer just support – it's a strategic profit engine. Danilo Zatta provides a clear and actionable framework for transforming spare parts pricing into a robust revenue stream.

Zatta speaks the language of senior management: the book bridges pricing theory with practical execution, showing how to modernize pricing strategies, implement smart tools, and lead cultural change. It offers concrete use cases.

For general managers, pricing leaders, and operational heads tasked with driving EBIT improvements in parts-heavy businesses, *Smart Parts Pricing* is not just insightful – it's a strategic playbook for sustainable profit growth."

JJ Heldt, *Sales Director, Bosch Rexroth*

"Danilo doesn't just explain spare parts pricing; he redefines it as a strategic advantage. He delivers a holistic methodology, blending rigorous analytics with customer-centric narrative, to transform aftermarket margins. As Manager Pricing at MS Motorservice International, I can attest that these insights will empower any team to build a strategy with sustainable processes and workflows, that will lead to a predictable, high-growth revenue stream."

Frank Runde, *Pricing Manger,*
MS Motorservice International – Rheinmetall Group

"*Smart Parts Pricing* by Danilo Zatta is an essential, pragmatic guide that distills complex aftersales pricing strategies into actionable insights, empowering companies to unlock hidden profits, boost competitiveness, and achieve spare parts pricing excellence."

Johanna Sandbichler, *Senior Service Pricing Manager and Operational Pricing Team Lead, INNIO Jenbacher Gas Engines*

"Spare parts pricing is not just about aftersales—it shapes the entire customer journey, influencing future equipment sales and long-term brand loyalty. This book brings light on a critical yet often overlooked topic, providing a strategic framework to turn spare parts into a powerful business advantage."

Alexandr Mitin, *Spare Parts Revenue Management Team Manager, Sidel*

"As a specialist in pricing strategy myself, I can confidently say that the insights and frameworks presented in this book are not only spot-on but also perfectly aligned with the best practices in our industry. Danilo's expertise shines through as he navigates the complexities of pricing in the automotive sector, offering practical solutions and strategies that are both innovative and actionable. This book is an invaluable resource for professionals looking to enhance their understanding of pricing dynamics and drive profitability in the automotive parts market. Highly recommended!"

Jean de Oliveira Salim, *Pricing Manager Marketing & Aftersales, Nissan Motor Corporation*

"Danilo Zatta's *Smart Parts Pricing* is a masterclass in unlocking hidden value in the aftermarket. With clear insights and real-world strategies, this book gives after-sales leaders exactly what they need to transform pricing into a true competitive advantage. A must-read for anyone serious about driving profitability through pricing."

Claire Rychlewski, *Chief Revenue Officer, Syncron*

Smart Parts Pricing

After-sales pricing has become a key priority of every company that manages parts operations. Written in a simple and readable way, *Smart Parts Pricing* is a concrete guide to support the transition to a modern and robust pricing strategy for parts and after-sales pricing.

In *Smart Parts Pricing*, pricing expert Danilo Zatta explains how to boost profitability and build a competitive advantage, transforming the way companies set and manage after-sales prices. It uncovers all the key aspects of monetization: price strategy, price setting, price implementation, price steering, and price enablers. It also includes parts pricing quick wins that can be actioned immediately. Concrete use cases from a diverse range of industries are presented, as well as how to gain insights about competitors' prices and how to successfully use parts pricing software.

This practical manual provides a clear guide to everyday decisions on parts pricing and is particularly relevant for companies with after-sales business units, consultants offering part pricing services, and market research companies offering parts benchmarks.

Danilo Zatta is one of the world's leading advisors and thought leaders in the field of pricing and topline excellence. As a management consultant for more than 20 years, he advises and coaches many of the world's best-known organizations. The *Financial Times* defined him as "one of the world's leading pricing minds."

Smart Parts Pricing

How to Price in After-Sales to Maximize Profitability

Danilo Zatta

Routledge
Taylor & Francis Group

LONDON AND NEW YORK

Designed cover image: Getty Images

First published 2026
by Routledge
4 Park Square, Milton Park, Abingdon, Oxon OX14 4RN

and by Routledge
605 Third Avenue, New York, NY 10158

Routledge is an imprint of the Taylor & Francis Group, an informa business

For Product Safety Concerns and Information please contact our EU representative
GPSR@taylorandfrancis.com. Taylor & Francis Verlag GmbH, Kaufingerstraße 24,
80331 München, Germany.

British Library Cataloguing-in-Publication Data
A catalogue record for this book is available from the British Library

ISBN: 978-1-041-08891-2 (hbk)
ISBN: 978-1-041-07790-9 (pbk)
ISBN: 978-1-003-64741-6 (ebk)

DOI: 10.4324/9781003647416

Typeset in Minion
by Newgen Publishing UK

To my family and friends,

your constant support, love, and encouragement have been the cornerstone of my journey in writing this book. Your belief in me, through every late night and weekends, has lifted me higher than I could have ever imagined. Thank you for your patience, understanding, and for always being my greatest cheerleaders. This book is as much yours as it is mine.

With deepest gratitude,

Dan

Contents

About the Author   xiii
Preface   xv
Acknowledgments   xvii
Prologue   xxi

Part I   After-Sales Profit Relevance   1
1   Spare Parts Pricing: The Hidden Profit Source   3
2   Four Pillars of Parts Price Setting   13
3   Transforming Spare Parts Pricing: From Foundation to Foresight   20
4   The Seven Sins of Spare Parts Pricing   25

Part II   Ten Quick Wins in Spare Parts Pricing   29
5   Hierarchical Pricing   31
6   Rounding Routines   37
7   Outlier Elimination   44
8   Low-Margin Optimization   49
9   Tail Pricing   54
10 Lifecycle Pricing   59
11 Market Intelligence   64
12 Minimum-Order Threshold   69
13 Price Quantity Breaks   73
14 Capacity Planning and Optimization   77

Part III   Learning from Parts Pricing Transformations   81
15 Philips Healthcare: Customer-Centric Parts Pricing   83
16 Terex: Parts Pricing Excellence with RGM, Data, and Technology   96
17 Ariston Group: Automation in Parts Pricing   105

18 Tenneco: Adapting Value Communication to Evolving Parts
    Purchase Decision-Makers   116

19 OPTIMA: Market Intelligence for Proactive Parts Distribution 121

20 Nokia Hardware Services: Shift to a Value-Centric Commercial
    Strategy   127

21 Mercedes-Benz: Advancing Parts Pricing Maturity via a Unified
    EU Spares Strategy   133

22 Maserati: From Cost Plus to Value Pricing   140

PART IV   How to Win in Parts Pricing   149

23 Getting Started   151

24 From Excel to State-of-the-Art Pricing Software   158

25 From Intransparency to Market Visibility   163

26 The Future of Spare Parts Pricing   169

About the Author

Danilo Zatta is one of the world's leading advisors and thought leader in the field of pricing and topline excellence, with significant experience in spare parts pricing.

As a management consultant for more than 20 years, he advises and coaches many of the world's best-known organizations.

The *Financial Times* defined him as "one of the world's leading pricing minds."

Dan was defined as one of the "TOP 50 globally leading Marketing & Sales Thought Leaders."

He has also been recognized amongst the *Top 5 Pricing Thought Leaders* on LinkedIn, in the list of the most engaging and impactful pricing thought leaders globally. The leading Italian business newspaper defined him as "as one of the most recognized monetization authors in the world."

He has led hundreds of projects in parts pricing for players in automotive, consumer electronics, industrial equipment and machinery, aerospace and defence, healthcare and medical devices, home appliances, telecommunication, energy and utilities, marine and shipping, agriculture, and many more.

Dan has also written 20 books including the international best seller *The Pricing Model Revolution* (2022), translated into 10 languages, *The 10 Rules of Highly Effective Pricing* (2023), translated into 3 languages, *At the Heart of Leadership* (Routledge, 2023), *Pricing Decoded* (Routledge, 2024) and *Revenue Management in Manufacturing* (2016). He has published hundreds of articles in different languages and regularly acts as keynote speaker at conferences, events, associations, and at leading universities. He also supports as personal topline coach several CEOs of leading companies.

Dan graduated with honours in economics and commerce from Luiss in Rome and University College Dublin in Ireland. He got an MBA from INSEAD in Fontainebleau, France, and Singapore. Finally, he completed a PhD in revenue management and pricing at the Technical University of Munich in Germany.

Connect with Dan on LinkedIn at www. linkedin.com/in/danilo-zatta

If you would like to talk to Dan about any advisory work or speaking engagements, please contact him via email at: zatta.danilo@gmail.com

Preface

"The true mystery of the world is the visible, not the invisible."

—Oscar Wilde

There is a quiet poetry in spare parts.

They do not boast. They do not dazzle in shop windows. You will not find them gracing the covers of glossy magazines. And yet—when the engine halts, the conveyor belt stalls, the aircraft waits grounded under a slate-grey sky—it is these silent sentinels that hold the key to motion, to continuity, to life.

To speak of spare parts pricing, then, is to enter the realm not only of numbers and margins, but of meaning. It is to engage in an act of interpretation, much like a philologist deciphering ancient runes. Each part bears its own story: of value created, perceived, contested. Each price, a palimpsest of history, strategy, and belief.

There is a moment in *The Name of the Rose*, Umberto Eco's great ode to semiotics and power, where the protagonist says: "Books are not made to be believed, but to be subjected to inquiry." So it is with prices. They are not commandments. They are hypotheses. And the parts we price? They are not merely goods. They are fragments of a promise.

For too long, the world of spare parts has lived in the shadow of the new.

We exalt the latest product launch, the gleaming innovation. But behind every product is a lifecycle, and behind every lifecycle, a legacy of care, repair, and reliability. The parts business is the silent custodian of this legacy—a lighthouse in the fog of obsolescence.

In the quiet murmur of a warehouse aisle, in the dim light of a workshop at dawn, value is not invented—it is revealed. Like a cartographer tracing the forgotten rivers of an old map, those who work with parts pricing uncover the contours of meaning where others see only maintenance.

Consider the paradox: that which is most enduring is often what is least seen.

To price a part well is not to impose a value, but to unveil it—like the conservators of Renaissance frescoes, peeling back centuries of grime to reveal a hidden masterpiece beneath. Michelangelo's ceiling was always there. It only needed light.

And light, in this context, is attention. Not the spotlight of spectacle, but the steady beam of care, of inquiry, of intention. Pricing is not just commerce. It is cartography. It is curation. It is craft.

This book, *Smart Parts Pricing*, is an invitation to illuminate.

You will find in these pages not a system, but a sensibility.

Not a formula, but a framework.

Its insights are drawn from the field—not the sterile lab of theory, but the muddy trenches where supply chains break and customers wait. It is written for those who see pricing not as a department, but as a discipline.

A way of thinking.

A way of being.

We are heirs to a long lineage of builders, traders, inventors—those who understood that every cog carries consequence. That the smallest decision, made with precision, can shift the direction of a company, even a century.

As Heraclitus reminded us, "You cannot step into the same river twice." Every pricing decision is context-specific, time-bound, a moment suspended between yesterday's logic and tomorrow's necessity. Our task is not to fix it once and for all. Our task is to stay awake—to adapt, to align, to evolve.

This is not a book only for pricing professionals. It is for leaders, strategists, thinkers. For those who understand that the future of business is not just about what we sell, but about how we value—and how we make others see that value.

Because in the end, pricing is not a consequence. It is a choice. And like all meaningful choices, it carries with it a worldview.

The journey begins, as always, with the smallest detail.

A washer. A seal. A spring.

And from there, a world.

Please let me know how you liked this book and feel free to reach out to me to share your thoughts. I also would love to hear your opinion on the parts pricing quick wins as well as your own experiences. You can reach out via the email below or connect with me and approach me on LinkedIn.

Keep in touch,

Dan

Rome/Munich, October

2025

zatta.danilo@gmail.com

www.linkedin.com/in/danilo-zatta

Acknowledgments

The journey of writing *Smart Parts Pricing* has been both enlightening and rewarding. Along the way, I have been fortunate to receive generous support, valuable insights, and encouragement from many individuals and organizations. I would like to take this opportunity to express my heartfelt gratitude to everyone who contributed to this project.

CLIENTS AND FRIENDS

I am deeply grateful to my clients and friends, whose trust and collaboration have been instrumental in shaping the content of this book. Your openness in sharing your experiences and challenges has provided rich, real-world context and deepened my understanding of the complexities of parts pricing. Thank you for being true partners in this endeavour.

- Armando Bigliocchi, Worldwide After Sales Marketing Manager a.d., Maserati

- Lorenzo Caravati, Business Development and Product Management Parts, Ariston Group

- Andrea Capello, Group Head of Parts Business Unit, Ariston Group

- Daniel Cho, Head of the Strategic Pricing Centre of Excellence, Philips Healthcare

- Viktoria Der, Director of Customer Service Strategic Pricing and PM Excellence, Philips Healthcare

- Ada Harka, Director, Head of Spares Europe, APAC & MEA, Electrolux Group

- Rafal Janaczek, EMEA Strategic Pricing Leader, Tenneco

- Jonas Kiene, Team Leader Service Parts Management, OPTIMA Packaging Group

- George Mauro, Aftersales Director a.d., Maserati

- Bronagh McConnell, Price Analyst, Terex

- Kai Ostendorf, Director, Parts, Sales & Pricing, Terex

- Paolo Pascarella, After Sales Business Development Manager, Mercedes-Benz

- Marco Piovano, Vice President, Parts & Solutions, Terex

- Saeed Qadri, Head of Portfolio Commercial Management, Nokia

- Chandra P. Singh, Commercial and Product Manager, Nokia
- Marco Zaccarelli, Marketing Expert a.d., Maserati

COOPERATION PARTNERS

To my cooperation partners: your encouragement, critical feedback, and professional generosity have played a pivotal role in this process. Thank you for helping identify relevant case studies, challenging assumptions, and supporting me as I explored the nuances of pricing strategies. Your insights have been truly invaluable.

A special thanks goes to the following companies, who supported this project through the contributions of many dedicated colleagues, listed here in alphabetical order:

SYNCRON

- Claudine Bianchi
- Gemma Brown
- Mathilde Hagander
- Rob Jospeh
- Kimberly Long
- Lisa Mercer
- Michelle Newton
- Geoffrey Reinaers
- Sarah Schöllgen
- Qasim Shabir
- Eliza-Marie Spatz
- Stephanie Swart
- Marco Warrens
- Claire Rychlewski

The Syncron team, representing one of the world's leading parts pricing solution vendor, shared insights, solutions and helped liaising me with several of their parts pricing clients across geographies and industries, enriching the contents of the book also with case studies.

EUCON

- Marc Bauer
- Dr. Philipp Borgstedt
- Osvaldo Celani
- Katrin Dagott
- Philip Harborth
- Matthias Matula
- Daria Nagel
- Patrick Schulte-Loh
- Dr. Alexander Timmer
- Jens Völker
- Kai Zippmann

The Eucon team, representing the world's leading automotive parts pricing data vendor, shared insights and solutions, enhancing the depth and quality of the book's content.

MARKT-PILOT

- Stephen Fauth
- Krystell Fuguet
- Alena Heinle
- Amin Oumhamdi
- Tobias Rieker
- Martin Ruth

The MARKT-PILOT team, representing the world's leading industrial parts pricing data vendor, shared insights and solutions, contributing valuable insights that shaped the book's substance. Also with case studies.

ENDORSERS

Throughout the development of this book, numerous C-level executives, presidents, managing directors, vice presidents, directors, and managers reviewed early manuscript versions. Your generous feedback, thoughtful suggestions, and candid discussions have been essential in shaping the final work.

A special thank you to those who also endorsed the book and whose quotes are featured in the *Praise for Smart Parts Pricing* section.

I'm deeply grateful to the incredible team at Routledge, and especially to my Publisher, Rebecca Marsh, and my Editor, Grace Collier. Bringing this book to life after *Pricing Decoded* and *The Heart of Leadership* feels truly special and beyond rewarding.

Above all, I want to thank my family and close friends—your endless love, encouragement, and support have carried me through every step of this journey. I couldn't have done this without you.

This book is a reflection of a collective journey—one built on collaboration, curiosity, and shared commitment to improving the way we approach parts pricing. I hope *Smart Parts Pricing* proves to be a valuable resource, and I look forward to continuing this journey together in the future.

With sincere appreciation,

Dan

Prologue

THE STRATEGIC EVOLUTION OF APPLIANCE SPARES PRICING IN ERA OF CONNECTED ECOSYSTEM AND RIGHT TO REPAIR

In today's landscape, where interconnected homes weave digital threads into our consumer' daily lives, the significance of appliance spare parts extends far beyond their physical form. They are now crucial nodes in delivering a seamless experience, embodying our commitment within an environment increasingly shaped by the Right to Repair. For Electrolux Group, navigating the value proposition in this interconnected ecosystem demands a strategic evolution, fuelled by intelligent and transparent pricing, rather than mere incremental adjustments.

Our strategic journey commences with a comprehensive system check, an evaluation of our current position within a market where appliances are no longer seen as isolated units but as integral components of a dynamic connected home, necessitating a renewed perspective on maintenance and repair. A primary challenge we face is the persistent pressure of price erosion, amplified by the inherent transparency of connected platforms where price comparisons are readily available. Homeowners expect not only fair prices but also the autonomy to maintain their increasingly sophisticated connected appliances through seamless access to the necessary parts and information.

The natural lifecycle of our installed base of connected appliances necessitates a strategic recalibration of our spares pricing. Anticipating the evolving failure modes of these intelligent appliances, which may increasingly involve intricate electronic components and sensors, our pricing strategies are proactively adapting to ensure not just availability but equitable access for both individual consumers and the expanding network of independent repairers.

Electrolux Group views evolving regulations around eco-design, data privacy, and material sourcing not as limitations but as guiding principles. Our holistic approach ensures the longevity and repairability of connected appliances while robustly safeguarding user data and promoting sustainable practices. This includes transparent access to fairly priced spare parts and diagnostic intelligence, fostering a climate of trust in this technologically advanced context.

Our commitment to operational excellence necessitates a sophisticated and agile infrastructure capable of seamlessly managing both physical spare parts and vital digital resources such as software updates and advanced diagnostic tools. Efficient and streamlined spare parts logistics, coupled with readily available digital repair resources, are not just desirable—they are essential for ensuring timely and cost-effective access to solutions for both individual consumers and repair professionals navigating the complexities of connected devices.

Elevating our direct-to-consumer (D2C) pricing within the connected ecosystem demands a customer-centric strategy integrating spare part information with sophisticated appliance diagnostics and support. Our online platforms evolve into dynamic hubs offering competitive pricing, intuitive troubleshooting guides, error code explanations, and remote diagnostic tools, empowering homeowners and technicians with transparent product information, technical documentation, repair manuals, and software compatibility details, justifying the value of genuine spares.

The pricing paradigm for spares is now intertwined with appliance interconnectedness and the Right to Repair, impacting market dynamics, regulations, internal capabilities, and empowered consumer expectations. A traditional "cost-plus" approach is insufficient. We are implementing a sophisticated methodology prioritizing transparency, fair pricing, and seamless integration of spares within the connected ecosystem.

Our response to price erosion involves a deeper focus on value-driven design and lifecycle costing, embedding repairability and long-term affordability into our connected appliances. We are refining our pricing structure for fairness across channels, exploring bundled service and spare part packages, and developing programmes to empower independent repair professionals specializing in connected devices—a commitment to the Right to Repair.

The strategic and insightful utilization of appliance usage data, connectivity diagnostics, and comprehensive customer data is the cornerstone of our success in navigating this intricate landscape. This data-driven approach propels us beyond reactive pricing adjustments, enabling a proactive and strategic framework that champions both the longevity of our appliances and seamless, equitable access to necessary components and critical information in an increasingly connected world.

In conclusion, the convergence of connected appliances and the Right to Repair presents not just intricate challenges but profound opportunities for Electrolux Group to lead with innovation. By embracing the principles of transparency, ensuring fair pricing, actively facilitating access to both physical spares and essential digital repair resources, and thoughtfully designing our connected appliances with repairability as a core tenet, we can not only exceed the evolving expectations of our tech-savvy homeowners and the vital independent repair sector but also significantly strengthen our brand reputation as a leader in both innovation and genuine consumer empowerment.

Ada Harka

Director, Head of Spares Europe, APAC & MEA

Electrolux Group

Part I

After-Sales Profit Relevance

"It is not down on any map; true places never are."
—Herman Melville, *Moby-Dick*

There is a moment, subtle and often overlooked, that happens right after the sale is closed. The deal is signed, the handshake exchanged, the product delivered. Most eyes move forward—chasing the next opportunity, the next number.

Yet something vital happens *after* this moment: the customer remains. The machine or vehicle begins its lifecycle. And quietly, profit begins to accumulate in the spaces no one is watching.

After-sales is the forgotten Ithaca in the Homeric map of modern business—a destination constantly longed for, yet misunderstood, delayed, or neglected. But like Odysseus' journey, it holds the deepest truths. It is in the post-sale terrain that reputations are cemented, margins are hidden in plain sight, and real loyalty is won or lost.

Profit in after-sales is not just financial—it is philosophical. It is about durability over disruption, about care beyond conquest. In a world obsessed with beginnings, we must rediscover the wisdom of endurance. This is where the *second story* begins—the one where companies do not merely *sell*, but *stay*.

Let us now pass through this quiet doorway—not with trumpets, but with curiosity—into a world where small parts yield great returns, and the back end becomes the true front line of strategic value.

We often think of pricing as numbers, columns, algorithms. Cold and rational.

But beneath the surface, pricing—especially in the realm of spare parts—is pure narrative. It is the story of how value is assigned, perceived, traded, and transformed. It is, as Italo Calvino might suggest, one of those "invisible cities" that builds itself quietly behind the scenes, shaping the visible world.

Like the builders of Gothic cathedrals who carved stone angels into the dark corners where no eye could see, those who work in parts pricing craft hidden value into the complex machinery of modern commerce.

DOI: 10.4324/9781003647416-1

To enter the world of parts pricing is not unlike embarking on a mythical journey. The hero's path—as told from Homer to Tolkien—always begins with the overlooked, the underestimated: a hobbit, a squire, a stowaway. In our case? A gasket. A filter. A bolt.

Yet from the smallest part can emerge the largest transformation.

Think of the butterfly effect: a single forgotten washer halting an entire assembly line. A misplaced decimal point on a part's price eroding trust, profits, and customer loyalty in a heartbeat. The detail *is* the whole.

As in the Tao Te Ching—"To know the great, start with the small."

In this first part, we will restore dignity and strategy to the humble world of spare parts pricing. This is not a manual of tricks, but a book of principles. A call to rethink parts not as expendable commodities, but as bearers of function, reliability, and brand promise. And as a relevant source of profitability.

Spare Parts Pricing
The Hidden Profit Source

Buried beneath bolts and serial numbers, somewhere between catalogues and warehouses, lies a treasure most companies overlook.

It's not a new market.

Not a breakthrough product.

It's already in the building.

Spare parts—those modest, replaceable pieces—carry more profit than the flagship machines they support. Yet, like all hidden treasures, they're often buried under layers of operational inertia.

THE PROFIT POWER OF AFTER-SALES

In many companies with an after-sales business unit, one surprising pattern consistently emerges: around 15% of total revenue comes from after-sales—but up to 50% of total profits originate there (see Figure 1.1). If not more.

Why? Because margins on spare parts are typically two to ten times higher than on new machines, vehicles, or equipment.

Spare parts pricing, however, presents a paradox. While it often delivers the most profitable revenue stream in the business, pricing strategies in this area are among the least developed. Even in companies where the profit contribution from after-sales is clear and decisive, leadership attention remains fixed on the main business—selling new machines, not managing the flow of parts that sustain them.

That's why spare parts pricing remains the hidden profit source—still undiscovered by many, and under-leveraged by most.

It can be referred to as the untapped gem in your business model: once discovered and well managed, it will boost profitability. Indeed, companies that dedicate the right amount of attention to smart spare parts pricing are the ones that enjoy above average profits.

Optimizing parts pricing can generate a 2%–10% increase in Return on Sales (RoS), depending on the company's pricing maturity—based on results from hundreds of after-sales transformation projects across industries. The best part? These

DOI: 10.4324/9781003647416-2

improvements are often driven by "quick wins" that deliver short-term payback, even before long-term changes are completed.

In most after-sales businesses, pricing also touches related services and digital products—such as remote diagnostics or connected equipment platforms. While this book focuses on spare parts, we will use the term "after-sales" to refer to the broader scope, including service and digital elements.

Spare parts pricing is a key topic across industries—from automotive and aerospace to construction, agriculture, industrial equipment, and healthcare. It drives profitability across geographies, channels, and customer types (see Figure 1.2).

WHY THE PRICING OPPORTUNITY IS MISSED

If parts pricing is so profitable, why isn't it prioritized?

The answer lies in complexity. The oversight affecting parts pricing is partly due to the high complexity inherent in managing a diverse and extensive spare parts inventory. Original equipment manufacturers (OEMs) frequently underestimate the pricing potential of this segment, even if the profit potential is substantial.

THE SIX PRICING CHALLENGES

Optimizing spare parts pricing is not a matter of tools alone—it's a strategic challenge shaped by complexity, invisibility, and inertia. Companies face six main hurdles on the road from pricing disorder to pricing power (see Figure 1.3). Each one deserves to be tackled with clarity and commitment.

Figure 1.1

After-sales pricing is more profitable than the core business

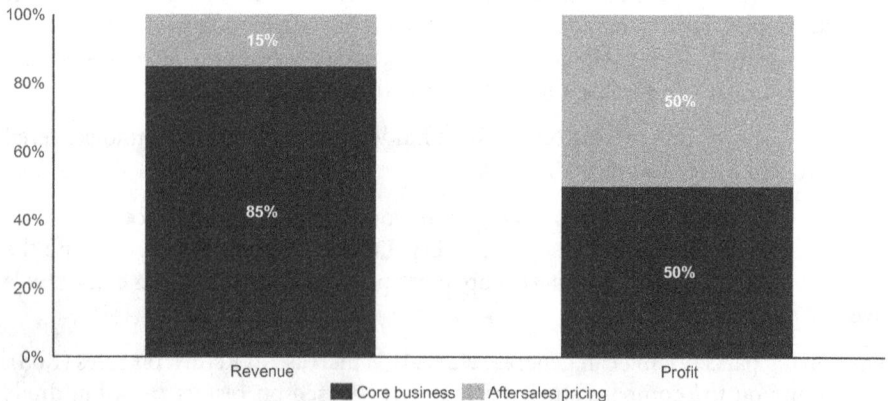

Scale and Diversity

Managing hundreds of thousands—sometimes over a million—stock keeping units (SKUs) across global supply chains is not uncommon. Each part differs in size, function, and demand behavior. Demand can be steady, seasonal, or erratic depending on product lifecycles or customer usage patterns.

The real challenge, however, lies in outdated systems. Manual processes and basic cost-plus pricing still dominate, missing critical variables such as demand elasticity, competitive pressure, or inventory cost. These systems cannot handle the complexity, leading to missed margin opportunities and slow reactions.

Opaque Competitive Landscape

For OEMs, navigating the competitive landscape in spare parts pricing is closely intertwined with the complexity of managing their vast and diverse inventories. Each spare part—differing in application, demand frequency, and lifecycle stage—may face a unique competitive environment, making comprehensive analysis a highly intricate task.

This complexity is further intensified by the presence of agile third-party suppliers. These competitors often focus on a narrower selection of high-demand parts, enabling them to operate leanly, adjust prices quickly, and aggressively target specific niches. As a result, OEMs must contend with a fragmented market where each SKU could be subject to a different set of competitors, necessitating distinct pricing strategies across the portfolio.

Additionally, spare parts fall into a variety of categories, each requiring its own pricing logic—warranty parts, "penny parts" (low-value items), price image-sensitive components, long- vs. short-tail parts, and end-of-lifecycle items. A one-size-fits-all pricing strategy is rarely effective.

Compounding the challenge is the lack of transparency and standardization in the spare parts market. Price benchmarking becomes difficult when third-party pricing data is fragmented, inconsistent, or unavailable. This opacity hampers OEMs' ability to understand true market positioning, making it harder to optimize prices and defend their value proposition in a competitive landscape.

Complex Distribution Channels

The distribution and sales channels for spare parts introduce an additional layer of complexity in assessing and managing end-user pricing. These channels—ranging from direct OEM sales and online platforms to intermediaries, independent distributors, buying groups, original equipment suppliers (OES), independent aftermarket (IAM) traders, and repair garages—each operate under their own pricing logic, market dynamics, and opacity (see Figure 1.4).

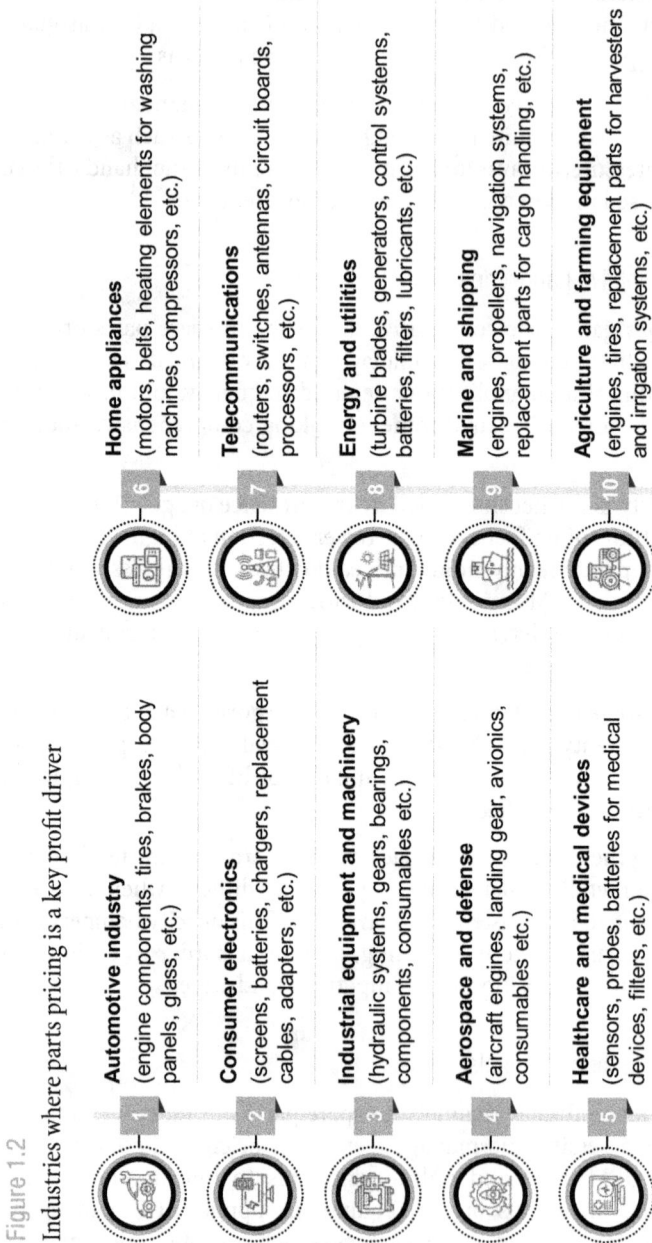

Figure 1.2

Industries where parts pricing is a key profit driver

Automotive industry
(engine components, tires, brakes, body panels, glass, etc.)

Consumer electronics
(screens, batteries, chargers, replacement cables, adapters, etc.)

Industrial equipment and machinery
(hydraulic systems, gears, bearings, components, consumables etc.)

Aerospace and defense
(aircraft engines, landing gear, avionics, consumables etc.)

Healthcare and medical devices
(sensors, probes, batteries for medical devices, filters, etc.)

Home appliances
(motors, belts, heating elements for washing machines, compressors, etc.)

Telecommunications
(routers, switches, antennas, circuit boards, processors, etc.)

Energy and utilities
(turbine blades, generators, control systems, batteries, filters, lubricants, etc.)

Marine and shipping
(engines, propellers, navigation systems, replacement parts for cargo handling, etc.)

Agriculture and farming equipment
(engines, tires, replacement parts for harvesters and irrigation systems, etc.)

Figure 1.3

The challenges in optimizing spare parts pricing

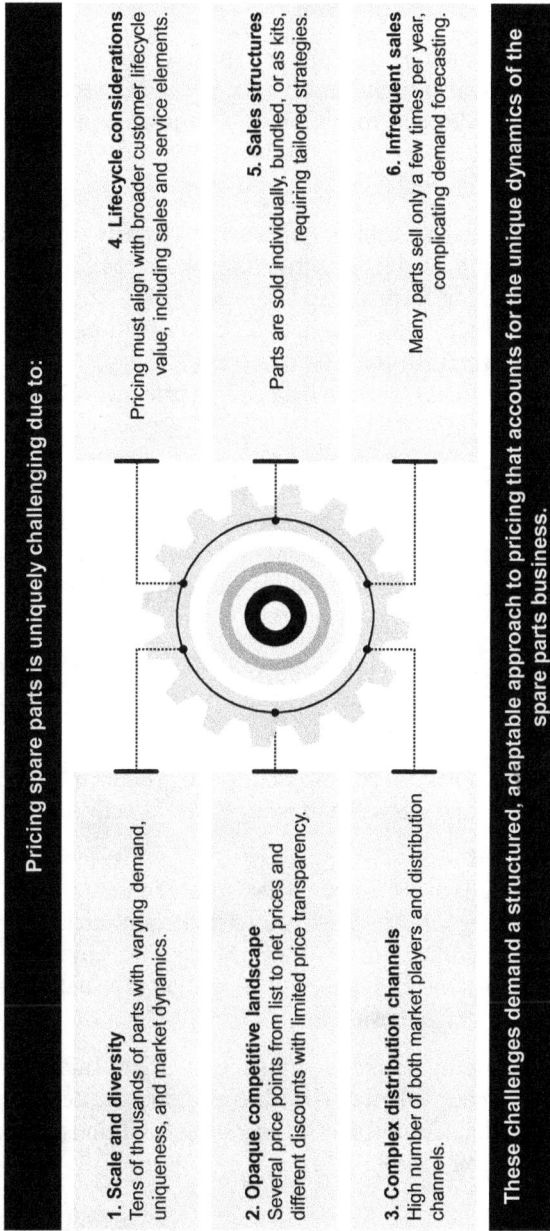

Pricing spare parts is uniquely challenging due to:

1. Scale and diversity
Tens of thousands of parts with varying demand, uniqueness, and market dynamics.

2. Opaque competitive landscape
Several price points from list to net prices and different discounts with limited price transparency.

3. Complex distribution channels
High number of both market players and distribution channels.

4. Lifecycle considerations
Pricing must align with broader customer lifecycle value, including sales and service elements.

5. Sales structures
Parts are sold individually, bundled, or as kits, requiring tailored strategies.

6. Infrequent sales
Many parts sell only a few times per year, complicating demand forecasting.

These challenges demand a structured, adaptable approach to pricing that accounts for the unique dynamics of the spare parts business.

This channel diversity often results in significant price discrepancies across touchpoints, making it difficult for OEMs to enforce a consistent and coherent pricing strategy. The lack of alignment can erode brand value, confuse customers, and create friction between sales partners.

Indirect channels—such as distributors and retailers—often set their own final prices, which can deviate significantly from the OEM's recommended pricing. This autonomy makes it difficult for OEMs to monitor the actual prices paid by end customers, potentially undermining the brand's perceived value and influencing customer purchasing behavior.

In addition, the involvement of multiple sales channels complicates the collection and analysis of sales data—an essential foundation for effective pricing strategies. Variations in reporting formats, update frequencies, and data granularity across channels make it challenging to consolidate information. As a result, OEMs often lack a comprehensive, real-time view of market dynamics and customer price sensitivity, limiting their ability to make data-driven pricing decisions.

Lifecycle Considerations

Spare parts pricing must be closely aligned with the broader concept of customer lifecycle value, encompassing both sales and service elements. However, one of the most pressing challenges in this domain is the need for frequent and responsive price adjustments, driven by a range of dynamic factors.

Firstly, spare parts demand is inherently volatile, influenced by unpredictable usage patterns, maintenance cycles, and external events—requiring pricing strategies that are both flexible and adaptive.

Secondly, rapid technological advancements and product obsolescence continuously reshape the lifecycle and relevance of many parts, directly impacting their value and sales potential.

In parallel, fluctuations in procurement, logistics, and storage costs necessitate regular price reviews to safeguard margins and ensure commercial viability. Competitive pressure is another critical driver—new pricing moves by rivals or the emergence of third-party alternatives can quickly shift market expectations and force OEMs to recalibrate their own price positions.

Finally, macroeconomic and regulatory shifts—such as trade tariffs, environmental regulations, or currency volatility—further reinforce the need for agile, data-driven pricing processes that can respond to changing conditions without compromising customer trust or profitability.

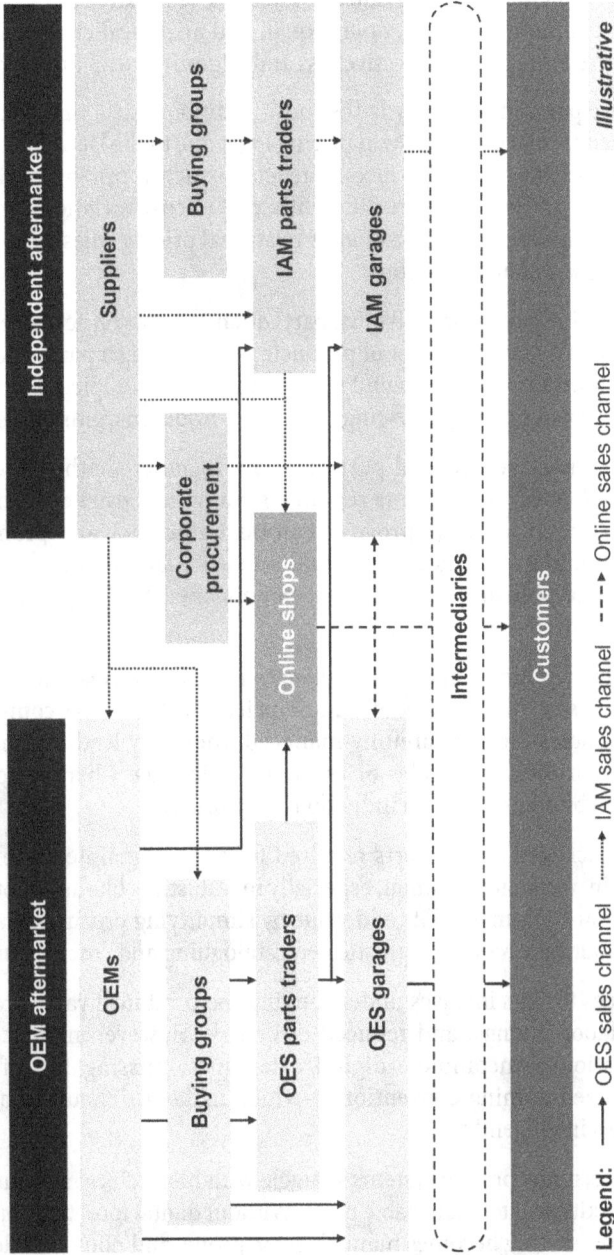

Figure 1.4
Distribution and sales channels—Example of an automotive aftermarket structure

OEM aftermarket

OEMs

Buying groups

OES parts traders

OES garages

Independent aftermarket

Suppliers

Buying groups

Corporate procurement

Online shops

IAM parts traders

IAM garages

Intermediaries

Customers

Illustrative

Legend: ⟶ OES sales channel   ⋯⋯▶ IAM sales channel   ---▶ Online sales channel

Sales Structures

Spare parts pricing is significantly influenced by the way in which parts are offered to the market—whether sold individually, bundled, or as part of kits. Each sales structure presents unique strategic, operational, and analytical challenges that must be addressed to ensure pricing effectiveness and alignment with broader business goals.

Selling spare parts individually is the most traditional structure. While straightforward, it often results in suboptimal pricing logic due to the lack of contextual linkage between parts. This can lead to inconsistencies—such as pricing left-hand and right-hand versions of the same part differently due to cost variations or volume-based distortions. Without standardization or relational pricing rules, customers may perceive pricing as unfair or arbitrary.

Moreover, setting prices for individual parts often depends on accurate cost allocation, but in many cases, the true cost of producing or sourcing a part is not well-defined. Overhead absorption, shared manufacturing lines, or incomplete supplier data can all obscure real costs, leading to pricing that either erodes margins or discourages sales.

In bundled structures, several parts are sold together—either due to functional dependency (e.g. all components required for a basic repair) or to create perceived value. This structure can improve operational efficiency and promote upselling. However, bundling introduces complexities in price allocation: how should the total bundle price be split among individual components? Which part drives value, and which is merely complementary?

Additionally, bundling can create challenges in price transparency. Customers may struggle to assess the fairness of bundle pricing if they can't compare individual prices. If bundles are not carefully managed, they may lead to cannibalization of higher-margin individual sales or create price leakage when customers demand discounts on bundles based on individual item prices.

Kits—pre-packaged sets of parts required for specific maintenance or installation tasks—are increasingly common, especially in industries like automotive, aerospace, and industrial equipment. Kits add value by simplifying procurement and reducing downtime, but they require sophisticated cataloguing and cost accounting.

Setting prices for kits involves understanding the combined value proposition: convenience, labor savings, and reduced error risk. However, many companies face data limitations—incomplete digital catalogues, missing Bill of Materials, or unstandardized naming conventions—which make it difficult to design kits and assign prices intelligently.

Furthermore, many pricing systems struggle with hierarchical structures, where kits include sub-kits or interchangeable parts. Without digital tools that can manage these relationships, pricing becomes manual, error-prone, and non-scalable.

Sales structures are also impacted by how parts are distributed—through direct sales, dealer networks, online platforms, or third-party service providers. Each channel may have different discount structures, service expectations, and cost bases. A consistent pricing strategy across channels requires clear pricing governance, which is often lacking in organizations with fragmented sales operations.

For instance, if a dealer receives a better price than an end customer due to legacy agreements or margin stacking, channel conflict can arise, damaging trust and reducing profitability. This is especially true when sales teams have significant autonomy in negotiating discounts without centralized oversight.

A recurring challenge in all sales structures is the lack of reliable data. Many spare parts catalogues are still not fully digitized, leading to outdated or inconsistent information. If cost data is missing or unreliable, it becomes extremely difficult to apply consistent pricing logic across parts or bundles. This leads to inefficiencies, such as overpricing low-value components or underpricing critical spares, ultimately affecting customer satisfaction and financial performance.

Infrequent Sales

Spare parts pricing is not a one-time decision but a multi-period strategy that must evolve alongside the product lifecycle and the customer relationship lifecycle. As machines, vehicles, or systems age, the demand, perceived value, and availability of spare parts change—requiring tailored pricing approaches that reflect both commercial objectives and customer needs.

Spare parts follow the lifecycle of the equipment they support, and each phase—launch, growth, maturity, and decline—has distinct implications for pricing:

Launch phase: During this early stage, parts availability is limited, and costs are often high due to lower volumes and initial production inefficiencies. Pricing strategies here may involve premium positioning, especially for captive parts that customers can't source elsewhere. Transparency and responsiveness are key to building trust.

Growth and maturity: As demand stabilizes and economies of scale improve, prices can be optimized based on cost-efficiency and market competition. This is also the phase where bundling, kits, and value-based strategies are most effectively applied, as the customer base and installed product population grow.

Decline or obsolescence: For aging products, parts may become scarce or expensive to produce. At this point, pricing must consider inventory liquidation, substitution options, or even planned obsolescence strategies. Decisions must balance profitability, customer service continuity, and brand reputation.

Beyond the equipment, pricing must be in tune with the total customer lifetime value (CLV). Parts pricing plays a critical role in shaping the customer experience over the long term—impacting perceptions of cost of ownership, service quality, and brand loyalty.

Smart pricing strategies can play a pivotal role in retaining customers by offering competitive prices during both warranty and post-warranty phases, tailoring value-based pricing for high-lifetime-value customers, and introducing initiatives such as loyalty programs or volume discounts to incentivize repeat purchases. This lifecycle-centric approach shifts the pricing mindset from being merely transactional to one focused on nurturing long-term relationships, where the overall revenue potential of each customer or fleet becomes a key consideration.

However, lifecycle pricing brings operational complexities, particularly in the need for frequent and agile price reviews. With market dynamics, raw material costs, technological advancements, and customer expectations constantly evolving, staying static in pricing can result in adverse effects. These include margin erosion due to inflation or increased production costs, customer dissatisfaction if prices become misaligned with perceived value or competitive offerings, and inefficiencies stemming from surplus or obsolete inventory.

To implement effective lifecycle pricing, companies must forecast future demand for parts and align pricing strategies accordingly. This involves identifying critical parts likely to fail at specific stages in the product lifecycle, planning for price adjustments during new product introductions and end-of-life transitions, and leveraging telemetry and usage data to anticipate wear patterns and pre-empt demand spikes.

By proactively responding to these lifecycle shifts, companies can better manage parts availability and pricing—ultimately enhancing both profitability and service levels.

This book addresses these four challenges indicating how to overcome these hurdles.

SUMMARY

Spare parts pricing is the untapped gem in industrial business models. After-sales often represents just 15% of revenues—but contributes up to 50% of profits. Despite this, it is often overlooked, underfunded, and underserved.

Six major challenges keep companies from realizing the full potential of parts pricing:

1 Scale and diversity

2 Opaque competitive landscape

3 Complex distribution channels

4 Lifecycle considerations

5 Sales structures

6 Infrequent sales

Overcoming them yields outsized returns: improvements of 2%–10% in RoS, driven by fast-acting quick wins and deeper long-term capability.

The treasure is there. The question is whether leadership is ready to dig.

2

Four Pillars of Parts Price Setting

In the art of pricing, there is no single compass. Each company navigates with its own set of tools—some inherited, some improvised. But in the world of spare parts, where volume meets variety and perception meets precision, four paths consistently emerge. Like pillars supporting a house, these approaches offer structure, elevation, and strategic balance. The question is not which one to choose—but when, where, and how to use each.

Spare parts pricing is a strategic element that plays a critical role in balancing profitability, customer satisfaction, and market competitiveness. Different businesses adopt different pricing methodologies depending on their level of pricing maturity, internal capabilities, and market dynamics.

In this chapter, we explore the four foundational approaches to parts pricing: cost-plus pricing (the bookkeeper's formula), smart cost-plus pricing (the architect's upgrade), competitive pricing (the market mirror), and value-based pricing (the strategist's compass). Each model serves a distinct purpose and comes with its own set of advantages and challenges.

COST-PLUS PRICING: THE TYPICAL STARTING POINT

Cost-plus pricing is the most basic and commonly used approach—most companies started here, and many still rely on it today. It involves determining the selling price of a spare part by simply adding a fixed markup to its cost.

This method is straightforward, internally transparent, and easy to implement. It ensures that costs are covered and is often manageable even without sophisticated pricing infrastructure.

But simplicity has its cost. Cost-plus pricing ignores external factors such as customer perception, market dynamics, and the strategic value of different parts. As a result, it can lead to illogical outcomes—underpricing of high-value parts or overpricing of commodity components.

At one OEM I advised, the price of the left and right rear-view mirrors differed significantly. The left mirror, being more prone to breakage, had higher volumes and thus lower production costs—making it cheaper under cost-plus logic. But to the customer, both mirrors looked identical. Dealers and customers alike questioned

DOI: 10.4324/9781003647416-3

the logic. The fix? We aligned the price to reflect perceived parity, raising the lower price. Complaints disappeared—and profits rose, without affecting sales volume (see Figure 2.1).

In another case, a tractor cabin manufacturer priced small vineyard cabins higher than large tractor cabins. Why? Because the smaller ones were produced in lower volumes and had higher unit costs. The outcome: customers were confused—expecting the larger product to cost more. After reviewing market conditions and elasticity, we increased the price of the larger cabin to reflect its true value. The result: no volume loss, higher margins, and a price that made sense to the market (see Figure 2.1).

SMART COST-PLUS PRICING: THE UPGRADE

But cost-plus, in all its simplicity, wears thin when portfolios grow and customers ask why one bolt costs more than another. The next step? Adding intelligence without adding complexity.

Smart cost-plus pricing builds upon the traditional model by introducing logic and segmentation to the markup. Instead of applying a flat percentage, margins are adapted based on part type, demand pattern, geography, lifecycle stage, or inventory risk.

For example, a company might apply higher markups to fast-moving parts or slow movers nearing obsolescence, while lowering margins for commodity or high-visibility components. Geographic multipliers can reflect local market conditions. This approach remains simple to manage but significantly increases pricing precision—especially for companies with large, diverse portfolios.

It's a practical bridge between basic cost-plus and more sophisticated models—a way to move forward without getting overwhelmed (see Figure 2.2).

COMPETITIVE PRICING: THE MARKET MIRROR

Where smart cost-plus looks inward, competitive pricing turns outward—to the battlefield of market perception.

Competitive pricing sets or adjusts prices based on what competitors are charging. It's essential in markets with high transparency—such as e-commerce platforms or independent aftermarket channels—where customers can compare prices instantly.

This approach requires constant monitoring of competitor pricing, local market dynamics, and rapid response capability. Tools for competitive intelligence and benchmarking are vital here.

But there's a risk: mirror too much, and you forget who you are. Blindly chasing the lowest price can erode margins and trigger a race to the bottom. Used in isolation, competitive pricing can become reactive and unsustainable. The best companies combine it with cost or value logic to ensure margin discipline and brand integrity.

Figure 2.1

Distortions caused by cost-plus pricing and actions to optimize prices

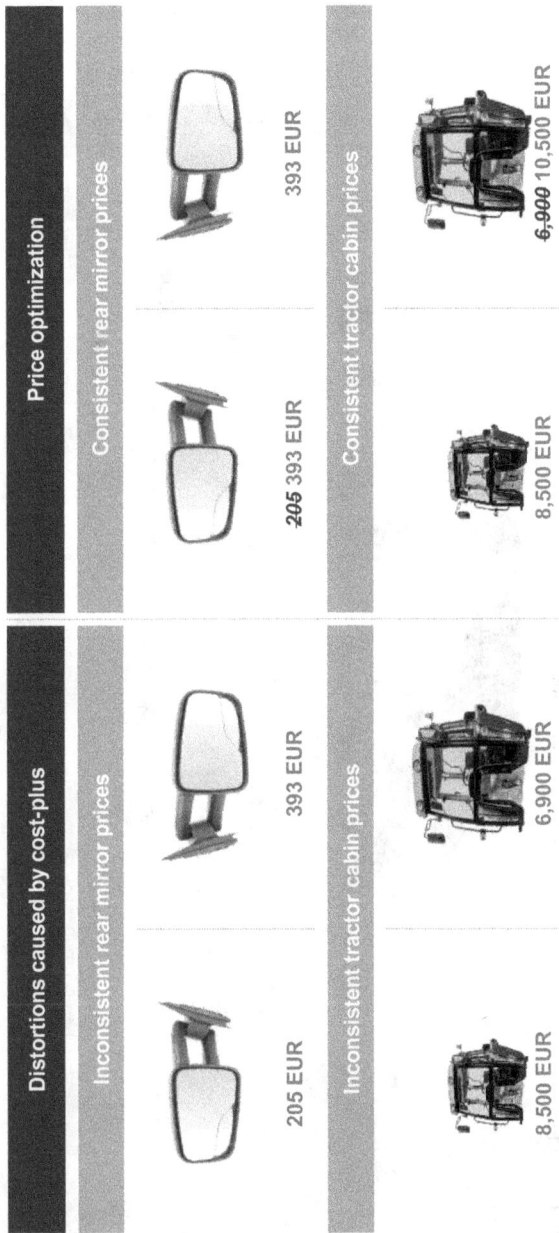

Figure 2.2

Examples of price drivers within the smart cost-plus approach

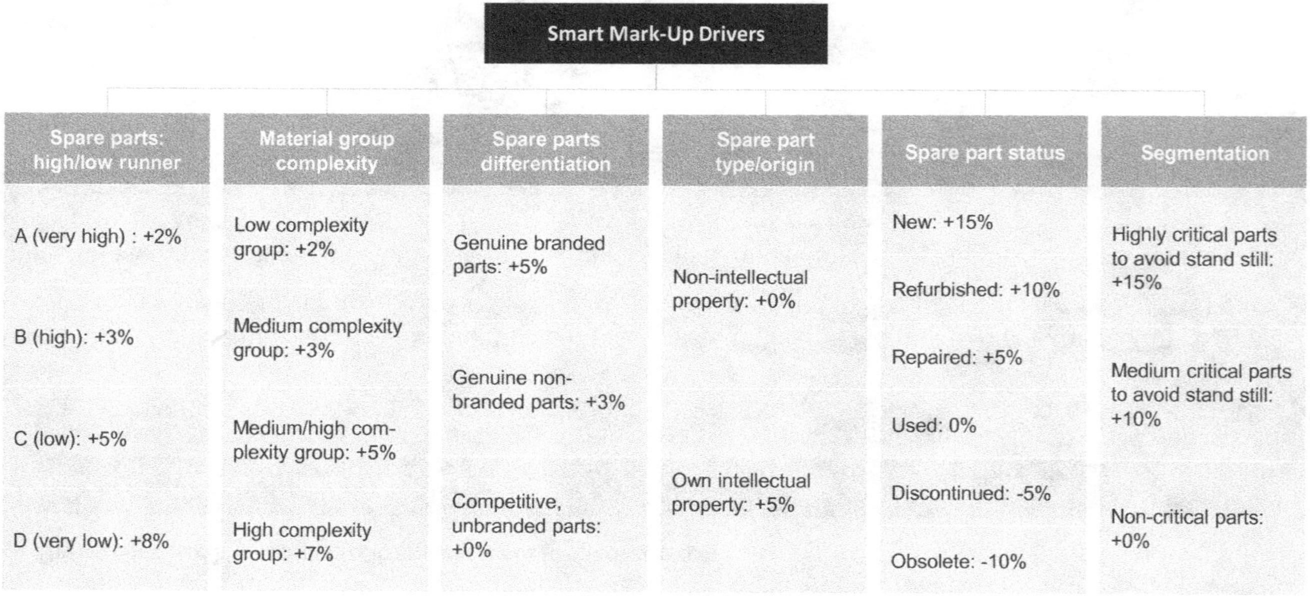

Smart Mark-Up Drivers

Spare parts: high/low runner	Material group complexity	Spare parts differentiation	Spare part type/origin	Spare part status	Segmentation
A (very high) : +2%	Low complexity group: +2%	Genuine branded parts: +5%	Non-intellectual property: +0%	New: +15%	Highly critical parts to avoid stand still: +15%
B (high): +3%	Medium complexity group: +3%	Genuine non-branded parts: +3%		Refurbished: +10%	
C (low): +5%	Medium/high complexity group: +5%		Own intellectual property: +5%	Repaired: +5%	Medium critical parts to avoid stand still: +10%
D (very low): +8%	High complexity group: +7%	Competitive, unbranded parts: +0%		Used: 0%	
				Discontinued: -5%	Non-critical parts: +0%
				Obsolete: -10%	

VALUE-BASED PRICING: THE STRATEGIST'S COMPASS

Value-based pricing is the most advanced and strategic approach. Here, the price of a part is set based on its perceived value to the customer—not its cost, and not the competition.

This model requires a deep understanding of how a part contributes to uptime, safety, efficiency, or brand trust. It accounts for factors such as criticality, ease of replacement, brand reputation, and willingness to pay.

For example, a safety-critical component that prevents downtime is worth far more to the customer than a cosmetic panel—even if both cost the same to produce. Value-based pricing captures this gap.

Implementing it requires cross-functional collaboration, data maturity, and analytical horsepower. It often involves building value models, quantifying benefits, and testing price thresholds. The reward? Greater margin control, stronger brand positioning, and tighter alignment with customer needs.

For new and existing parts, value-based pricing can integrate value drivers, competition insights, and internal guardrails into a structured retail price (see Figure 2.3).

CHOOSING THE RIGHT APPROACH

Each of the four pricing models has its place in a company's pricing journey. Cost-plus pricing offers a foundation for organizations beginning to formalize their pricing strategies. Smart cost-plus provides more control and refinement while remaining relatively easy to scale. Competitive pricing becomes essential in markets where visibility and pricing pressure are high. And value-based pricing, while complex, represents the gold standard—enabling companies to maximize margins and align prices with what customers truly value (see Figure 2.4).

In practice, companies often blend these approaches. A basic cost-plus logic might be used for low-value, long-tail parts; competitive pricing might govern fast-moving, high-visibility components; and value-based pricing might be reserved for high-impact or branded parts where the customer experience is central. The most successful organizations evolve through these pricing strategies over time, gradually embedding more intelligence, automation, and customer insight into their pricing systems.

SUMMARY

Each of the four pricing models offers a different balance between simplicity, market sensitivity, and profit potential. Cost-plus is easy to apply but lacks nuance. Smart cost-plus introduces segmentation and basic intelligence. Competitive pricing ensures market alignment but can erode value if not balanced. Value-based pricing, while the most complex, is also the most powerful, enabling companies to truly capture the value they deliver.

Each of the four pricing models offers a different balance between simplicity, market sensitivity, and profit potential:

Cost-Plus Pricing is the most straightforward method, adding a fixed markup to costs to ensure margins. However, it ignores customer perception and market dynamics, often resulting in illogical pricing and lost value opportunities.

Smart Cost-Plus Pricing enhances the traditional approach by applying differentiated margins based on segmentation and strategic criteria. It remains operationally simple while offering more refined control over profitability and alignment with part characteristics.

Competitive Pricing adjusts prices based on competitor benchmarks and is essential in highly transparent markets. While effective for maintaining market positioning, it risks price wars and margin erosion if not complemented by internal cost and value considerations.

Value-Based Pricing sets prices according to the perceived value to the customer, considering factors like criticality, brand, and impact on uptime. Though complex and resource-intensive, it offers the greatest potential for profit and customer satisfaction by truly aligning prices with willingness to pay.

Smart parts pricing is not about choosing one approach permanently—it's about evolving your pricing capabilities over time and combining them, as, e.g., a view on competitiveness is always needed and is very helpful if combined with other pricing approaches. The right mix depends on product complexity, market maturity, and organizational capabilities.

Figure 2.4

Comparison between parts pricing approaches

Pricing Approach	Simplicity	Market Sensitivity	Profit Optimization	Maturity Level
Cost-Plus Pricing	★★★★★	★☆☆☆☆	★☆☆☆☆	Basic
Smart Cost-Plus Pricing	★★★★☆	★★☆☆☆	★★☆☆☆	Developing
Competitive Pricing	★★★☆☆	★★★★☆	★★★☆☆	Intermediate
Value-Based Pricing	★★☆☆☆	★★★★★	★★★★★	Advanced

Figure 2.3

Value-based pricing approach for the brake disc of a BMW 5 series

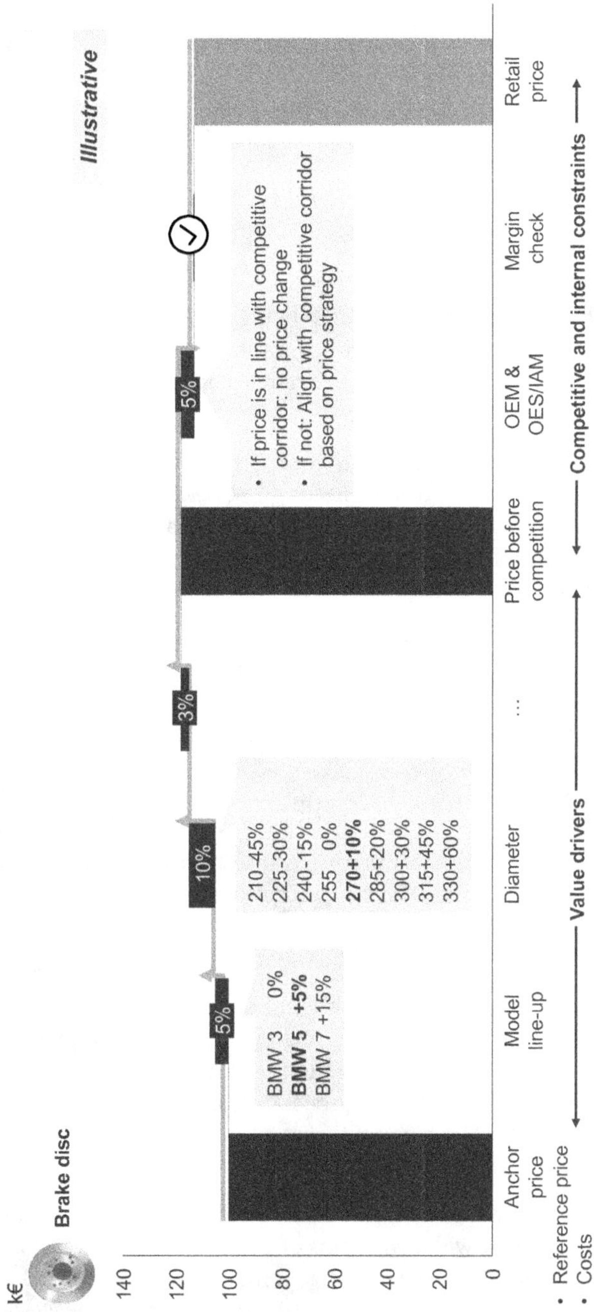

Illustrative

Brake disc

k€

| Value drivers | | | Competitive and internal constraints | | |

Anchor price — Model line-up (5%) — Diameter (10%, 3%) — Price before competition (5%) — OEM & OES/IAM — Margin check — Retail price

• Reference price
• Costs

Model line-up:
BMW 3 0%
BMW 5 +5%
BMW 7 +15%

Diameter:
210 -45%
225 -30%
240 -15%
255 0%
270 +10%
285 +20%
300 +30%
315 +45%
330 +60%

• If price is in line with competitive corridor: no price change
• If not: Align with competitive corridor based on price strategy

3

Transforming Spare Parts Pricing
From Foundation to Foresight

In the Alps, climbers say: "The mountain reveals itself step by step." Spare parts pricing is much the same. You don't jump to the peak—you earn it, layer by layer. First you gather tools, then you gain altitude. Eventually, if your footing holds, you reach the summit. And from there, pricing becomes not only a lever—but a vantage point to see what others can't.

Spare parts pricing is not a static activity. It is a maturity journey—one that evolves as capabilities, systems, and business needs grow. Most companies start with basic cost-plus logic and gradually move towards advanced, data-driven, and customer-centric pricing approaches. The transformation, however, is not an overnight change—it typically unfolds in three stages of altitude.

These stages are not rigid. Some companies might move faster in some areas, slower in others. Yet the path from pricing chaos to pricing excellence follows a predictable pattern. This chapter outlines a practical roadmap for transforming spare parts pricing in three strategic stages: Basecamp, Ascent, and Summit (see Figure 1.1).

STAGE 1: BASECAMP—BUILDING THE PRICING FOUNDATION

The first step in a spare parts pricing transformation is about building the structural core of parts pricing. Many organizations operate with limited transparency, fragmented ownership, and manual processes. Before advanced tools or tactics can deliver results, the foundation must be solid.

The transformation begins by clearly defining a pricing strategy. At this stage, leadership must define the overarching pricing philosophy that aligns with the company's commercial goals. Will the organization stick with cost-plus logic, move to value-based pricing, or apply a hybrid approach? Clear strategic goals—margin expansion, price consistency, market competitiveness—must be articulated and shared across departments.

This is also the moment to initiate structured segmentation of the parts portfolio. Since spare parts vary widely in terms of volume, criticality, visibility, and lifecycle, applying a one-size-fits-all pricing logic is inefficient. Not all parts are created equal. Segmenting the portfolio based on volume, value, visibility, lifecycle stage, or strategic importance helps define differentiated pricing strategies. For example, fast-moving

DOI: 10.4324/9781003647416-4

Figure 3.1

The spare parts pricing maturity stages

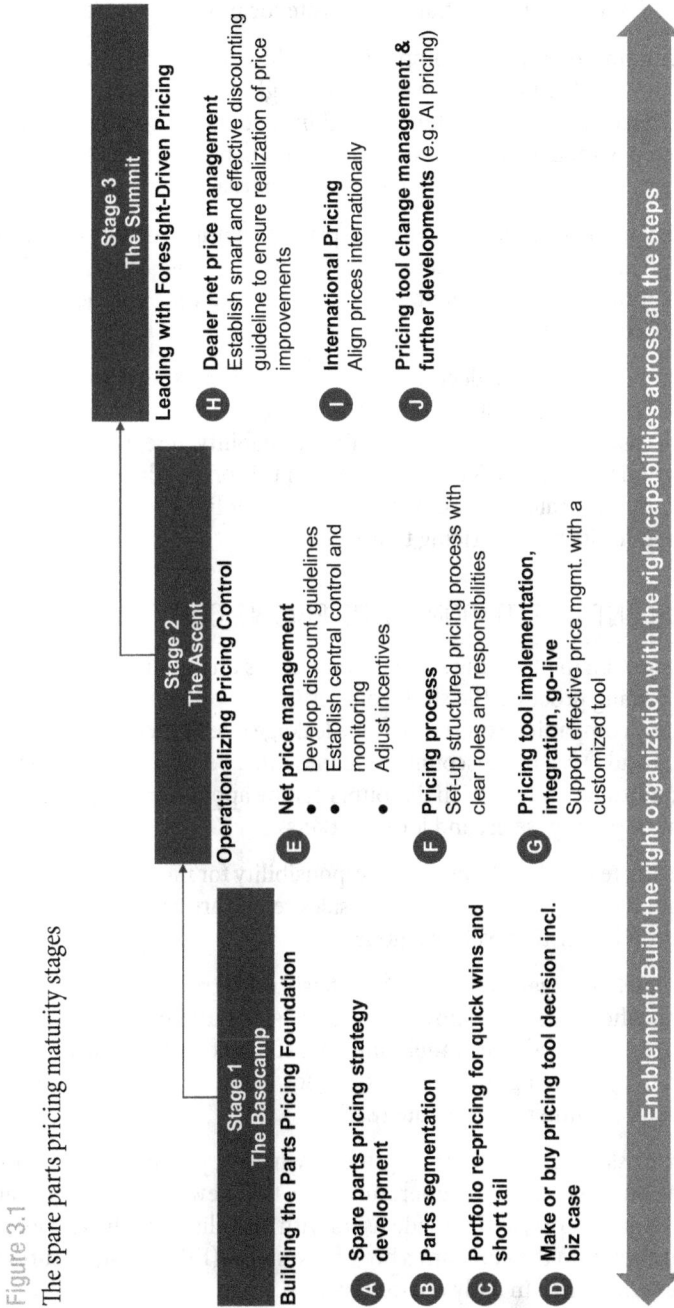

Stage 1
The Basecamp

Building the Parts Pricing Foundation

Ⓐ **Spare parts pricing strategy development**

Ⓑ **Parts segmentation**

Ⓒ **Portfolio re-pricing for quick wins and short tail**

Ⓓ **Make or buy pricing tool decision incl. biz case**

Stage 2
The Ascent

Operationalizing Pricing Control

Ⓔ **Net price management**
- Develop discount guidelines
- Establish central control and monitoring
  - Adjust incentives

Ⓕ **Pricing process**
Set-up structured pricing process with clear roles and responsibilities

Ⓖ **Pricing tool implementation, integration, go-live**
Support effective price mgmt. with a customized tool

Stage 3
The Summit

Leading with Foresight-Driven Pricing

Ⓗ **Dealer net price management**
Establish smart and effective discounting guideline to ensure realization of price improvements

Ⓘ **International Pricing**
Align prices internationally

Ⓙ **Pricing tool change management & further developments** (e.g. AI pricing)

Enablement: Build the right organization with the right capabilities across all the steps

or safety-critical parts might follow different pricing logic than long-tail or cosmetic components. Segmenting parts based on these characteristics enables differentiated pricing strategies and is an essential prerequisite for more advanced tactics.

Once segmentation is in place, companies should launch a re-pricing wave across selected portions of the portfolio, particularly high-volume or high-revenue parts. This often surfaces clear inconsistencies and immediate margin opportunities that can be corrected without disrupting sales volumes. Such quick wins build momentum and demonstrate the value of a more structured approach.

This is also the moment to identify internal "pricing champions"—people who understand both the business and the value of disciplined pricing. These individuals may sit in finance, product management, or operations, and they will become key allies as the journey continues.

In parallel, the company must decide whether to invest in a specialized pricing tool or to continue using existing systems. This make-or-buy decision should be supported by a business case that outlines expected ROI, scalability, integration potential, and impact on organizational efficiency. At the end of this phase, the organization should have a clear pricing strategy, a segmented parts portfolio, a roadmap for re-pricing, and a direction for its future pricing toolset.

STAGE 2: ASCENT—OPERATIONALIZING PRICING CONTROL

With the foundation in place, the second step focuses on building discipline and control into the pricing process. The shift from setting list prices to managing net prices is critical. Many companies experience value leakage due to excessive or unstructured discounting. To address this, discount guidelines must be created and enforced. These define the conditions under which discounts can be applied and create transparency between central pricing, sales, and local markets.

A central pricing team typically assumes responsibility for monitoring these rules and ensuring compliance, while incentives for sales teams are recalibrated to encourage price realization rather than volume alone.

At the same time, the organization must establish a clear pricing process. This process should define who owns what, how pricing decisions are made, how delegation of authority is regulated and which tools and data support them. It introduces governance into pricing, ensuring that changes are not based on intuition or negotiation, but on logic and alignment with strategy.

With this process defined, the pricing tool—whether purchased or built—enters implementation. Its role is to operationalize the new pricing logic, automate calculations, store history, and provide users with visibility into the rationale behind prices. Integration into the company's broader systems (ERP, CRM) ensures that pricing becomes embedded in daily operations.

This is where the organization needs its "pricing process builders"—cross-functional, respected professionals who can implement governance with empathy and authority. These individuals bring sales, product, and finance into alignment, translating pricing strategy into pricing behavior.

Once the tool goes live, the organization transitions from ad-hoc price updates to structured and data-driven pricing management. But this step is not only about systems—it's also about adoption. Teams must be trained, aligned, and committed to using the new process and tools in a consistent and collaborative way.

STAGE 3: SUMMIT—LEADING WITH FORESIGHT-DRIVEN PRICING

The third step of the journey brings spare parts pricing to a strategic level, focusing on scaling capabilities, refining tools, and embedding advanced pricing logic into the business. One of the most important areas of focus is dealer net price management. At this stage, companies move beyond setting good list prices to ensuring that those prices are effectively realized in the market. A robust and logic-based discount structure is key to avoiding margin erosion and to ensuring that dealer relationships are managed fairly and transparently. Effective dealer pricing helps translate pricing strategy into actual profitability, especially when volume-based rebates and local negotiations are involved.

As companies expand globally, international pricing becomes a crucial topic. Uncoordinated local pricing often leads to parallel imports and customer frustration. A mature pricing organization introduces a globally aligned pricing framework where prices are set centrally but adapted through structured multipliers to fit local conditions. This ensures consistency while preserving local competitiveness.

Meanwhile, pricing tools continue to evolve. What began as a rule-based engine can now integrate AI-driven recommendations, lifecycle pricing logic, and real-time data from connected products. Companies begin to implement more predictive pricing models, adjusting prices proactively based on usage patterns, market shifts, or stock levels. The focus shifts from managing the present to anticipating the future.

At the Summit, pricing becomes a source of foresight. The organization empowers "pricing storytellers"—leaders who can articulate why prices are what they are, and how they reflect strategic intent. These people elevate pricing from a calculation to a conviction.

ENABLEMENT ACROSS ALL STEPS

Throughout the three phases of transformation, continuous improvement is critical. As pricing practices evolve, they must be measured, refined, and optimized on an ongoing basis. Companies begin to treat pricing as a key performance area, supported by well-defined key performance indicators (KPIs) and regular performance reviews. Governance structures develop into formalized pricing excellence functions with a clear mandate to drive value. These functions are empowered through advanced analytics and data visibility, allowing them to influence commercial decisions pro-actively. At this stage, pricing is no longer viewed merely as a financial lever—it becomes a strategic tool that enhances customer experience, strengthens brand positioning, and reinforces market competitiveness.

For this evolution to take root and deliver sustainable results, the organization must also invest in the right talent and culture. Establishing a dedicated pricing team— whether centralized or operating in a hybrid model—is essential. This team must be staffed with individuals who bring a balanced mix of analytical capabilities and business insight. Alongside structural setup, building skills is a continuous priority. Companies should implement tailored development programs, including formal training, workshops, and certifications, to ensure the team keeps pace with evolving tools and methods.

To embed pricing deeply into the business, change management must be delib-erate and ongoing. Since pricing decisions intersect with various functions, success depends on fostering consistent collaboration across departments such as sales, product management, finance, and IT. Only through this cross-functional alignment can pricing transformation become an integrated and lasting part of the company's operational DNA.

SUMMARY

Spare parts pricing transformation is a step-by-step evolution. It begins at Basecamp, where strategy and segmentation provide the footing. It advances through the Ascent, where structure, governance, and systems give pricing discipline. It culminates at the Summit, where global consistency, predictive tools, and strategic clarity transform pricing into foresight.

Each stage delivers measurable improvements in revenue, margin, and organizational capability. And across all phases, building the right organization with the right talent remains the ultimate success factor.

Smart parts pricing is not just a tool—it is a mindset. And like any mindset, it becomes power only when it is shared. Climb with strategy, and the summit becomes more than a view—it becomes a vantage point from which to lead.

4

The Seven Sins of Spare Parts Pricing

Every hero's journey begins in shadow—before claiming the mountaintop, one must descend into the valley. So too in the world of spare parts pricing: before and during a parts transformation as describe in Chapter 3, we must confront the unspoken errors that sabotage progress from the start.

Spare parts pricing is not merely about markups or percentages. It is a theatre of urgency, perception, lifecycle stages, and unspoken expectations. It is where operational excellence and emotional decision-making collide.

In this section, we expose the "seven sins of spare parts pricing"—common, deeply embedded, and surprisingly human errors. They are not always dramatic. Sometimes they are quiet. But they are always costly. Naming them is the first step to overcoming them. These need to be kept in mind when planning a transformation journey as illustrated in Chapter 3.

THE ICARUS SYNDROME

Overpricing without Perceived Value

> "You flew too close to the sun, and now your wings are melting."
> —*Prometheus*, Ridley Scott

Some companies price their spare parts high simply because they always have. Legacy brand strength, engineering quality, and past success all seem to justify the premium. But the aftermarket has evolved. Customers compare prices. Distributors negotiate harder. Independent service providers buy globally.

When the price is no longer supported by a clear perception of value, the wax wings melt. The customer walks away. And someone else steps in—usually a cheaper, faster, or more transparent competitor.

DOI: 10.4324/9781003647416-5

THE HAMLET COMPLEX

Chronic Fear of Raising Prices

> "To raise, or not to raise—that is the question."

In many organizations, even the smallest price increase triggers paralysis. Product managers worry about backlash. Sales teams resist change. Executives over-analyze.

Meanwhile, inflation rises. Inventory costs grow. And margins quietly disappear. In a spare parts catalog with thousands of SKUs, inertia is the real enemy. Action, even small and deliberate, creates momentum. Pricing courage is not reckless—it is responsible.

THE JEDI FALLACY

Believing Parts Pricing Is a Matter of Instinct

> "Use the force, Luke!"
>
> —Obi-Wan Kenobi

Too often, list prices are determined by intuition: a quick glance at a competitor, a markup formula, or someone's "gut feeling." But spare parts pricing is far more complex than it seems. A single bolt might be used across 12 machine models. The downtime it prevents could be worth thousands.

Instinct is valuable. But it must be supported by method. Lifecycle segmentation, price elasticity, demand frequency—these are the new tools of the trade. You don't guess your way to pricing excellence. You build it.

THE TOWER OF BABEL

Organizational Misalignment on Pricing

> *"Chaos isn't a pit. Chaos is a ladder."* — *Littlefinger, Game of Thrones*

Pricing sits at the crossroads of sales, product, engineering, finance, and operations. When these teams aren't aligned, confusion takes over. One team offers discounts to hit volume. Another pushes for margin. A third invents a "temporary" offer that becomes the new standard.

Customers experience this not as strategy, but as noise. And noise erodes trust. A pricing architecture must be coherent. And that coherence begins with governance and internal harmony.

THE DON QUIXOTE DELUSION

Trying to Win Every Deal at Any Cost

> *"Facts are the enemy of truth." — Don Quixote*

Some pricing teams chase every order. They react to every competitor move. They slash prices for legacy machines and fear losing a single unit to a cheaper alternative.

But not every customer is strategic. Not every part is worth saving. Winning on volume alone in a saturated, low-growth aftermarket is a fool's errand. The smart path is knowing when to walk away—and when to defend margin like a castle under siege.

THE MATRIX ILLUSION

Mistaking the List Price for the Real Price

> *"There is no spoon." — The Matrix*

On the spreadsheet, margins appear solid. But buried beneath layers of discounts, promotions, rebates, and special conditions, the reality is often far less pretty.

In spare parts—where adjustments are frequent and pricing is often localized—the gap between list price and realized price can become a canyon. And if no one tracks it, no one fixes it. True pricing power begins with visibility. You cannot improve what you don't measure.

THE MACBETH ERROR

Sacrificing Long-Term Price Integrity for Short-Term Wins

> *"I am in blood stepped in so far." — Macbeth*

To meet quarterly targets, businesses slash prices "just this once." To close a deal, they offer a discount "just for today." Over time, temporary exceptions become the new normal. Channel partners expect it. Customers wait for it. The brand weakens.

Like Macbeth, these companies gain the crown but lose the soul. In spare parts—where trust is built over time—pricing consistency is not a detail. It is your reputation.

SUMMARY

These sins are not fatal—but they must be faced before and during a spare transformation. In spare parts pricing, more than in most domains, habits are inherited. Processes become rituals. "That's how we've always done it" becomes strategy.

> "What we do in life, echoes in eternity."
>
> —Maximus, *Gladiator*

The Icarus Syndrome shows us the danger of overconfidence. The Hamlet Complex reveals how hesitation can be fatal. The Jedi Fallacy warns us against relying on instinct over structure. The Tower of Babel exposes the cost of internal misalignment. The Don Quixote Delusion illustrates the futility of chasing every deal. The Matrix Illusion reminds us that perception and reality often diverge. And the Macbeth Error highlights the price of sacrificing tomorrow for today.

Recognizing these seven sins is the first act of strategic clarity.

Pricing, ultimately, is a message. It's a story we tell the market about who we are, and what we believe our value to be. If the story is confused, the market tunes out. But if it's clear, consistent, and courageous—the market listens.

Now that we've crossed the inferno of missteps, we can begin the ascent.

Part II

Ten Quick Wins in Spare Parts Pricing

"There is nothing more deceptive than an obvious fact."
—Arthur Conan Doyle, *The Boscombe Valley Mystery*

Sometimes, the treasure is not buried at the end of the map, guarded by dragons or puzzles, but lies quietly at our feet—obscured only by the dust of habit. In our obsession with grand strategies and sweeping digital overhauls, we often forget the humble power of small, intentional acts. But the world is not changed by fireworks alone. Sometimes, it is changed by the tightening of a single screw.

In pricing, as in life, the smallest hinge can swing the heaviest door. The smallest insight can unlock a new architecture of value. The "quick win" is not a trivial gesture, but the crack of light through which the whole structure is illuminated. It is not speed that defines it, but *precision*. A quick win is not a shortcut—it is a lever. A fulcrum. It is Archimedes whispering, "Give me a place to stand, and I will move the Earth."

When Sherlock Holmes uncovers a crime through the arrangement of footprints in the garden or the subtle scent of tobacco on a sleeve, it is not magic. It is *attentiveness*.

The difference between the mediocre and the master lies in what they notice.

And how they act on it.

These next chapters are your lens: they teach you where to look, what to shift, and when to act.

Do not mistake these actions for quick fixes. They are not bandages, but acupuncture points. Tactical, yes—but surgical in their impact. Each chapter here is a keystone. Like the first notes of Beethoven's Fifth, the motif may be simple. But it contains within it the structure of the entire symphony. Like the opening moves of a chess master, these are not random tactics, but the unfolding of strategy in miniature.

What you will encounter are techniques born not from theory, but from lived experience—collected on factory floors, in parts warehouses, in after-sales departments. They are drawn from the conversations behind the scenes, from the workshops where pricing directors roll up their sleeves and adjust the gears.

DOI: 10.4324/9781003647416-6

These quick wins are not universal formulas, but rather universal awakenings. Like a brush dipped in ochre on a fresco wall, they may seem insignificant—until you step back and witness the masterpiece emerging on the ceiling of the Sistine Chapel.

And so, take this section not as a checklist, but as a *journey through insight*. Imagine you are walking beside Leonardo da Vinci in his cluttered studio, watching him sketch flight on a piece of parchment. Or with Machiavelli among the olive groves of San Casciano, plotting the nature of power not through force, but through understanding. The wisdom of the Renaissance was always this: that grandeur begins with precision.

What we call "quick" is not rushed.

What we call "small" is not insignificant.

This is not the fast lane.

It is the fine blade.

Like all true craftsmanship, these spare parts pricing wins ask only one thing:

That you pay attention.

5

Hierarchical Pricing

Not all parts are created equal—and neither are the machines they serve. In spare parts pricing, value isn't just embedded in the part—it's shaped by where and how it's used. Customers buying premium vehicles or equipment expect superior performance, service, and support. They also show a higher willingness to pay for the parts that keep their investments running. Yet most pricing models ignore this, charging identical prices for parts used in both entry-level and top-tier machines. Hierarchical pricing corrects this imbalance—and unlocks a quick-win opportunity for boosting margin without touching the product itself.

THE CONCEPT OF HIERARCHICAL PRICING

Hierarchical pricing is the practice of aligning parts prices with the value tier of the machine, vehicle, or system they support. It reflects not just the physical cost of the part, but the context of its use—customer expectations, brand positioning, and perceived value.

Products—whether vehicles or machines—are often sold in tiered line-ups. Each tier attracts different customer segments, with varying expectations, performance needs, and price sensitivities. For example, a customer purchasing a premium MAN TGX truck or an Audi A1 hatchback anticipates higher quality and service—and is typically prepared to pay more for parts compared to buyers of entry-level models like the MAN TGL or a lower positioned Seat Ibiza.

Yet many manufacturers still price shared parts (like brake pads or discs) uniformly across models, ignoring these differences. This flattens the pricing potential and leaves value on the table. Hierarchical pricing corrects this by adjusting part prices based on the application tier.

Let's consider a practical example from the commercial vehicle sector: MAN Truck & Bus produces a range of trucks including the TGL, TGM, and TGX.[1] Each model serves a distinct use case and has a different price positioning:

- TGL: A compact light-duty truck for urban and short-haul logistics (7.5–12 tons), starting at approximately €50,000.

DOI: 10.4324/9781003647416-7

- TGM: A medium-duty truck ideal for regional distribution and public utility work (12–26 tons), priced around €70,000.

- TGX: A heavy-duty, long-haul truck for international freight (18–44 tons), costing up to €100,000.

Customers who purchase a TGX expect higher performance, reliability, and support—and they're willing to pay more for parts that support this high-end product. Yet, in many cases, parts such as brake discs or pads are priced uniformly across models. This means that a customer who paid twice as much for a TGX is offered the same price for a shared part as someone who bought a TGL.

This is a missed opportunity.

MONETIZING WILLINGNESS TO PAY WITH HIERARCHICAL PRICING

Consider a brake disc priced at €90, applied uniformly across TGL, TGM, and TGX. The TGM, being a more robust and expensive truck, justifies a higher price due to the greater value perception and usage context. Adjusting the price to upwards for TGM or TGX applications, as visualized by the upward arrow in Figure 5.1, captures more value without changing the part itself.

Similarly, if a set of brake pads is priced at €129 for all three models, then the pricing strategy is failing to reflect the tiered vehicle value. The price should increase incrementally for TGM and even more significantly for TGX to reflect both the purchase price of the vehicle and the customer's expected total cost of ownership.

APPLYING THE CONCEPT ACROSS BRANDS

The same logic applies when comparing products across brands within the same product segment. Take the Volkswagen Group as an example, which includes Seat, Volkswagen (VW), and Audi—all offering small hatchbacks like the Ibiza, Polo, and A1 respectively.[2]

Despite these models sharing similar mechanical platforms, their brand positioning and customer segments differ substantially:

- Seat Ibiza: Entry-level, budget-conscious buyers.
- VW Polo: Mid-range customers expecting more refinement.
- Audi A1: Premium buyers seeking design, technology, and prestige.

If a brake disc is priced at €60 across all three, Audi and VW are underpriced relative to the perceived value their brands offer. Customers paying a premium for an Audi are implicitly prepared to pay more for its maintenance—provided the brand

Figure 5.1

Model hierarchy of a truck line-up to be reflected in parts prices

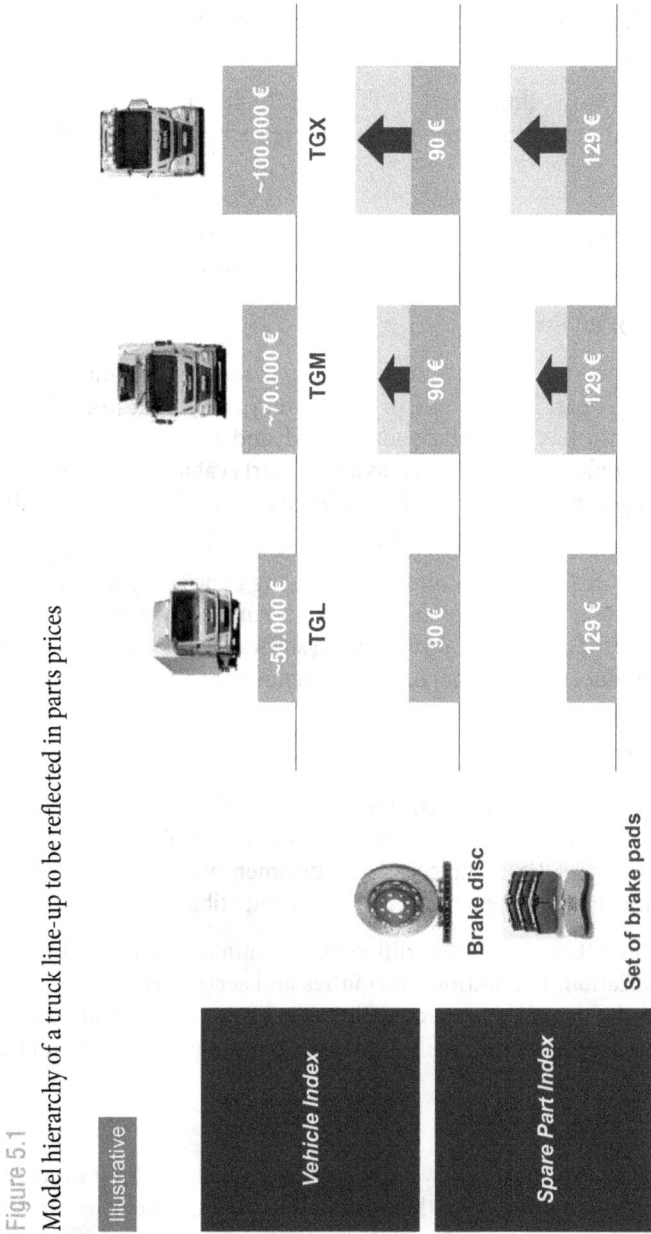

Illustrative

experience remains consistent. Failing to reflect this in parts pricing means leaving value untapped.

Again, identical components used across economy, mid-range, and premium vehicles fail to reflect the value differentiation customers already accept in their vehicle purchase decisions.

This differentiation is illustrated in Figure 5.2, showing how brand and model hierarchy should guide parts pricing tiers—even when the physical component is identical.

OVERCOMING THE CHALLENGES OF HIERARCHICAL PRICING

Managing Increased Complexity

The primary downside of hierarchical pricing is increased complexity. Instead of managing a single part number and price, you may need to create multiple entries: a brake pad for TGL, a second brake pad for TGM, and a third brake pad for TGX. This fragmentation multiplies quickly across a large parts catalogue and introduces operational challenges in inventory, pricing maintenance, and system integration.

However, this complexity is manageable—and worthwhile—especially with modern pricing systems that allow for conditional pricing logic and part differentiation by application. Several automotive and industrial companies have overcome similar challenges by introducing centralized pricing software and coordinating across sales, pricing, and product management under a Revenue Growth Management framework.

Preventing Part Substitution

Another potential risk is part substitution, where independent workshops or price-sensitive customers source the cheapest available version of a shared part, regardless of the intended model. For instance, a TGX customer might use the lower-priced TGL brake disc if the part numbers or fitments are compatible.

To mitigate this, OEMs can assign different part numbers for the same component based on application. In addition, warranties and service agreements can be made contingent on the use of the correct application-specific parts. Some manufacturers also employ packaging or traceability markers to differentiate premium parts.

SUMMARY

Hierarchical pricing is a powerful yet underutilized quick win lever in spare parts pricing. By aligning part prices with the value of the machines, vehicles, or systems they support, companies can better capture the willingness to pay of premium customers. When parts are priced uniformly across different product tiers, opportunities for higher margins are missed—especially in sectors like automotive, trucks, and industrial equipment where product line-ups span a wide value range.

Figure 5.2

Model hierarchy of cars in the same segment with different brands to be reflected in parts prices

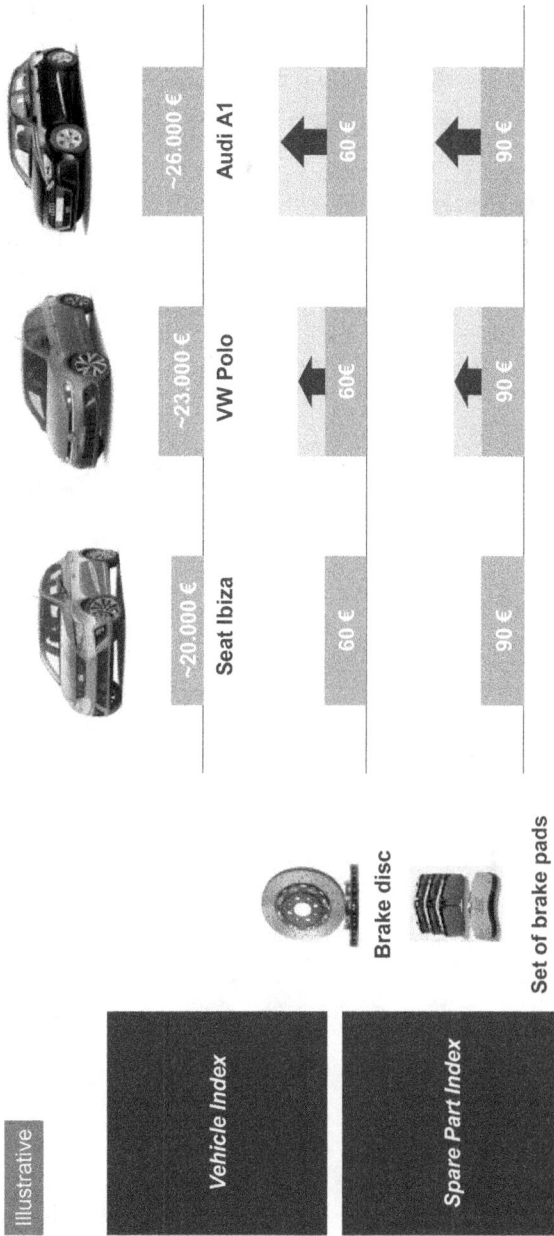

Illustrative

	Seat Ibiza	VW Polo	Audi A1
Vehicle Index	~20.000 €	~23.000 €	~26.000 €
Spare Part Index — Brake disc	60 €	60€	60 €
Set of brake pads	90 €	90 €	90 €

Implementing hierarchical pricing helps monetize brand and product positioning, supports strategic revenue uplift, and aligns pricing with customer expectations. While this approach introduces additional complexity—such as managing more price records and preventing part substitution—the benefits often outweigh the challenges. With modern pricing tools and strong governance in place, companies can apply hierarchical pricing effectively and turn it into a quick win for aftermarket profitability.

NOTES

1 Example made up to explain the concept of hierarchical pricing.
2 Example made up to explain the concept of hierarchical pricing in the context of more brands.

6

Rounding Routines

In spare parts pricing, strategic complexity often overshadows tactical opportunity. Yet one of the most underrated levers for revenue and profit uplift lies in the smallest of numbers—cents and decimals. Rounding routines, when applied intelligently, transform scattered prices into clean, psychologically compelling price points that resonate with customers and deliver results fast.

Spare parts pricing teams frequently focus on strategic levers like segmentation or competitor benchmarking but overlook how much impact can be made by simply rounding prices more intelligently. Rounding routines are one of the most tactical yet high-ROI quick wins available.

This chapter explores how rounding routines, when applied systematically, can optimize price points to maximize revenue, support psychological pricing thresholds, and maintain an acceptable price image. Done right, rounding is not just cosmetic—it's strategic.

THE CONCEPT OF ROUNDING ROUTINES

Let's start with a familiar consumer example: a package of chewing gum priced at €0.90. If analysis shows that the price threshold—the point at which demand begins to fall—is €1.00, the price can be increased up to €0.99 without impacting demand or brand perception.

The additional 9 cents are not only additional revenues. They are at the same time additional profits, as costs did not change.

> Why does this work? Because the price remains below the psychological ceiling of €1.00. This is known as "just-below pricing." Customers perceive a price of €0.99 as meaningfully lower than €1.00, even though the difference is marginal. This pricing psychology is well-documented in behavioral economics and is proven to improve purchase intent—even in B2B transactions.

The same concept applies in spare parts pricing. After a uniform percentage-based price adjustment, price points often become messy and inconsistent (e.g. €242.37, €17.86, €1.03). These prices may miss thresholds or erode perceived value. That's

DOI: 10.4324/9781003647416-8

where rounding routines come into play—to clean up pricing, align with customer expectations, and fully capture willingness to pay.

Rounding routines work by adjusting spare part prices upward in a structured way that captures additional value without triggering customer resistance. The approach varies depending on the price level of the part, as different price ranges call for different rounding strategies (see Figure 6.1).

By applying the appropriate rounding logic across each price band, companies can enhance price consistency, strengthen brand perception, and generate incremental revenue with minimal risk of customer pushback.

MONETIZING WILLINGNESS TO PAY THROUGH ROUNDING

To effectively capture customers' willingness to pay, different rounding routines can be applied depending on the value of the spare part. These routines aim to align prices with psychological thresholds while ensuring that no unnecessary margin is left on the table.

For higher-priced spare parts, rounding usually focuses on the second digit from the right, such as the tens place. For example, a part priced at €246 can be rounded to €250, creating a cleaner and more strategic price point. Another option is to use the number nine as a rounding anchor—bringing a price like €272 up to €290 (see Figure 6.1). This method is particularly suited to premium items, where avoiding decimals maintains a perception of quality and professionalism.

In the mid-price range, rounding shifts to the first digit, or the units place. Here, setting nine as the rounding target would turn a price like €42.56 into €49.00. Alternatively, you might define several rounding points—such as three, five, and nine—and round prices up to the next available one. For instance, applying this method to €42.56 would round the price to €43.00. This type of rounding maintains coherence and simplicity for parts priced in the moderate range.

When it comes to lower-priced items, particularly those between €10 and €50, rounding tends to focus on the first decimal place. Choosing a rounding point such as nine means a price like €9.26 would move to €9.90. If you define both five and nine as rounding digits, then a price of €9.24 would round up to €9.50. These small adjustments, while seemingly minor, can yield significant revenue when applied across high-volume SKUs.

For very low-priced items, especially those under €1, the rounding focuses on the second decimal. Even in this range, setting a rule such as rounding to nine can create measurable improvements. For example, a price like €0.13 would be adjusted to €0.19—still affordable for the customer, but more aligned with willingness to pay and value capture.

Figure 6.1

Price rounding approach differentiated by digits—An example

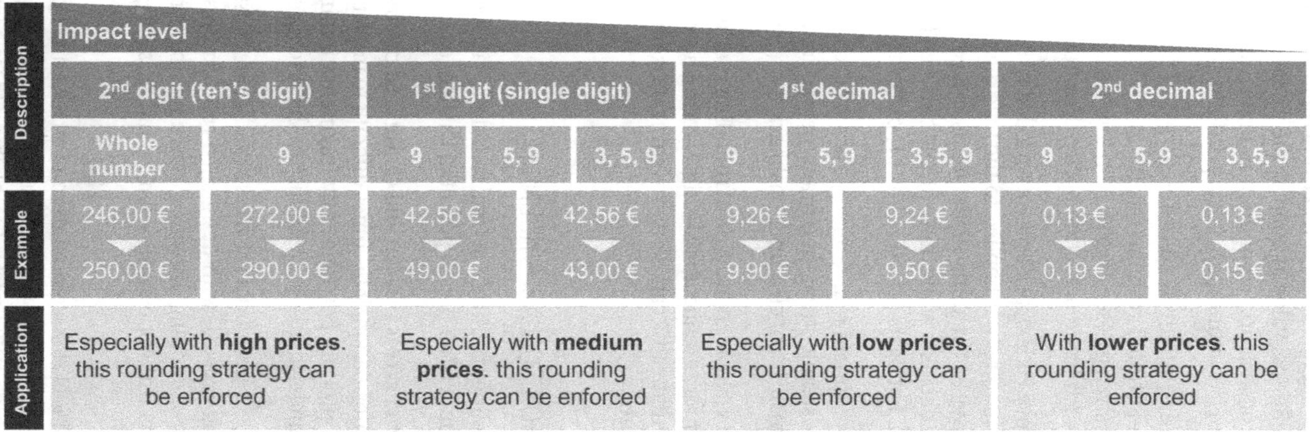

Impact level	2nd digit (ten's digit)		1st digit (single digit)			1st decimal			2nd decimal		
Description	Whole number	9	9	5, 9	3, 5, 9	9	5, 9	3, 5, 9	9	5, 9	3, 5, 9
Example	246,00 € → 250,00 €	272,00 € → 290,00 €	42,56 € → 49,00 €		42,56 € → 43,00 €	9,26 € → 9,90 €		9,24 € → 9,50 €	0,13 € → 0,19 €		0,13 € → 0,15 €
Application	Especially with **high prices.** this rounding strategy can be enforced		Especially with **medium prices.** this rounding strategy can be enforced			Especially with **low prices.** this rounding strategy can be enforced			With **lower prices.** this rounding strategy can be enforced		

APPLYING THE CONCEPT: A CASE STUDY

Implementing rounding routines often delivers rapid financial impact, as companies begin capturing additional value as soon as the updated prices go live. This was the case for a leading construction equipment manufacturer, which applied structured rounding logic across its entire spare parts portfolio and saw immediate results.

By tailoring rounding methods to different price tiers, the company generated over €850,000 in additional revenue—without changing the physical products or the overall pricing strategy (see Figure 6.2). The success came from introducing a differentiated approach based on defined price thresholds.

For parts priced above €6,500, prices were rounded to the nearest hundred. Between €700 and €6,500, rounding was applied to the tens digit. For parts between €80 and €700, rounding targeted the units place. Items priced between €10 and €80 were rounded at the first decimal, while those priced between €1 and €10 were adjusted at the second decimal. For parts priced below €1, prices remained unchanged.

By applying the appropriate rounding logic across each price band, companies can enhance price consistency, strengthen brand perception, and generate incremental revenue with minimal risk of customer pushback.

This structured and scalable application of rounding routines proved to be an efficient and low-effort lever for revenue uplift—highlighting how even small changes, when implemented systematically, can deliver significant gains across large and diverse spare parts catalogues.

REQUIREMENTS FOR SCALABLE ROUNDING

To apply price rounding effectively, several foundational elements need to be in place, along with a clear understanding of potential challenges.

First, companies need access to clean and centralized pricing data. Without accurate and consolidated information, it becomes difficult to implement rounding rules consistently across the product portfolio. Any fragmentation in price management can lead to errors and undermine the credibility of the pricing structure.

A strong governance framework is also essential. There must be clearly defined ownership of the pricing process, with designated roles and responsibilities to manage, approve, and oversee rounding decisions. When pricing is managed across multiple functions or regions without coordination, rounding strategies may become inconsistent or diluted.

Another prerequisite is the segmentation of price bands or thresholds. Rounding is most effective when it follows a structured approach, applying different routines to low-, mid-, and high-value parts. Establishing these segments in advance allows

Figure 6.2

Realization of 850+ k€ additional revenues by applying price rounding differentiated by price threshold

Price Thresholds	Rounding Logic	Example		Price Increase
> 6.500 €	3rd digit (hundred) to 3, 5, 7, 9	6.720 €	6.900 €	Ø +1.2%
>700 €	2nd digit (tens) to 3, 5, 7, 9	789 €	790 €	Ø +1.0%
> 80 €	1st digit (single) to 3, 5, 7, 9	87.73 €	89.00 €	Ø +0.9%
>10 €	1st decimal to 3, 5, 7, 9	15.76 €	15.90 €	Ø +1.1%
>1 €	2nd decimal to 3, 5, 7, 9	3.77 €	3.79 €	Ø +0.6%
>0 €	Keep status quo	0.39 €	0.39 €	Ø +0.0%
Total additional revenues				**850+ k€**

pricing teams to apply the most appropriate rounding rules and better align them with customer expectations.

The technical ability to automate rounding is equally important. Attempting to apply rounding logic manually across thousands of SKUs is inefficient and prone to mistakes. Companies need ERP systems or pricing tools that can execute rule-based rounding and apply logic across product categories and price levels with minimal effort.

Equally critical is commercial alignment. Sales, marketing, and other customer-facing functions need to understand the purpose of rounding and support the strategy. Without this buy-in, well-intended pricing changes can face resistance, leading to miscommunication or mistrust within the organization and with customers.

CHALLENGES TO WATCH FOR

Despite these prerequisites, several challenges can arise during implementation. One common issue is customer sensitivity, especially at lower price points. Even small increases can provoke negative reactions if they cross psychological thresholds or lead to comparisons with competitors' prices.

Another challenge is maintaining price credibility. If rounding appears inconsistent or arbitrary, it can damage the brand's price image. Customers expect logical, coherent pricing, and unexpected jumps—however small—can erode trust.

Operational complexity is another concern. Differentiated rounding by product use, region, or customer segment can result in multiple price entries or even additional part numbers. This can create inventory and data maintenance issues if not carefully managed.

There's also the risk of over-rounding. If rounding rules are too aggressive or lack proper controls, prices may exceed customer expectations and reduce competitiveness. This is particularly risky in highly competitive markets or when parts are easily comparable across providers.

Lastly, without proper testing or simulation, it's difficult to predict how rounding changes will impact revenue, volume, and customer behavior. A lack of data-driven insight can lead to decisions that look good in theory but underperform in practice.

By preparing for these requirements and anticipating the associated risks, companies can turn rounding from a tactical adjustment into a reliable and scalable pricing lever.

SUMMARY

Rounding routines can be a strong quick-win lever in spare parts pricing. Often overlooked, smart rounding can significantly enhance revenue and profit by aligning prices with psychological thresholds and perceived value—without affecting customer demand.

By applying different rounding methods based on price tiers—from adjusting decimals in low-priced items to rounding whole digits in high-value parts—companies can monetize willingness to pay while improving price clarity and consistency.

To implement rounding effectively, companies must have clean pricing data, clear governance, segmented price bands, the right tools for automation, and internal alignment across commercial functions. Challenges such as customer sensitivity, perceived inconsistency, operational complexity, and the risk of over-rounding must be carefully managed.

When applied with discipline and precision, rounding routines deliver measurable financial impact with minimal disruption—making them a practical, high-ROI component of any aftermarket pricing strategy.

Rounding is more than clean-up—it's conversion optimization for B2B. When scaled with discipline, it becomes one of the fastest, least disruptive ways to lift spare parts profitability.

7

Outlier Elimination

In the complex and data-heavy world of spare parts pricing, the volume of items can overwhelm even the most experienced pricing teams. While structured strategies like rounding and hierarchical pricing capture systemic value, a significant opportunity often lies hidden in plain sight: eliminating pricing outliers.

Outlier elimination is one of the most effective and least disruptive ways to drive immediate revenue and margin gains—simply a great quick win. It targets pricing inconsistencies—parts that deviate significantly from predicted or comparable values—without changing product features or risking customer dissatisfaction. When properly implemented, this method delivers clean, justifiable price adjustments that align with internal logic and market expectations.

THE CONCEPT OF OUTLIER ELIMINATION

Given the breadth of spare parts in most catalogues, even the best pricing teams cannot manually detect every inconsistency. Outlier detection uses logic and automation to pinpoint where prices fall out of sync with technical attributes, comparable parts, or predictive models—highlighting profit gaps that would otherwise go unnoticed.

Let's consider the example illustrated in Figure 7.1: a part family with five components. Based on a predicted price derived from internal specs (like weight, diameter, or material) or external market benchmarks, four of the five parts—A, B, D, and E—align well with the pricing model. But part C is priced far below its predicted value: €31.99 instead of €51.12.

This €19.13 gap represents pure profit waiting to be captured. No additional cost, no engineering change, no customer backlash—just a missed opportunity.

In practice, this scenario is not rare. In a global pricing optimization project with a leading automotive OEM, hundreds of such pricing outliers were identified—hidden within a catalogue of several hundred thousand SKUs. Once corrected, the result was over €750,000 in additional revenue within weeks, with minimal volume impact and no measurable customer dissatisfaction.

Why? Because the new prices simply brought the parts in line with logic and expectations—restoring internal price consistency and perceived fairness.

DOI: 10.4324/9781003647416-9

MONETIZING WILLINGNESS TO PAY THROUGH OUTLIER ELIMINATION

Outlier elimination is not just about correcting mistakes—it is about monetizing untapped value in a way that customers often accept without hesitation. It aligns pricing with what feels logical, removing pricing noise and reinforcing price credibility.

Every customer group, whether dealers or end users, has a built-in expectation of what constitutes a reasonable price for a spare part. These expectations are typically formed by experience, market comparisons, and the relationship between price and technical value. When a price significantly deviates from this expected range—particularly on the low end—it often represents an untapped opportunity to increase revenue and profit without compromising sales volume or customer satisfaction.

To successfully capitalize on these opportunities, companies must first establish a baseline or reference price for each spare part. This can be achieved through predictive pricing models that analyze internal attributes such as weight, material, and production complexity, as well as external signals like competitor pricing or industry benchmarks. Once the predicted price is defined, it becomes possible to assess how far each actual list price deviates from this reference.

The next step is identifying and grouping comparable parts into logical families. These families can be based on similar technical features, application types, or usage contexts. Within each group, prices should follow a consistent logic—parts that serve similar functions and have similar costs should be priced in a similar range. When one part stands out significantly—either below or above the group—it becomes a candidate for closer review.

A systematic approach to identifying pricing outliers involves setting thresholds that determine what qualifies as a deviation. For example, if a part is priced more than 20% below its predicted value, it might be flagged for correction. However, even smaller discrepancies can be worth addressing when applied across a large volume of transactions.

Clean and reliable data is essential for this process. If product attributes are incomplete or outdated, or if pricing history is inconsistent, the system might either miss real outliers or produce false positives. Therefore, maintaining high data quality and a consistent pricing logic is foundational.

What truly unlocks the power of outlier elimination is automation. With modern pricing tools and software, companies can scan their entire catalogue of parts in seconds, identify deviations, and simulate pricing corrections across thousands of items. This scalability makes the approach particularly effective for organizations managing large and complex spare parts portfolios.

Equally important is internal alignment. Sales teams, product managers, and pricing functions must all be on the same page about the purpose of the initiative. Outlier correction is not a random price increase—it is a correction of legacy inconsistencies, bringing prices back in line with logic and expectations. When this alignment

Figure 7.1

Pricing consistency assessment identifies deviations within similar products, eliminating outliers

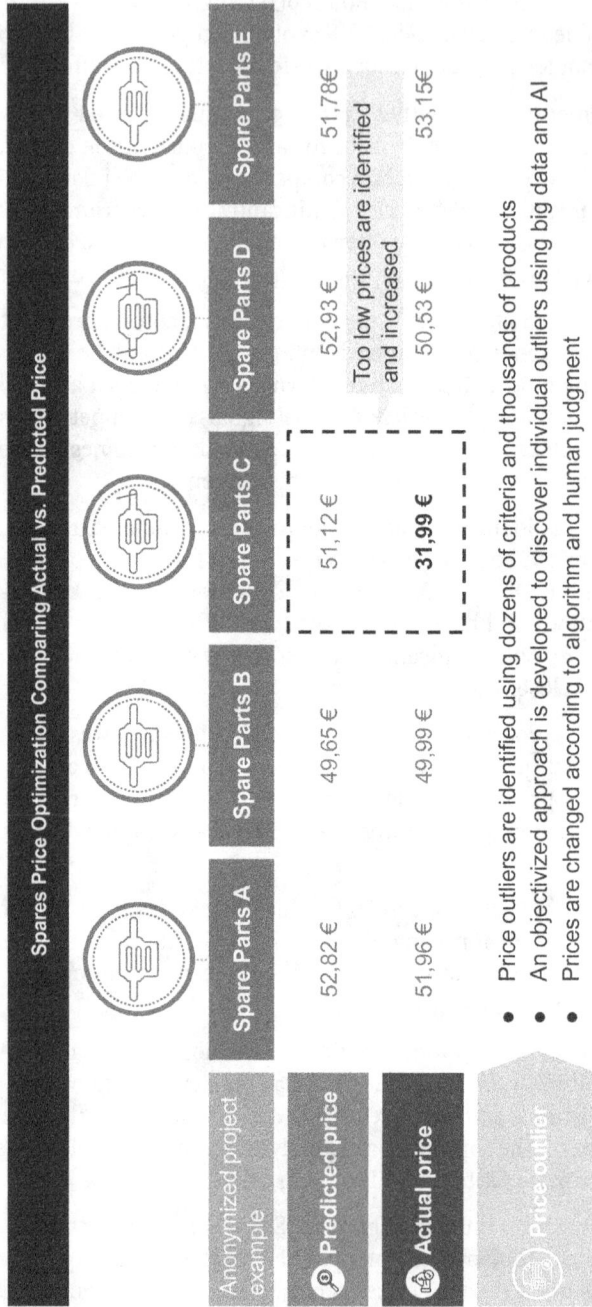

Spares Price Optimization Comparing Actual vs. Predicted Price

Anonymized project example	Spare Parts A	Spare Parts B	Spare Parts C	Spare Parts D	Spare Parts E
Predicted price	52,82 €	49,65 €	51,12 €	52,93 €	51,78€
Actual price	51,96 €	49,99 €	**31,99 €**	50,53 €	53,15€

Too low prices are identified and increased

- Price outliers are identified using dozens of criteria and thousands of products
- An objectivized approach is developed to discover individual outliers using big data and AI
- Prices are changed according to algorithm and human judgment

Price outlier

is achieved, the organization can act quickly and decisively, correcting hundreds or even thousands of outliers with confidence.

The impact is immediate. Adjusting underpriced items to their predicted or fair value allows the company to capture revenue that would otherwise be lost. Since these corrections are often below psychological price thresholds and still within a competitive range, customer pushback is rare. In most cases, the price change is seen as justified—especially when it brings similar parts into a consistent price band.

By applying this approach across the catalogue, companies are able to systematically monetize willingness to pay. The results often show up quickly in the bottom line, with revenue uplifts that translate directly into profit, as costs remain unchanged and volume effects are negligible. In this way, outlier elimination becomes one of the most direct and effective methods of value capture in spare parts pricing.

APPLYING THE CONCEPT: A CASE STUDY

A leading global manufacturer in the logistics and material-handling equipment industry provides a strong reference case. With over 110,000 SKUs sold in just three years and more than 1 million active list prices, manual price reviews were impossible. Despite decades of experience, price inconsistencies slipped through.

By implementing a centralized pricing software connected to multiple data sources—item specs, cost history, sales data, and competitor benchmarks—the company systematically surfaced outliers. These included parts that were priced well below their technical or competitive peers, often due to legacy errors, uncoordinated updates, or overlooked attributes.

In one instance, a seemingly minor bracket was priced at €8.90—while similar brackets in the same family were consistently selling for €19–22. Adjusting the price not only aligned it with logic but also avoided raising any customer complaints.

Over a short period, hundreds of similar corrections were implemented, yielding an uplift of over €550,000—virtually all of it incremental profit. The updated pricing logic was then embedded into a recurring governance process to catch future outliers before they reached the market.

SUMMARY

Outlier elimination is a high-impact, low-risk pricing quick win. It requires no changes to the product or commercial policy—only the willingness to bring discipline and data to bear on price consistency.

By combining data, automation, and internal alignment, companies can correct undervalued parts, reinforce internal logic, and capture margin—all without triggering customer pushback or volume loss.

While other pricing tactics focus on strategy, segmentation, or brand positioning, outlier elimination is a practical housekeeping lever—yet one that can yield six-figure gains in weeks, making it a must-have in any aftermarket pricing playbook.

When scaled across large portfolios, this simple practice becomes one of the most direct and cost-effective tools in the pricing arsenal.

8

Low-Margin Optimization

In the realm of spare parts pricing, it's tempting to focus attention on the big-ticket items or the highest-selling SKUs. But hiding beneath the surface of every aftermarket portfolio lies a category of parts that quietly drain profitability—low-margin products that haven't seen a pricing update in years. These parts often slip through the cracks of traditional pricing strategies and, as a result, accumulate across the catalog, slowly eroding overall performance.

Yet, not all low-margin parts are lost causes. In fact, when combined with a second dimension—price sensitivity—many of them emerge as prime candidates for improvement. Specifically, parts that have both low margins and low price elasticity present one of the most compelling pricing opportunities. These are the quiet achievers of pricing quick wins: items whose prices can be increased without jeopardizing sales volumes or customer relationships.

This chapter explores how spare parts with low margins and low elasticity can be strategically identified, repriced, and transformed into margin boosters with minimal disruption and high returns.

THE CONCEPT OF LOW-MARGIN OPTIMIZATION

The power of this approach lies in the intersection of two pricing truths: first, that some parts are chronically underpriced; second, that many of these parts can absorb increases without triggering customer pushback. Combining these two insights creates a powerful targeting mechanism for quick and measurable margin uplift.

At the core of this quick win is a simple yet powerful insight: a part that generates low margins but is also insensitive to price changes is a missed opportunity waiting to be captured. When companies analyze spare parts using only one dimension—such as margin—they often overlook important behavioral dynamics. But when margin analysis is layered with a second lens—price elasticity—it becomes possible to identify specific parts that are both underpriced and underappreciated.

Imagine plotting all spare parts across two axes: one for margin, the other for elasticity. The quadrant where low-margin meets low-elasticity is where the greatest untapped potential resides. These parts are priced too low to generate meaningful profit but do not trigger resistance or volume loss when prices rise. In other words,

DOI: 10.4324/9781003647416-10

they represent "safe bets" for price increases. This applies to spare parts of Group 1 in Figure 8.1.

This opportunity emerges frequently in large spare parts catalogs, especially when legacy pricing methods—such as flat mark-ups or cost-plus models—have persisted over time. Items like washers, pins, clips, gaskets, filters, or hardware brackets are often essential to machine function, relatively inexpensive, and purchased regularly by customers who value speed and availability over price scrutiny. Because of their small ticket size and routine nature, they rarely raise pricing objections, making them ideal candidates for optimization.

MONETIZING WILLINGNESS TO PAY WITH LOW-MARGIN OPTIMIZATION

Low-margin optimization works not by being aggressive, but by being precise. Small price changes on stable parts compound quickly—and when aligned with customer behavior, they go largely unnoticed while improving the bottom line.

The beauty of this approach lies in its simplicity. By slightly increasing prices on low-margin, low-sensitivity parts, companies can dramatically improve margin performance—without touching product design, changing service levels, or risking customer loyalty. But to do this effectively, it's necessary to follow a structured process anchored in data and logic.

It begins with a detailed margin analysis, isolating parts that consistently deliver poor profitability. This step alone often reveals dozens or even hundreds of parts priced with minimal or even negative margins, especially in catalogs that span multiple regions, currencies, or cost structures.

Next, the elasticity of these parts must be evaluated. This can be done using a combination of indicators such as historical price-volume behavior, frequency of purchase, customer complaint data, and market comparability. Parts that maintain stable sales volumes over time, are rarely questioned by customers, or have few direct substitutes are typically price-inelastic. These are the parts where price changes will go largely unnoticed—yet deliver real gains.

Once these candidates are identified, the pricing team can define new target prices that lift profitability while remaining within psychological thresholds. A filter priced at €1.20 that sells 50,000 units a year might be repriced at €1.50—a 25% increase in margin with no effect on volume. When multiplied across similar parts, this can result in hundreds of thousands of euros in additional profit per year.

Importantly, the process should not be positioned internally as a random price hike. Instead, it should be framed as a structured correction of underperforming pricing, based on data, fairness, and alignment with market value. When communicated properly, these changes are easily justified both inside and outside the organization.

APPLYING THE CONCEPT: A CASE STUDY

A global manufacturer of agricultural machinery—let's call it AgriMax—faced a familiar challenge in its aftermarket business. While its flagship tractors and harvesters were known for durability and performance, the company's spare parts division had not kept pace with modern pricing practices. A recent audit revealed that more than 15,000 active parts were contributing minimal or even negative margins. Many of these items were priced using outdated cost-plus logic, with little consideration for customer behavior or demand patterns.

The pricing team at AgriMax decided to dig deeper. By analyzing three years of transactional data, they discovered a subset of parts that consistently showed high and stable volumes despite repeated price updates—or, in some cases, despite no changes at all. These were maintenance-critical components: gaskets, couplers, nozzles, and fasteners. Despite their low price points, they were indispensable to customers and ordered regularly, often bundled with larger service jobs.

What made these parts stand out wasn't just their low profitability—but the fact that demand for them remained unaffected by past price changes. The data showed that even when similar parts had seen price increases of 10%–15%, order volumes held steady, and customer behavior remained unchanged. This was a clear sign of low price elasticity.

With this insight, AgriMax launched a low-margin optimization initiative. First, they identified all parts with margins below a defined internal threshold and flagged those with stable volume trends. Then, using a combination of cost data, competitive intelligence, and transactional insights, they created a revised pricing logic that applied moderate but targeted price increases.

For example, a hydraulic hose coupling that was previously priced at €3.80 with a slim 0.8% margin was repriced at €4.99. A set of sealing rings, sold in packs of ten at €1.05 per unit, was moved to €1.49 per unit. These new prices remained well below psychological or competitive thresholds, yet the margin impact was substantial. Because the parts were frequently bundled into repair kits or service packages, the price change blended into the total cost with little resistance.

Over the course of six months, AgriMax rolled out these adjustments across a catalog of 1.200 low-margin, low-elasticity SKUs. The result was a significant increase in profitability: gross margin for this product cluster rose by 5.6%, generating a net gain of over €1.2 million annually—with no detectable decline in sales volumes or customer satisfaction.

Just as importantly, the initiative gained full buy-in from commercial and product teams. Because the changes were supported by clear data, aligned with customer behavior, and did not disrupt service operations, the rollout was fast, disciplined, and repeatable. AgriMax has since incorporated this logic into its ongoing pricing governance model, using it as a recurring tool to identify and correct low-margin leakage before it impacts financial performance.

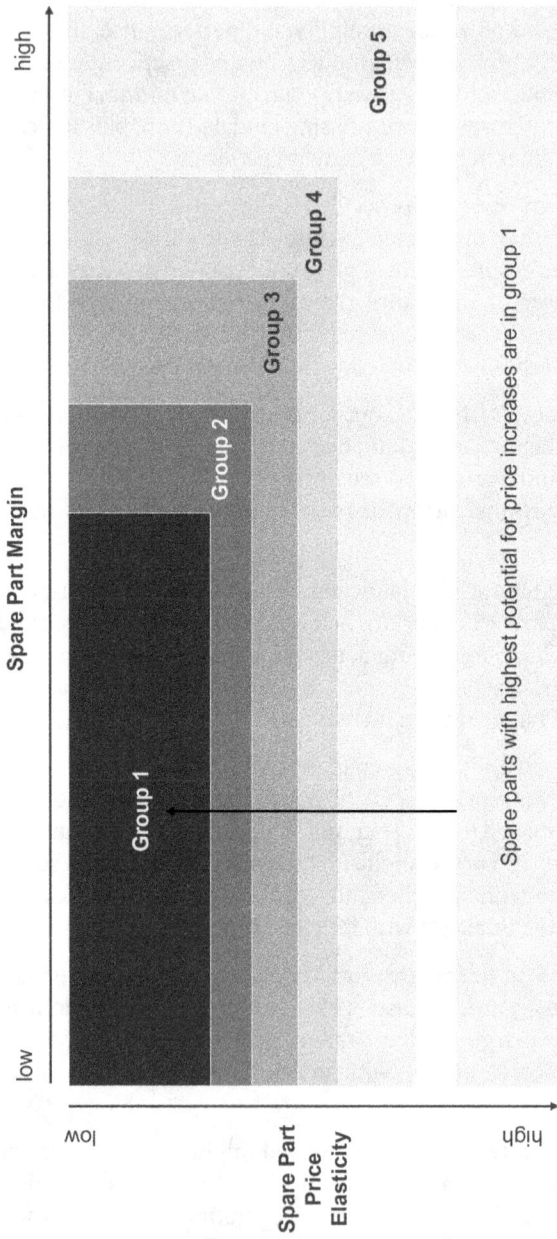

Figure 8.1

Low-margin optimization: Spare parts with a low margin and low price sensitivity have optimization potential

This case demonstrates that low-margin optimization isn't about aggressive pricing—it's about precision. It's about identifying which parts customers truly depend on, understanding their behavior, and aligning pricing to reflect the value delivered, all while preserving trust and continuity in the aftermarket experience.

SUMMARY

Low-margin optimization is a straightforward yet powerful pricing quick win. It doesn't require a change in product or channel strategy, nor does it rely on complex algorithms or lengthy negotiations. What it does require is visibility: visibility into margin contribution, elasticity signals, and internal alignment across teams.

When approached methodically, this strategy turns low-performing parts into high-return pricing actions. By targeting parts with low margins and low sensitivity, companies can execute clean, justifiable price increases that generate immediate profit—without risking volume, damaging customer relationships, or creating pricing inconsistencies.

Among all quick wins in spare parts pricing, low-margin optimization is perhaps the most quietly effective. It flies under the radar but hits directly at the bottom line—proving that even the smallest parts, when priced correctly, can drive some of the biggest gains.

9

Tail Pricing

In spare parts pricing, focus naturally gravitates toward the most visible and frequently sold items. These "short-tail" products dominate conversations, reports, and strategies because they are the ones that customers recognize, challenge, and compare. But while these high-profile parts shape the price image of a company, they often represent only a fraction of the total spare parts universe.

Beyond the short tail lies the long tail: an expansive collection of slow-moving, low-visibility items that together make up the bulk of the SKU count—and often hold significant untapped pricing potential. While the short tail demands surgical precision and competitive awareness, the long tail invites a different approach: automation, smart logic, and value-based increases that won't disrupt customer perception or loyalty.

Companies can systematically optimize pricing across the full tail of their spare parts catalog, using differentiated strategies for visibility-driven short-tail parts, margin-leaking long-tail parts, and a third critical area—profit pricing—where structural actions are required to ensure baseline profitability.

THE CONCEPT OF SHORT- VS. LONG-TAIL PRICING

Spare parts portfolios typically follow a power law distribution: a small percentage of parts generate the majority of sales volume and revenue, while a large majority of parts sell infrequently and contribute marginally to topline figures. This creates three distinct zones within the pricing strategy landscape (see Figure 9.1).

The short tail includes fast-moving, high-visibility items—those that distributors and end customers know by heart. These parts are purchased repeatedly and often compared against competitors. Because of their visibility, they heavily influence the perceived fairness and overall price image of the company. Overpricing these parts can lead to immediate backlash—whether in the form of reduced orders, negotiation pressure, or brand damage.

Therefore, these parts must be priced competitively and with caution, often using advanced competitive benchmarks and elasticity models to find the sweet spot between value capture and customer satisfaction.

DOI: 10.4324/9781003647416-11

By contrast, the long tail consists of slow-moving items, rarely purchased and usually only as part of a very specific maintenance or repair event. Customers typically lack price awareness here, and comparison across brands is infrequent or even impossible. This gives pricing teams more freedom. In theory, prices for these parts could be doubled or tripled without raising concern. However, there's a hidden danger: if the accumulation of long-tail price hikes leads to a significantly higher total cost of ownership over time, it may discourage customers from reinvesting in the next machine or vehicle model.

The effect is subtle but damaging—a reduced repurchase rate due to inflated maintenance costs. This is why price increases in the long tail should still be guided, not random. Smart algorithms, value thresholds, and upper caps can allow companies to lift margins while preserving long-term customer relationships.

The third zone is what we refer to as the profit pricing segment. This is not defined by volume or visibility, but by margin leakage. It includes parts that are priced so low that they generate little to no profit—or worse, create losses. These items require immediate correction. This could involve a price increase to meet a defined minimum margin threshold, or structural changes such as introducing minimum order quantities, charging low-order surcharges, or even delisting parts with chronically negative margins. The aim here is to stop profit erosion and bring discipline to the lower end of the catalog.

Each of these zones—short tail, long tail, and profit pricing—requires a tailored strategy. A one-size-fits-all pricing method risks either overexposing the brand or leaving massive value on the table.

MONETIZING WILLINGNESS TO PAY WITH DIFFERENTIATED TAIL STRATEGIES

Short-tail pricing is about perceived fairness. Long-tail pricing is about contextual urgency. Profit pricing is about internal logic. Understanding these mental models is key to unlocking value without introducing risk.

Willingness to pay manifests differently across the short and long tail of a spare parts catalog. In the short tail, customers are conscious of price. Their willingness to pay is defined not just by the part's value, but also by market comparisons, price history, and relationship dynamics. It must be monetized carefully—by optimizing psychological thresholds, aligning to competitors, and leveraging purchase data to test tolerance.

In the long tail, willingness to pay is more abstract—less about competitive pressure and more about availability, urgency, and value-in-use. A customer may happily pay three times the baseline price for a niche electronic sensor simply because it's needed to get a critical asset back online. In this context, price becomes secondary to availability and reliability. That's where companies can capture hidden value—by pricing for importance, not just cost or volume.

The profit pricing zone is less about willingness to pay and more about internal pricing hygiene. In this category, monetization comes from eliminating waste, enforcing discipline, and ensuring that no part erodes margin through neglect or outdated pricing logic.

Together, these three zones form a complete pricing model for spare parts catalogs that embraces complexity without becoming chaotic—and allows companies to extract value proportionally across their full portfolio.

APPLYING THE CONCEPT: A CASE STUDY

A compelling example comes from a global manufacturer of professional cleaning systems, which we'll refer to as CleanTech Solutions. With a portfolio of over 80,000 spare parts across floor scrubbers, industrial vacuums, and autonomous cleaning robots, CleanTech was struggling to balance pricing rigor across such a vast assortment.

Historically, the pricing team focused almost exclusively on the top 5% of parts by volume—belts, brushes, filters, and wheels. These fast movers were priced competitively, carefully benchmarked against peers, and regularly reviewed. However, the remaining 95% of the catalog received little attention. Pricing for these items had remained largely unchanged for years, resulting in inconsistent margins and missed opportunities.

A portfolio-wide pricing scan revealed three clear issues. First, short-tail parts were priced too defensively, leaving value untapped. Second, long-tail parts included thousands of low-visibility SKUs priced below logical thresholds—even though customers showed no price sensitivity. And third, nearly 8% of parts were sold below cost, creating negative margins that added up to a six-figure annual loss.

To address these issues, CleanTech implemented a three-zone pricing strategy.

In the short tail, prices were optimized using elasticity indicators and competitor benchmarks, bringing select increases to parts with higher perceived value while maintaining market alignment. For the long tail, the team introduced smart guardrails: parts were grouped by function and importance, and prices were gradually increased using a tiered logic that included caps to avoid runaway pricing. In the profit pricing zone, minimum margins were enforced systematically. Where price increases alone wouldn't suffice, minimum order quantities and surcharges were applied, and in a few cases, parts were discontinued entirely.

The results were significant. Short-tail optimization led to a 2.4% uplift in contribution margin, while the long-tail pricing initiative generated an additional €900,000 in annual profit—without a single recorded customer complaint. The profit pricing actions alone stopped €450,000 in yearly margin leakage. But beyond the numbers, CleanTech also achieved something less tangible but equally powerful: pricing clarity

Figure 9.1

Differentiating pricing for various segments in the spare parts portfolio

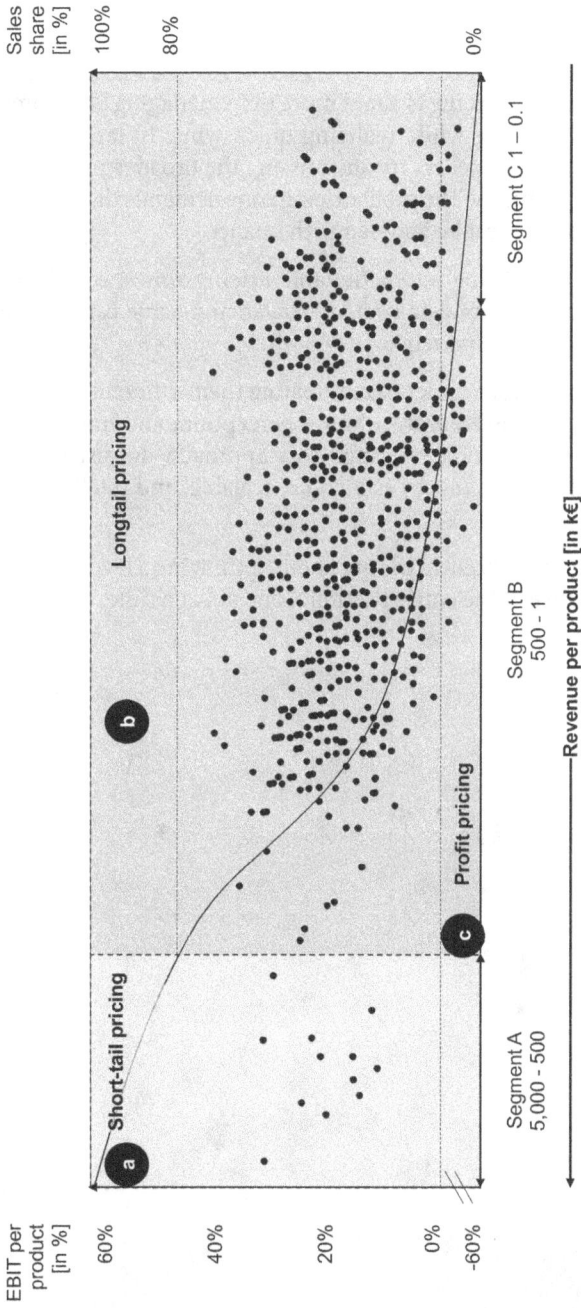

across the portfolio. Each part now had a clear logic, a defined margin corridor, and a strategy behind it.

SUMMARY

Short- vs. long-tail pricing is about more than managing SKU complexity—it's about pricing with purpose while realizing quick wins. In large spare parts portfolios, focusing only on top sellers means missing the broader picture. The long tail offers volume of opportunity. The profit pricing zone demands discipline. And the short tail, while influential, must be handled with nuance.

By splitting the catalog into actionable pricing zones, companies can move from reactive pricing to strategic control—balancing value capture with brand consistency and customer experience.

By recognizing these segments and treating them differently, companies can balance customer expectations, protect brand perception, and unlock hidden profit across their entire aftermarket offering. This approach doesn't just maximize pricing potential—it builds a more sustainable, scalable, and intelligent pricing system for the future.

In the end, pricing excellence is not about optimizing a few parts—it's about elevating the performance of the entire portfolio, one tail at a time.

10

Lifecycle Pricing

Spare parts don't just support machines—they follow them across decades of use, service, and reinvention. Lifecycle pricing is about aligning price logic with the age, ownership phase, and strategic value of the product as it matures. It's not just about cost and competition—it's about timing, retention, and brand loyalty.

Pricing can shift over time to match the evolving context of the product and the customer. From warranty periods to old-timer collectability, pricing should flex with purpose—not remain fixed across decades.

THE CONCEPT OF LIFECYCLE PRICING

Lifecycle pricing means tailoring spare parts prices to where the product is in its lifecycle—from launch and ramp-up to maturity, phase-out, and heritage. This approach recognizes that the same part can play a very different role—and justify a different price—depending on whether it's in a warranty context or supporting a 25-year-old legacy machine.

Consider the example of a vehicle. In the early stages of its life, while still under warranty, price increases for covered parts should be avoided. The reason is simple: during warranty repairs, OEMs reimburse dealers a percentage of the list price. A higher list price, in this case, directly increases the OEM's internal cost without adding margin. It's value leakage—not capture.

In contrast, for parts not covered by warranty in the same early lifecycle phase, there is an opportunity to charge higher prices. At this point, the vehicle is still new, and the owner is usually loyal to the OEM's service network. The perceived value is high. However, this pricing window must be handled carefully. Pushing prices too far may accelerate customer defection to independent channels or lead to early dissatisfaction.

As the vehicle ages and production ends, the situation shifts. This "end-of-production" phase, often referred to as the decennial phase, brings new challenges (see Figure 10.1). Customer loyalty starts to erode, and price sensitivity increases. Here, retention becomes the top priority. Owners will compare OEM parts with lower-cost alternatives from independent providers. Pricing must adapt. The goal is no longer maximizing margin—but maintaining relevance. Competitive pricing helps retain

DOI: 10.4324/9781003647416-12

Figure 10.1

Pricing strategy differentiated for warranty, decennial, and heritage parts

Part category	Strategy	Benefits
Warranty Part *Example:* *electronic control unit* 	• **Keep** the margin relatively low during the warranty period • **Increase** it when the warranty period is over	• Contained warranty expenses • Reduced taxes and duties • Reduced handling costs
Decennial Part *Example:* hood cover 	• **Adapt** prices for parts of vehicles that went out of production 10-25 years ago • Avoid loosing sales to independent workshops	• Higher revenues & profits with typically disloyal clients • Traffic generation at dealers
Heritage Part *Example:* Shock absorber 	• **Increase** prices for classic parts of vehicles that went out of production 25+ years ago • **Capture** willingness to pay: with the increasing value of the car the part price increases as well	• Higher revenues and profits through genuine parts • Traffic generation at dealers

service traffic in authorized garages and avoids losing customers to the independent aftermarket.

Eventually, the vehicle reaches a new stage: heritage. Typically beginning around 20 years after the start of production (though this varies by brand and region), the vehicle becomes a classic. Parts take on new meaning. They are no longer just functional—they are authentic, original, and emotionally valuable. Owners care about originality and preserving the legacy of their vehicle. As a result, genuine parts can command a premium again. Scarcity and brand identity justify a new price tier, one that celebrates—not discounts—the passage of time.

MONETIZING WILLINGNESS TO PAY OVER TIME

Lifecycle pricing allows companies to unlock willingness to pay at the right moment. Early in the vehicle's life, when trust is high and performance is paramount, customers are ready to pay more for parts—especially those not covered by warranty. In the post-warranty phase, pricing must balance value capture with retention risk. If prices are too aggressive, customers will begin shifting to third-party providers.

During the end-of-production phase, owners are often less loyal and more price-sensitive. This is when strategic reductions on key SKUs help keep service revenue flowing. It's less about unit margin and more about customer lifetime value. Finally, in the heritage phase, emotional value takes precedence. Prices can rise again—gently but deliberately—to reflect the uniqueness of original parts and the status of the vehicle as a collector's item (see Figure 10.2).

Lifecycle pricing is not static. It's dynamic pricing in sync with the evolution of ownership, usage, and identity.

APPLYING THE CONCEPT: A CASE STUDY

A mid-sized premium US-based OEM offers a clear example of this strategy in action. The company had an SUV that ended production in 2008. From 2005 to 2008, during its warranty period, the OEM kept list prices stable. This helped avoid higher internal reimbursement costs.

After the warranty phase, from 2009 to 2015, the OEM selectively increased prices on high-demand, non-warranty parts by up to 15%. Customers were still loyal, and early lifecycle engagement was strong.

Between 2016 and 2022, the landscape changed. Competitive pressure increased. Independent garages offered cheaper alternatives. To protect market share, the OEM adjusted prices downward for key fast-moving parts, especially those exposed to competitive benchmarks. This helped retain customers and prevented service volume from collapsing.

Figure 10.2

Pricing strategy along the spare parts lifecycle

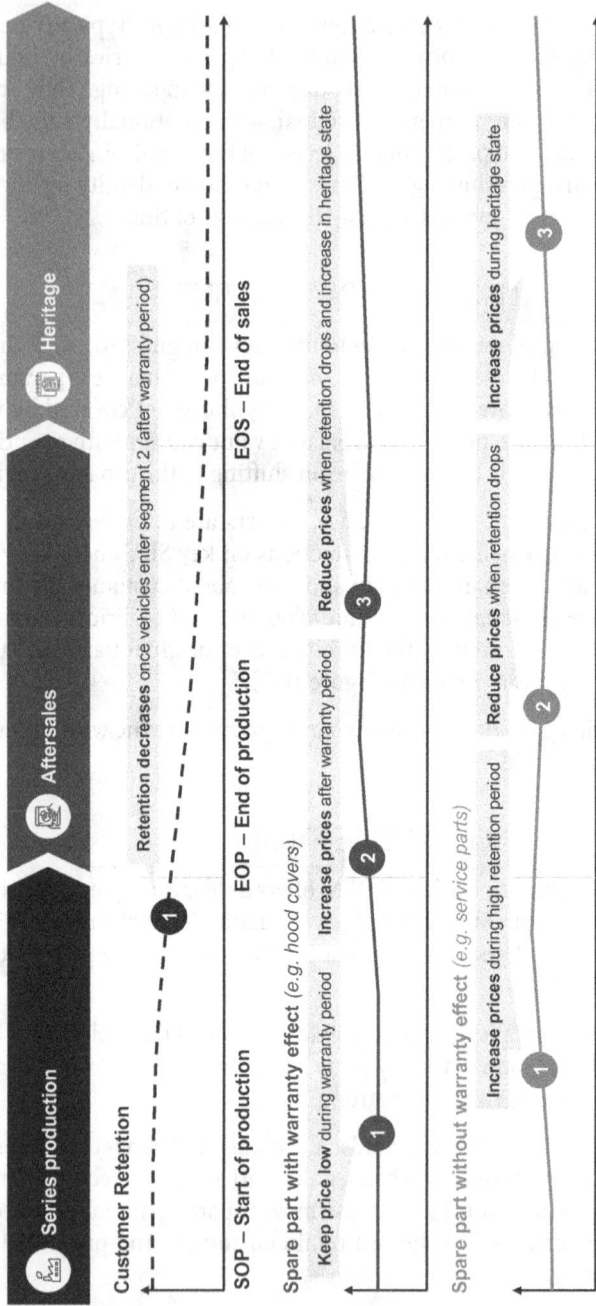

By 2023, the SUV had gained status as a future classic. Owners were proud of their vehicles and eager to preserve them. The OEM shifted gears again. Prices for original trim pieces, emblems, and rare components were adjusted upward to reflect their collectable value. These increases were well-accepted, as owners perceived the parts not just as functional items but as restorers of originality.

This strategy, applied over time, aligned price with purpose—maximizing profit when possible, maintaining retention when needed, and monetizing legacy when it mattered most.

SUMMARY

Lifecycle pricing transforms time into a pricing lever.

When pricing aligns with lifecycle stages, it turns age into advantage—lowering costs, protecting loyalty, and celebrating legacy.

When pricing adapts to the maturity stage of the product, it can reduce internal costs during warranty, boost margins in early non-warranty phases, protect retention at end-of-production, and reclaim premium positioning in the heritage phase.

There is no single "correct" price for a spare part. There is only the right price for this moment in its life. Lifecycle pricing recognizes this—and turns it into a quiet but powerful lever for sustainable aftermarket value.

11

Market Intelligence

Spare parts pricing does not exist in a vacuum. No matter how optimized your internal logic may be—a number of customers will always compare prices externally. That's why understanding your competitive position isn't optional. It's essential.

Market intelligence via price benchmarking transforms competitor insights into strategic pricing action. By identifying where your prices stand relative to the market, you can uncover margin opportunities, flag pricing risks, and defend your price positioning with data.

Done right, benchmarking isn't about following competitors blindly—it's about using the external landscape to sharpen your internal pricing power and realize quick wins.

THE CONCEPT OF MARKET INTELLIGENCE

Market intelligence refers to the systematic comparison of your spare parts prices with those of external reference points—typically direct competitors or original equipment suppliers (OES). The goal is simple: to detect and act on pricing gaps.

There are multiple ways to structure this comparison. In some cases, benchmarking focuses on direct competitors—companies that sell similar products or operate in the same customer segment. In others, the comparison is between genuine OEM parts and functionally equivalent parts produced by the same supplier (OES) and sold independently under a different label.

In both cases, the analysis is meant to reveal pricing opportunities and guardrails.

For example, when benchmarking against higher-positioned brands, your spare parts should rarely be priced higher—unless justified by a significant product advantage or service inclusion. If your part is technically comparable or inferior, yet priced above a better-known premium competitor, there's a mismatch—and likely a volume or perception issue.

Conversely, when benchmarking against OES alternatives, genuine OEM parts can—and often should—be priced at a premium. Take Mercedes-Benz's AMG carbon fiber brake discs, which are priced above the equivalent Brembo units supplied to the

DOI: 10.4324/9781003647416-13

independent aftermarket. The higher price reflects exclusivity, warranty, branding, and the total experience. This kind of premium is justified, but it must be monitored carefully to avoid overreach.

The benchmarking process itself is repeatable. It starts by defining a representative basket of parts—ideally across key product categories, value tiers, and usage types. Then, competitor prices are collected, structured, and compared. Most leading companies repeat this exercise every six to twelve months to ensure their pricing remains market-relevant.

Specialized providers support this process with technology and data aggregation.

In the automotive sector, Eucon is the market leader, providing price comparison intelligence for both passenger and commercial vehicle segments with offices in Europe, North and Latin America, and Asia-Pacific, serving more than 250 customers.

The market leader in the industrial space is MARKT-PILOT, offering digital benchmarking services tailored to OEMs with offices in Europe and North America serving more than 100 customers.

MONETIZING WILLINGNESS TO PAY WITH BENCHMARKING

Price benchmarking isn't just a defensive move—it's a proactive strategy to monetize willingness to pay. By identifying parts that are underpriced compared to market alternatives, companies can implement targeted price increases with minimal risk.

Customers are already exposed to market prices. If your brake disc is 20% cheaper than competitors' equivalents—without a strategic reason—you're leaving margin on the table. A small, data-driven price increase in such cases is often perceived as fair.

On the flip side, benchmarking protects customer trust. If your prices are significantly above similar offerings from trusted OES suppliers, customer confidence can erode. Adjusting prices downward in such cases—especially for highly comparable or commoditized items—can improve competitiveness without sacrificing brand value.

Importantly, benchmarking also enhances internal alignment. It gives sales and pricing teams a shared reference point. Instead of debating abstract pricing logic, discussions can focus on data: "How does this compare to the market?" That transparency builds confidence and speeds up decision-making.

APPLYING THE PARTS BENCHMARKING: AUTOMOTIVE CASE STUDY

A premium European automotive manufacturer partnered with Eucon to evaluate its pricing consistency against both direct competitors and OES parts.

Figure 11.1

Automotive market intelligence provided by Eucon (Source: Eucon)

Market Data Engine

Data: IAM Sales Data

Market and Parts Potential Dashboard

OE Part No.	OE Product Group	Aftermarket Cat.	extrapol. IAM Sales **this period**	extrapol. IAM Sales last period	IAM Sales Development	IAM Competitor w/ highest sales
					IAM Sales Data	
93185370	3421 MUFFLER	Wear	560	700	↘ -20%	ERNST
95189390	4232 RELAY	Electric	130	140	↘ -7%	VEMO
90083300	5362 SHOCK ABSORBER	Wear	210	190	↗ +11%	SACHS
93295379	8632 COMPRESSOR	Heating/ AC	50	45	↗ +11%	VALEO
90135329	9563 DOOR FR LEFT	Body/ Accident	40	40	→ 0%	VAN WEZEL
90006363	7632 SLIDING DOOR RR	Body/ Accident	5	4	↗ +25%	VAN WEZEL

OE Part No.	OE Product Group	Own Sales
93185370	3421 MUFFLER	XXXXX
95189390	4232 RELAY	XXXXX
90083300	5362 SHOCK ABSORBER	XXXXX
93295379	8632 COMPRESSOR	XXXXX
90135329	9563 DOOR FR LEFT	XXXXX
90006363	7632 SLIDING DOOR RR	XXXXX

Actual sales figures of your IAM competitors per OE part number

Monthly sales figures development

Main IAM competitor

Compare with own sales figures

Figure 11.2

Industrial market intelligence provided by MARKT-PILOT (Source: MARKT-PILOT)

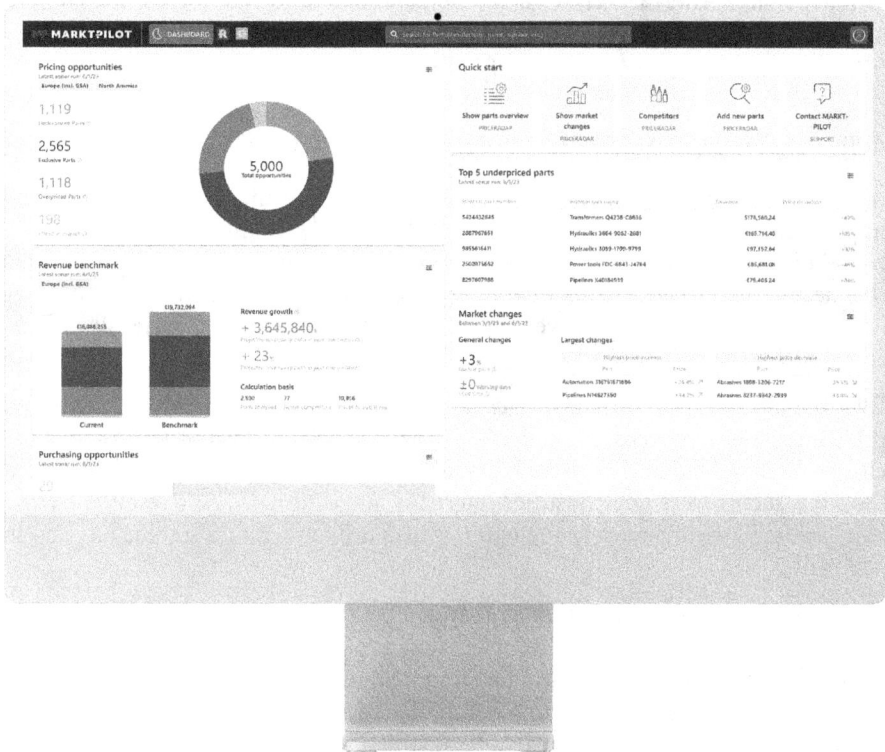

The experts proceeded in a two-step approach: first Eucon delivered an analysis of the complete parts portfolio of the OEM to show the competitive threat on part number level. This mass data analysis of the around 400,000 OEM part numbers was based on intelligent cleansing processes to ensure high-quality data.

The outcome allowed to derive overall pricing rules for the full portfolio as well as a parts basket of 500 high-volume SKUs for further benchmarking. This second step gave a detailed understanding of the most important parts like brake pads, filters, wiper blades, and spark plugs.

The analysis revealed that certain fast-moving parts were priced above comparable premium-brand competitors—posing a potential risk to the brand's price perception. Meanwhile, other parts—particularly those where the OEM brand offered clear value-added services or longer warranties—were found to be underpriced relative to their value proposition.

Additionally, extrapolated sales data of OES/IAM competitor parts proved valuable for analyzing the market situation based on OEM part number level where IAM, or Independent Aftermarket, refers to the market for automotive parts, accessories, and services sold by companies not affiliated with the original vehicle manufacturer (OEM). Figure 11.1 presents this analysis using a representative example.

APPLYING THE PARTS BENCHMARKING: INDUSTRIAL CASE STUDY

A leading industrial equipment manufacturer operating across 60 countries implemented price benchmarking using MARKT-PILOT. The company selected a basket of 2,000 frequently sold parts across product categories. The analysis showed that nearly 40% of these items were priced significantly below market—sometimes by as much as 25%. The gaps were especially pronounced in categories like filters, couplings, and wear parts.

Over the following two pricing cycles, the manufacturer implemented incremental price increases—between 5% and 15%—on those underpriced SKUs. Because the changes were rooted in real market comparisons, the pricing team felt confident and the adjustments were easily justified internally and externally. As a result, the company achieved an annual revenue uplift of €1.2 million with no significant drop in volume.

At the same time, parts that were already competitively priced—especially those in highly transparent segments—were left unchanged. Benchmarking helped direct effort where it mattered most, avoiding unnecessary changes.

SUMMARY

Price benchmarking is a high-impact quick win in spare parts pricing.

It aligns pricing with market logic—not through imitation, but through intelligence. When done right, it turns visibility into profitability providing confidence and direction.

This approach helps avoid both overpricing that risks customer loss and underpricing that sacrifices margin. It supports smarter price adjustments, improves internal decision-making, and brings clarity to pricing strategy.

With the help of digital platforms like Eucon or MARKT-PILOT, benchmarking is no longer a manual, once-a-year task. It's becoming a strategic rhythm—one that helps keep your pricing aligned with the world outside.

12

Minimum-Order Threshold

In spare parts pricing, profit opportunities often hide in operational inefficiencies. One such inefficiency is the high cost of handling and delivering small, fragmented orders—particularly in B2B distribution models involving dealer networks. The solution? A minimum-order threshold.

By setting a financial threshold below which a surcharge applies, OEMs can not only recover logistics costs but also influence dealer ordering behavior. The result is a combined quick wins of improved profitability, operational streamlining, and better service for the end customer.

THE CONCEPT OF MINIMUM-ORDER THRESHOLD

The minimum-order threshold is a pricing mechanism designed for OEMs selling spare parts via dealers. It defines a financial minimum for each order—usually based on the total invoice amount. If a dealer places an order below this threshold, a fixed surcharge is applied.

This fee structure serves two key purposes. First, it monetizes low-value orders that are disproportionately expensive to fulfill. Second, it nudges dealers toward more efficient ordering behavior—either by combining orders, increasing volumes, or adjusting order timing.

By implementing a minimum threshold and associated fee, OEMs can realize a previously untapped profit pool. At the same time, inventory and delivery operations are optimized. Fewer small orders mean fewer fragmented deliveries, better use of logistics resources, and more stable warehouse operations.

What makes this approach particularly powerful is its behavioral impact. Dealers near the threshold often choose to increase their order size to avoid the fee—leading to more parts in stock at local level, which improves the speed and quality of service for end users.

In short, the minimum-order threshold isn't just a pricing tactic—it's a lever to reshape dealer behavior, improve service levels, and drive EBITDA uplift.

DOI: 10.4324/9781003647416-14

MONETIZING WILLINGNESS TO PAY AND ORDER BEHAVIOR

Dealers already accept minimum thresholds in other supplier relationships. When the rules are clear and the incentives fair, the majority adapt without resistance. In this context, willingness to pay is not just about product value—but about convenience, urgency, and habit.

Some dealers will accept the fee as the cost of convenience. Others, especially those near the threshold, will optimize their purchasing to avoid it. And still others will shift their order cadence to consolidate multiple small orders into fewer, larger ones—creating savings for both sides.

Importantly, this change leads to more parts being available closer to the customer. With higher on-shelf availability at dealer level, end users experience better service and faster repairs. The result is a true win-win-win across the chain: the OEM sees profit uplift, the dealer becomes more self-sufficient and improves service, and the end user benefits from reduced downtime and better availability.

APPLYING THE CONCEPT: A CASE STUDY

A leading manufacturer of robotic machinery relied on a global network of dealers to distribute spare parts. Until recently, the company had no minimum-order threshold in place. This led to a large number of low-value orders—each of them requiring individual processing, packaging, and shipping. The cumulative cost of managing these small orders reduced profitability and placed strain on logistics resources.

To address the issue, the OEM introduced a minimum-order threshold of €1,200. Any invoice below that amount would be subject to a flat surcharge of €150. After implementation, a significant portion of dealers—roughly 70% of those placing small orders—chose to accept and pay the surcharge. This adjustment alone created a new revenue stream, resulting in an annual profit uplift of approximately €250,000.

Not all dealers were willing to pay the fee. Among those who were close to the threshold, many adjusted their ordering behavior instead. About half of these dealers began adding extra parts to their orders to exceed the €1,200 limit and avoid the surcharge. As a result, overall parts sales increased, generating approximately €180,000 in additional revenue. This came without any increase in operational cost, as the deliveries were already planned.

At the same time, the surcharge and threshold policy prompted behavioral change in how orders were scheduled. About 40% of the orders that would have previously fallen below the minimum threshold were now being consolidated into fewer, larger shipments. This consolidation significantly reduced transportation frequency and improved delivery efficiency. The OEM was able to reduce transport-related costs and handling efforts, leading to a further €100,000 in annual profit improvement.

In total, the introduction of the minimum-order threshold resulted in a combined annual profit uplift of €530,000 (see Figure 12.1).

Figure 12.1

Benefits of the introduction of a minimum-order threshold for dealers

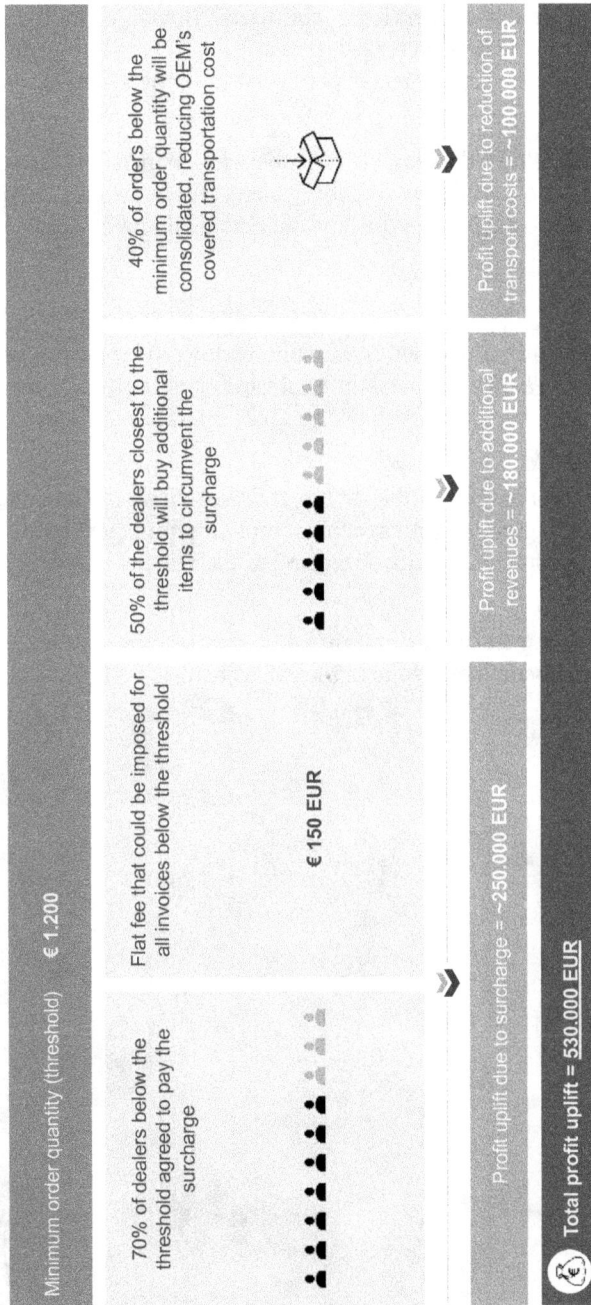

| Minimum order quantity (threshold) | € 1.200 |

70% of dealers below the threshold agreed to pay the surcharge

Flat fee that could be imposed for all invoices below the threshold

50% of the dealers closest to the threshold will buy additional items to circumvent the surcharge

40% of orders below the minimum order quantity will be consolidated, reducing OEM's covered transportation cost

€ 150 EUR

Profit uplift due to surcharge = ~250.000 EUR

Profit uplift due to additional revenues = ~180.000 EUR

Profit uplift due to reduction of transport costs = ~100.000 EUR

Total profit uplift = 530.000 EUR

More importantly, it led to smarter dealer behavior. Dealers who increased their order sizes began holding more parts in stock, which in turn enabled them to provide faster, more reliable service to end users. The OEM improved its operational performance, the dealers increased their sell-out potential, inventory availability as well as revenues, and customers experienced fewer delays due to better on-site part availability.

This approach delivered a tangible triple benefit: financial gain for the OEM, service improvement and upsell potential for dealers, and higher satisfaction for end users who had access to parts more quickly and reliably than before.

SUMMARY

The minimum-order threshold is a simple yet powerful quick win in spare parts pricing. By defining a clear financial threshold and applying a surcharge for orders below it, OEMs can change dealer behavior, reduce operational friction, and unlock new revenue streams.

This strategy works on multiple fronts: it drives direct fee income, increases parts sales by encouraging basket expansion, and cuts transport costs by consolidating orders. It also improves service speed and availability by boosting local inventory at the dealer level.

The result is not just higher margin—but smarter, more sustainable aftermarket operations that benefit everyone in the value chain.

13

Price Quantity Breaks

For OEMs selling via distributors, pricing strategy can do more than just protect margins: it can shape behavior. One of the most overlooked yet powerful levers for aligning incentives in B2B distribution is the use of price/quantity breaks. This tactic blends behavioral economics with operational efficiency: offering discounts only when the distributor's behavior creates measurable value for the OEM.

The essence of price/quantity breaks lies in rewarding dealers for behavior that simplifies operations and penalizing inefficiencies that drive up handling costs. Instead of offering unconditional discounts, OEMs can define clear quantity tiers that trigger better pricing. Dealers who align with these predefined batch sizes benefit from preferential terms. In this case it becomes a win-win. Those who don't may see higher prices, reflecting the additional cost their behavior imposes on the system.

This approach shifts the perception of discounts from being a guaranteed right to being a performance-based reward. It reframes pricing as a two-way street, where both sides benefit from cooperation and operational logic.

THE STRATEGIC LOGIC BEHIND PRICE/QUANTITY BREAKS

The central goal of this pricing method is to influence how dealers place orders, encouraging them to align their purchasing behavior with the OEM's predefined delivery quantities. These quantities are typically based on packaging units or shipping configurations that maximize logistical efficiency. When dealers comply, the system benefits from fewer pick-and-pack operations, optimized freight usage, and a more stable warehouse workload.

In doing so, price/quantity breaks also enable a shift in dealer expectations. Instead of viewing discounts as an entitlement, dealers begin to see them as rewards for contributing to overall efficiency. This subtle but important change in perception helps OEMs foster healthier, more aligned relationships with their distribution networks.

Beyond perception, the financial rationale is clear. Aligning dealer orders with OEM packaging units significantly reduces fragmentation, streamlines logistics, and ultimately creates measurable cost savings and profit improvements.

DOI: 10.4324/9781003647416-15

A PRACTICAL EXAMPLE: THE FORKLIFT OEM IN ASIA

Consider the case of an Asian affiliate of a European forklift manufacturer. This affiliate received spare parts from the central European warehouse in standard bulk quantities—for example, 10 oil filters, 30 fuel filters, or 250 small nuts per shipment. Despite this, downstream dealers routinely placed orders in broken quantities that disrupted the supply chain and increased handling costs.

To address the issue, the affiliate implemented a structured price/quantity break policy. Dealers who did not adhere to the recommended order quantities faced a 10% price increase for those noncompliant units. On the other hand, those who ordered according to the defined quantities were eligible for volume-based discounts.

The impact of this change was striking. The price increase applied to fragmented orders led to a revenue gain of approximately €1,300,000. At the same time, the volume-based discounts granted to compliant dealers amounted to a cost of €320,000. In parallel, the reduction in cost per order due to better alignment and reduced complexity resulted in savings of €120,000. Taken together, these effects generated a total profit uplift of €1,100,000 (see Figure 13.1).

This case also demonstrated a significant shift in dealer mindset. Through transparent communication—emphasizing a collaborative message such as "Our goal is to create a reciprocal partnership where mutually rewarding behavior brings value to both parties" – dealers began adjusting their behavior to avoid penalties and unlock discounts. The message was clear: aligned ordering behavior isn't just encouraged, it's rewarded. And a win-win for both.

BEYOND WILLINGNESS TO PAY: MONETIZING WILLINGNESS TO BEHAVE

What sets this pricing lever apart is its focus on behavior rather than just willingness to pay. Traditional pricing strategies are often designed to capture value from customers who are willing to pay more for speed, brand, or availability. Price/quantity breaks, by contrast, are about incentivizing operational compliance. Dealers aren't just paying for parts—they're paying (or saving) based on how they engage with the supply chain.

By introducing this model, OEMs effectively monetize a new variable: the dealer's willingness to align behavior with system efficiency. This creates a form of price discrimination that's not only fair but mutually beneficial. Dealers with optimized processes and planning capabilities are rewarded for their contribution to the system's performance. Those who create friction bear its true cost.

KEYS TO SUCCESSFUL IMPLEMENTATION

Implementing price/quantity breaks requires thoughtful preparation and internal alignment. First and foremost, OEMs must define the optimal delivery quantities

Figure 13.1

Benefits of the introduction of price/quantity breaks

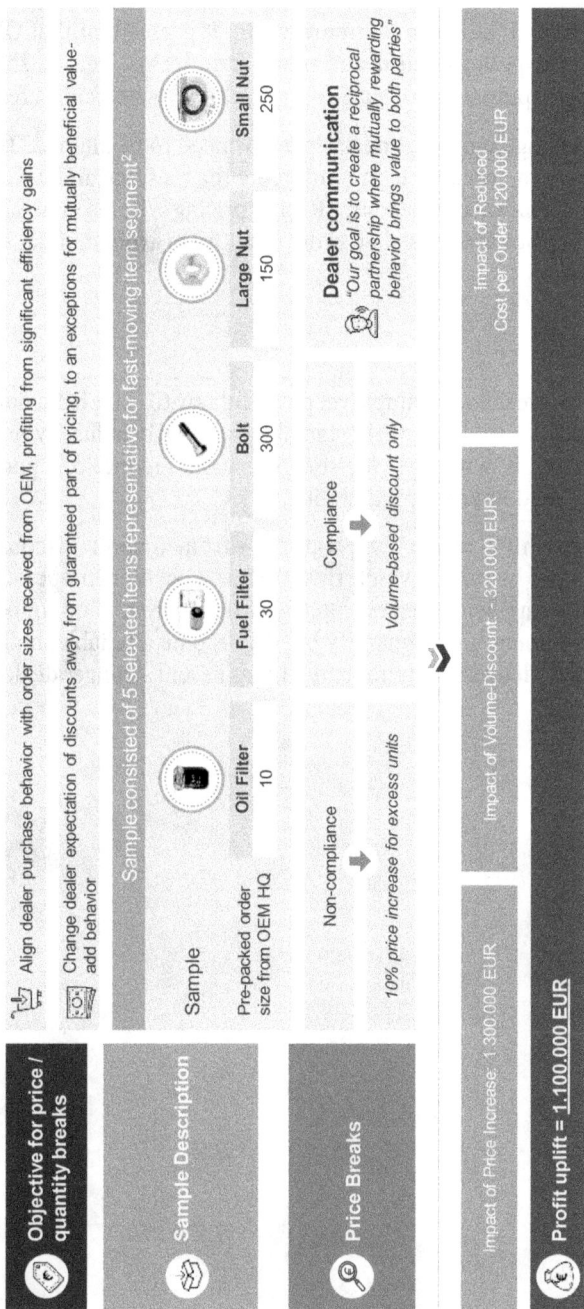

Objective for price / quantity breaks

- Align dealer purchase behavior with order sizes received from OEM, profiting from significant efficiency gains
- Change dealer expectation of discounts away from guaranteed part of pricing, to an exceptions for mutually beneficial value-add behavior

Sample Description

Sample consisted of 5 selected items representative for fast-moving item segment[2]

Sample

	Oil Filter	Fuel Filter	Bolt	Large Nut	Small Nut
Pre-packed order size from OEM HQ	10	30	300	150	250

Price Breaks

Non-compliance
10% price increase for excess units

Compliance
Volume-based discount only

Dealer communication
"Our goal is to create a reciprocal partnership where mutually rewarding behavior brings value to both parties"

Impact of Price Increase: 1.300.000 EUR

Impact of Volume-Discount: - 320.000 EUR

Impact of Reduced Cost per Order: 120.000 EUR

Profit uplift = 1.100.000 EUR

based on warehouse logistics, packaging units, or inbound freight structures. These should form the foundation of the pricing model.

Equally important is dealer communication. It is essential that OEMs explain the logic behind the policy in clear and transparent terms. Dealers should understand that this is not a punishment, but a framework for shared value creation.

Internally, pricing, logistics, and sales teams need to be aligned. The sales team, in particular, plays a crucial role in reinforcing the message and encouraging compliance. From a technical perspective, ERP and pricing systems must support automated application of price tiers based on order quantity to avoid manual errors and ensure transparency.

SUMMARY

Price/quantity breaks are a simple yet powerful way to drive behavioral change across the dealer network while delivering tangible financial benefits. By rewarding ordering behavior that aligns with OEM logistics, companies reduce cost per order, minimize inefficiencies, and improve profitability.

This strategy shifts dealer expectations—from default discounting to earned incentives—and helps reposition the OEM as a partner in operational excellence, not just a parts supplier. When executed with transparency and supported by the right tools and alignment, price/quantity breaks become a reliable, high-impact pricing lever—one that delivers both improved margins and stronger dealer relationships.

14

Capacity Planning and Optimization

Spare parts pricing isn't just about SKUs—it's about synchronizing supply, demand, and service readiness. Capacity-aware pricing is a next-generation lever that transforms idle service slots into revenue, customer satisfaction, and operational efficiency. It links pricing with planning—and value with timing.

Spare parts pricing isn't just about individual SKUs—it's about the ecosystem around them. In many industries, parts drive service visits, and service visits drive retention, satisfaction, and lifetime value. But what happens when service capacity goes underutilized? Pricing can step in.

This is a new frontier in aftermarket value creation: capacity-aware pricing. By using AI to anticipate service demand and align spare parts pricing accordingly, companies can proactively manage workshop utilization, boost revenue, and increase customer engagement. This is not just operational planning—it's a pricing quick win.

THE CONCEPT OF CAPACITY PLANNING AND CAPACITY OPTIMIZATION

At its core, capacity optimization through pricing is about timing the right offer with the right availability. It lets pricing steer customer behavior while smoothing operational peaks and troughs.

In other words capacity planning and optimization in the context of spare parts pricing is about aligning parts and service demand in a coordinated, predictive way. The goal is to optimize the use of authorized workshops by incentivizing service-linked purchases during periods of low utilization (see Figure 14.1).

The process begins with an AI model that forecasts future demand—both for parts and for the services associated with them. These models can account for seasonal cycles, usage data, product lifecycles, and even external variables such as weather conditions. For example, tire or battery replacements spike during temperature extremes. Anticipating this allows better inventory positioning and smarter pricing interventions.

When the AI model predicts a drop in service utilization—such as fewer appointments at authorized workshops—it triggers a pricing adjustment. Prices for selected spare parts that are closely linked to services (like brake pads, batteries, or tires)

DOI: 10.4324/9781003647416-16

are temporarily lowered or maintenance promotions offered to clients. These more attractive prices stimulate product purchases and indirectly drive customers into the service network.

At the same time, stock levels of these forecasted parts are set to optimal levels—balancing availability with cost. Workshops are prepared not just to fulfill service requests, but to handle them efficiently and profitably.

What makes this model effective is its ability to tailor offers based on forecasted free service capacity. If workshop slots are underbooked in a certain region or time window, the model recommends product-and-service bundles to help fill the gap. This is especially impactful when there is strong control over commercial channels—such as dealer networks or e-commerce platforms—allowing targeted execution of campaigns.

The result is a dynamic, responsive system where pricing helps to shape—not just follow—demand. This creates a win-win: increased workshop efficiency for the OEM or service provider, and better deals for customers when and where capacity is available.

MONETIZING WILLINGNESS TO PAY THROUGH CAPACITY OPTIMIZATION

Willingness to pay is not static. It shifts depending on urgency, availability, and perceived value. In the context of service-linked parts, pricing can be adjusted not only by competitive factors but also by workshop occupancy levels.

During periods of low utilization, customers have more flexibility—and may respond positively to incentives. A small price drop on a part like a battery, bundled with a discounted installation offer, can stimulate immediate demand without eroding brand perception.

Conversely, during peak service periods, prices can return to standard levels—or even increase slightly if justified by urgency or convenience. Customers booking service on short notice may accept higher pricing in exchange for availability.

This approach effectively monetizes the elasticity of demand around service appointments. It also leverages willingness to pay in a new way—not just based on product value, but on timing, convenience, and resource availability.

APPLYING THE CONCEPT: A CASE STUDY

A leading European commercial vehicle brand implemented this approach for winter tire changes. Based on historical patterns and real-time workshop booking data, the OEM's AI model predicted underutilization during mid-autumn—a period when many customers delay tire changes despite colder weather setting in.

Figure 14.1

Optimizing utilization of authorized workshops

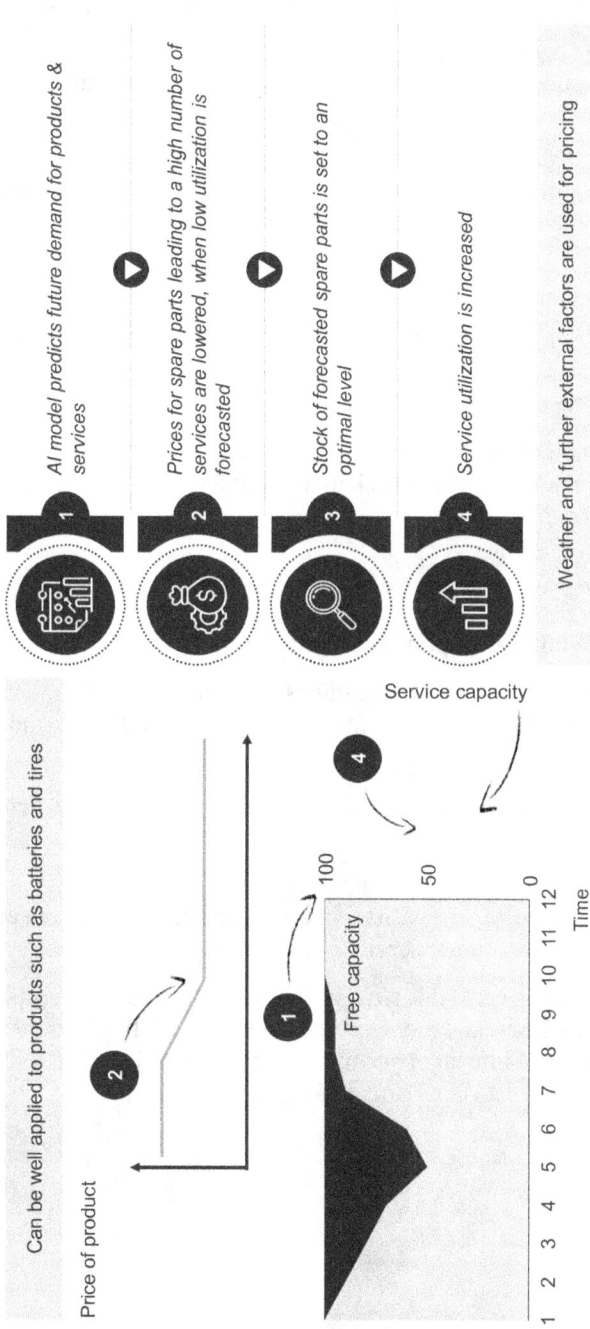

Can be well applied to products such as batteries and tires

Price of product

Service capacity

1. AI model predicts future demand for products & services

2. Prices for spare parts leading to a high number of services are lowered, when low utilization is forecasted

3. Stock of forecasted spare parts is set to an optimal level

4. Service utilization is increased

Weather and further external factors are used for pricing

Free capacity

Time

Instead of launching a generic discount, the OEM crafted a precise bundle—triggered only in regions where workshops had low bookings and high winter tire stock.

The model triggered a limited-time offer: a bundled package that included new winter tires, discounted installation, and a complimentary safety inspection. Prices for the tires themselves were slightly reduced—but only in regions and time slots where workshop capacity was forecasted to be low.

At the same time, regional stock levels of the relevant SKUs were automatically adjusted upward in affected warehouses, ensuring fulfillment readiness.

The result was a significant uplift in service bookings—23% above baseline in targeted regions. Workshops operated at higher efficiency, fixed-cost absorption improved, and tire sales increased without eroding margin. Because the discount was tied to spare capacity, it didn't become a blanket promotion—and didn't compromise pricing integrity.

This case shows how spare parts pricing can become a lever for operational optimization and a quick win, especially when integrated with demand forecasting and service scheduling.

SUMMARY

Capacity planning and optimization is a new pricing lever with high potential.

By tying pricing to operational readiness, companies can shift demand, smooth service flows, and drive margin—not just from parts, but from optimized capacity use.

Companies can dynamically adjust prices to smooth utilization, boost service bookings, and drive cross-selling using AI to forecast parts demand and service availability.

Unlike static promotions, this approach ties pricing to operational readiness. Parts that are linked to service visits—like tires, batteries, or brake components—can become triggers for timely service engagement.

When applied correctly, this strategy helps avoid service underutilization, improves workshop efficiency, and monetizes customer flexibility. It turns a hidden cost—idle service capacity—into an opportunity for value creation. And it does so with precision, timing, and data at its core. It is a great quick win!

Part III

Learning from Parts Pricing Transformations

"The past is never dead. It's not even past."
—William Faulkner, *Requiem for a Nun*

Every transformation begins as a whisper. A tension. A discomfort that grows in the silence of boardrooms, in the clutter of old spreadsheets, in the gut feeling that *something isn't working anymore.*

Before it becomes strategy, a transformation is simply a moment—one person asking the right question. What if? Why now? Why not differently?

This section is a collection of such moments. A gallery of transitions, each with its own landscape, climate, and weather. Some took place under pressure—like tectonic shifts during crises. Others unfolded slowly, like vines growing over forgotten architecture. Each story here is a map of becoming—and like all meaningful maps, it's messy. The territory was never charted in advance.

We speak of transformation, but what we really mean is metamorphosis. And like Kafka's Gregor Samsa, organizations often wake up one morning and find that they can no longer operate in the same skin. They must change—or crumble.

To learn from transformation is to participate in one of the oldest rituals known to humankind: the transmission of experience through story. Long before business schools and PowerPoints, there were fables, epics, and campfire tales. From *The Odyssey* to *The Arabian Nights*, from *Beowulf* to the *Book of Job*, we have always passed wisdom forward not through charts, but through narrative. Because data tells you what happened. But story tells you why it mattered.

In this part of the book, you will not find commandments carved in stone, nor silver bullets wrapped in consultancy-speak. Instead, you will find texture: tension, doubt, trial, surprise, and revelation. There are no perfect paths here, only courageous ones—and that, more than anything, is the soul of transformation.

Some companies began with skepticism. Others with hope. Many made mistakes. But all of them moved. They changed their relationship to parts pricing—and in doing so, changed their relationship to value, to their customers, to their future. These were not simply structural changes. They were ontological: changes in being.

DOI: 10.4324/9781003647416-17

Picture the ship of Theseus, rebuilt plank by plank while remaining afloat. Is it the same ship at the end of the journey? Or something entirely new? In these spare parts pricing transformations, the same paradox holds true. Each company retained its name, its legacy, its culture. But beneath the surface, something had shifted. Mindsets realigned. Silos dissolved. The quiet lever of spare parts pricing was elevated from tactical afterthought to strategic compass.

These stories come from the field: manufacturers, automotive producers, distributors, multinationals, and niche players alike. From the chaotic noise of spare parts to the silent revolutions unfolding in after-sales pricing offices across the globe.

And while the context differs, the heartbeat remains the same: the will to evolve. Not for the sake of fashion, but for survival. Not for profit alone, but for coherence.

We might even say that, in reading these stories, you become part of their unfolding. Because transformation, like myth, is participatory. You must enter it to understand it. Like Dante descending into the Inferno—not to marvel at the fire, but to ascend again with vision cleared. He could not reach paradise without first naming what had been lost.

Perhaps you, too, will see echoes of your own organization in these tales—a decision not yet taken, a lesson not yet learned. Or perhaps a new chapter waiting to be written.

Because transformation is not a concept. It is a narrative act.

And every act of transformation begins with the same phrase:

Let me tell you a story.

15

Philips Healthcare
Customer-Centric Parts Pricing

This case study was shared by Daniel Cho, Head of the Strategic Pricing Centre of Excellence at Philips Healthcare, and Viktoria Der, Director of Customer Service Strategic Pricing and Product Management Excellence at Philips Healthcare.

PHILIPS HEALTHCARE PROFILE AND PARTS PRICING CHALLENGES

Philips Healthcare, a €14-billion global business, is highly recognized as a pioneering leader in health technology. With the strategy to provide better care for more people, the company has consistently pursued innovative avenues to enhance the quality of life through its diverse array of medical devices, imaging systems, and healthcare solutions. Integral to this mission is the effective management of an extensive spare parts portfolio, encompassing more than 160,000 critical components essential for ensuring the uninterrupted operation of medical equipment that sustains vital healthcare services across numerous settings.

Historically, Philips Healthcare relied on an Excel-based cost-plus-margin model that did not adequately account for the varying critical importance of different parts and the nuanced demands of its diverse customer base. This approach led to inefficiencies and customer dissatisfaction, highlighting the need for a more customer-focused and strategically robust pricing strategy.

Over the past decade, Philips has made significant advancements in its parts pricing strategies. The introduction of innovative processes, systems, and automation has brought about a myriad of improvements in both the efficiency and accuracy of price creation and execution, benefiting hundreds of thousands of customers daily.

Before we delve into the improvements and implementations of recent years, it is important to first address the key challenges identified in our traditional price setting and execution methods.

Customers

Over the years, Philips has observed that some customers feel overwhelmed by its multichannel approach to accessing spare parts, often finding themselves confused about the optimal channel to use. We will address the challenges posed by our omni-channel strategy in the subsequent sections. The primary hurdle lies in the

DOI: 10.4324/9781003647416-18

Figure 15.1

Customer choices of the replacement of ultrasound probe (Source: Philips)

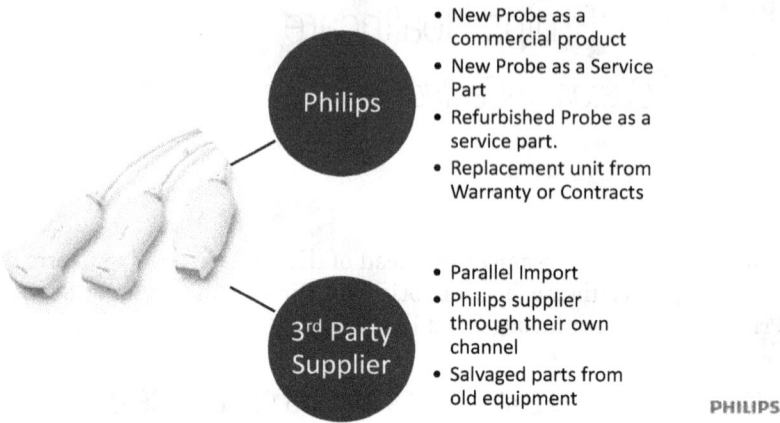

inconsistencies of our pricing, which are not sufficiently supported by clear differentiation. For instance, a customer may choose to purchase a brand-new ultrasound probe to replace a broken one; alternatively, they might opt for a brand-new service part, a refurbished probe, or avail a rebate by returning the old broken part when ordering a new service part. Furthermore, customers can acquire these parts from third-party suppliers who salvage components from old machines, or through parallel imports from other countries. Another available option is purchasing extended warranty or service contracts that cover parts in the event of a breakdown (see Figure 15.1).

Given the extensive variability in availability, expected quality, useful life, as well as pricing, it can be challenging for our customers to make informed decisions that best meet their needs. There is a pronounced need for better alignment of our offerings and prices, along with providing customers with a clear decision-making path to achieve the best value for their purchases. This necessitates a robust internal strategy, a compelling value proposition for customers, and comprehensive support materials to aid customers in making well-informed decisions.

Channel (Omni-Channel)

As previously mentioned, customers have multiple avenues through which they can access specific parts. Adding to this complexity is the concept of channels, which represents the customer touchpoints and denotes how we interact with customers to facilitate their purchase of spare parts. Philips offers several online purchasing portals, including a customer service portal available to all service contract holders, allowing them to buy parts at contractual discounts. Additionally, there is an electronic data interchange (EDI) system, providing customers with the most convenient means to search and order Philips parts directly from their own purchasing websites. Philips also maintains an e-store dedicated to spare parts. Beyond online options, customers can call our service hotline for quotations or engage with one of our many service engineers (see Figure 15.2).

The complexity arises when these varied channels present inconsistent prices, warranties, and shipment dates, potentially causing customers to feel deceived or frustrated if they discover they have made purchases under less favorable terms at higher prices.

How can we ensure customers receive a seamless experience regardless of the channel they use to obtain quotations and pricing? Moreover, how can we effectively meet their shipment time requirements while balancing it with the price they are willing to pay?

Competition

There are four major competitors that serve as viable alternatives for our customers should they choose not to purchase from Philips:

1. Original equipment manufacturer (OEM) companies that offer standard parts, such as displays, printers (e.g., HP), network components (e.g., Cisco), and supplies.

2. Suppliers to Philips who also sell independently.

3. Third-party service companies that sell refurbished parts obtained from old Philips equipment.

4. Parts suppliers that import Philips components from low-cost markets.

Figure 15.2

Challenges of aligning omni-channel offers to Philips Healthcares' customers (Source: Philips)

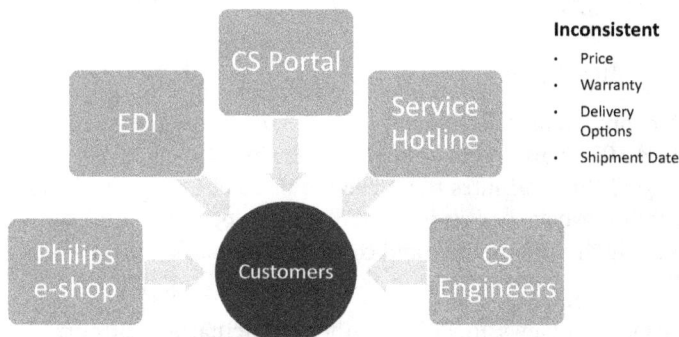

Figure 15.3

Differential value Philips need to provide to maintain leadership (Source: Philips)

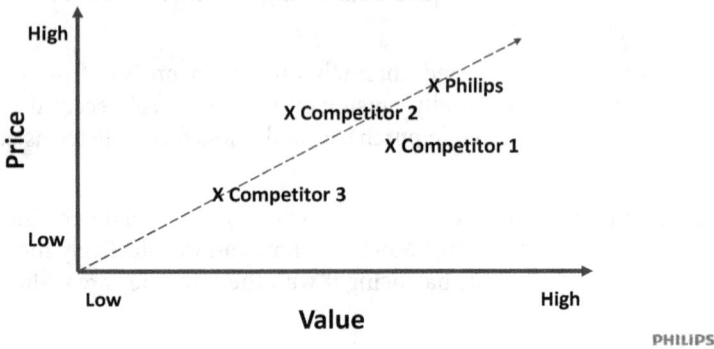

Customers are at liberty to select their preferred vendor, and so long as the parts meet the required quality standards and are safe for patient use, Philips does not have a mandate to prevent these competitors from selling. The most effective way to persuade customers to choose Philips is by offering superior value at competitive prices. This scenario is akin to purchasing original parts from Mercedes or Bosch, where a significant segment of customers still prefer the authenticity of parts provided directly by the car manufacturer.

Any successful strategy aimed at increasing market share hinges on delivering the most competitive offerings, creating an effortless customer experience, and providing top-tier delivery and return services. Key to maintaining brand preference and loyalty includes observing competitor actions, assessing customer satisfaction and net promoter score (NPS), and ensuring a customer-centric complaint-handling service (see Figure 15.3).

Observing and reacting to competitive moves should be an integrated part of a successful pricing strategy.

Processes, Systems, and Automation

Philips currently offers an extensive catalog of over 160,000 spare parts clustered in 14 business lines and 300+ parts types to its customers in 100+ countries. Given that it takes an average of three minutes to review the price of each part, the task demands at least 1,000 man-days per review cycle. Continuous price reviews are indispensable due to the highly competitive and cost-sensitive market we operate in (see Figure 15.4).

Factors necessitating price reviews include significant fluctuations in currency exchange rates, variations in supplier costs, or the imposition of special tariffs. While we have introduced a value-based pricing approach, which mitigates the need for

Figure 15.4
Philips spare parts in numbers (Source: Philips)

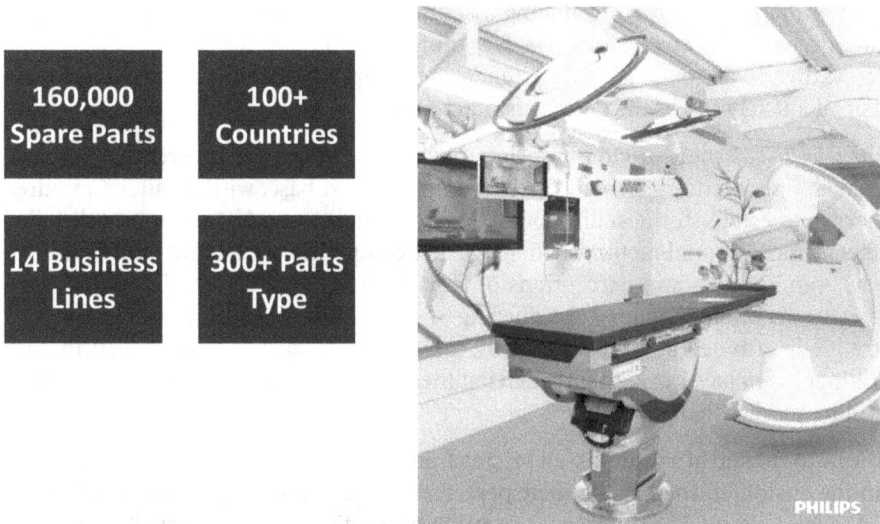

wholesale price adjustments following cost changes, the consistent monitoring of prices remains vital for maintaining customer loyalty, market share, and profitability. For instance, inflation can enhance customer willingness to pay, tariffs may be counterbalanced with surcharges or adjustments to promotions, and competitor price hikes could provide an opportunity for Philips to follow suit.

Historically, parts pricing at Philips was managed using a straightforward Excel-based cost-plus-margin model. Although simple, this model was deficient in capturing the nuanced customer perspectives and the strategic importance of various parts. Treating all parts uniformly—regardless of their criticality—resulted in inefficiencies and unacceptable levels of customer dissatisfaction.

Compounding these issues were prevalent inconsistencies in pricing analogous parts, such as differences between right-hand and left-hand components or screws varying in dimensions. These discrepancies not only perplexed customers but also introduced operational complexities for internal teams responsible for managing the vast inventory. Consequently, these challenges have highlighted the urgent need for a more strategic, customer-centric approach to parts pricing.

Philips must review spare parts prices several times a year, but allocating 1,000 mandays for this endeavor is unfeasible. Hence, there is a pressing necessity for automated systems that can efficiently set and update prices as required, thereby enabling us to respond promptly to market demands and maintain our competitive edge.

SOLUTION

Over the past decade, Philips has transitioned all of its spare parts to a value-based pricing model, thereby introducing a sophisticated layer of complexity to its pricing strategy. This nuanced approach acknowledges the varying perceptions of value across diverse customer segments, rendering it impractical to maintain a single price that adequately serves the entire customer base.

The legacy cost-plus pricing model employed by Philips was inherently simplistic in its design, predicated solely on the company's cost base, with an added required margin to establish the selling price. While straightforward, this approach failed to consider essential factors such as market competition, customer willingness to pay, brand loyalty, and perceptions of fairness. Moreover, the rigidity of the cost-plus model often precluded the offering of discounts, mandating the achievement of a predetermined margin. As a result, these prices frequently exceeded customers' willingness to pay, inadvertently driving them toward competitors and diminishing Philips' market share.

The introduction of a value-based pricing framework necessitates an intensified focus on the customer, specifically their perceived value and willingness to pay for that value. Addressing the differences in value perception and price sensitivity across various segments of the customer base becomes paramount. Establishing a comprehensive set of pricing policies is essential to strategically charge customers based on their perceived value while maintaining competitiveness within the market (see Figure 15.5 on a price waterfall, as a representation of such a pricing policy).

Monitoring and tracking price execution and the provision of discounts is integral to ensuring the efficacy of the value-based pricing model. Employing advanced analytics and deriving insightful metrics from this monitoring can significantly enhance both order growth and profitability for the business. Analytics offer a powerful tool for identifying trends, understanding customer behaviors, and optimizing pricing strategies to achieve sustainable business success.

PHILIPS SPARE PARTS PRICING APPROACH

In order to mitigate the myriad challenges previously outlined, Philips Healthcare made the strategic decision to redesign its pricing strategy, processes, systems, and policies, supported by a robust suite of analytics tools. This comprehensive overhaul was aimed at fostering a nuanced approach that effectively addresses the complexities inherent in value-based pricing.

Philips' transition to a value-based pricing model represents a sophisticated, customer-centric approach requiring meticulous policy formulation and comprehensive monitoring to ensure its effectiveness. By strategically aligning prices with customer-perceived value and leveraging advanced analytics, Philips has maintained its competitive edge, driven order growth, and achieved robust profitability while fostering long-term customer loyalty and satisfaction.

Figure 15.5

Pricing waterfall as basis of the new pricing policy (Source: Philips)

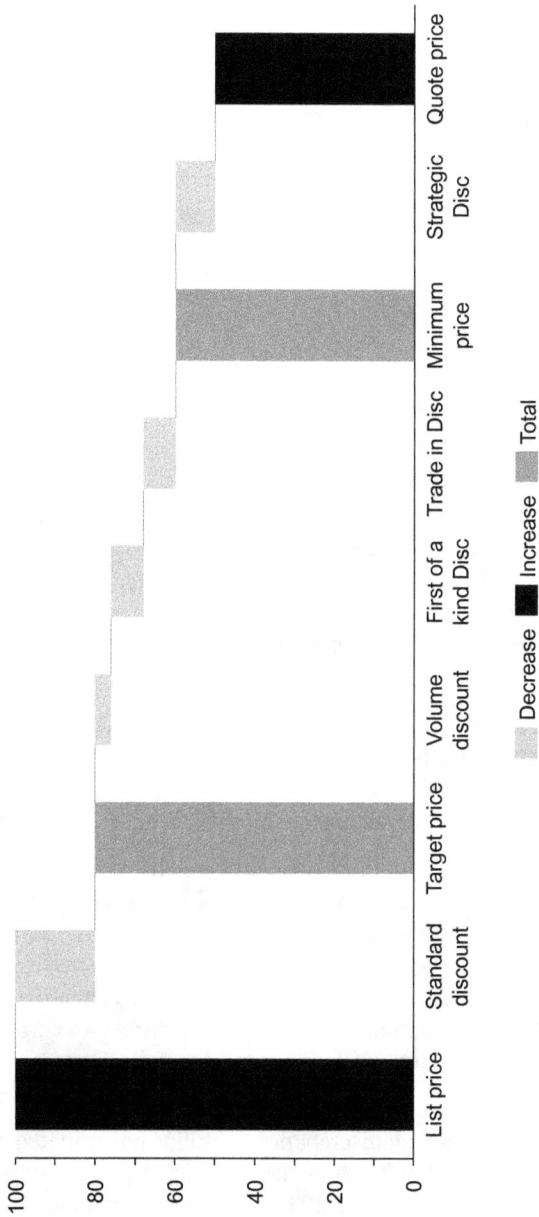

As a cornerstone of this strategy, Philips has developed differentiated discount policies tailored to distinct customer segments. These policies consider the value delivered to customers, their budget availability, and preferred delivery options. This targeted approach ensures that discounts are meaningful and reflect the nuanced requirements of various segments.

Additionally, Philips has adopted a type-based approach to categorize spare parts. The use of various attributes that represent different value points for customers was established. For example, availability levels are segmented into categories such as same-day delivery, 24-hour delivery, and 48-hour delivery. Parts that directly influence the uptime of essential equipment are valued higher by customers who are willing to pay more for expedited delivery of these critical components. Another significant attribute is the association of parts with different equipment. For instance, parts related to a multi-million euro Cath Lab are valued higher than those for a 3,000 euro cardiograph. Criticality and relevance are also key attributes that helped to group products into logical types (typology). These attributes are pivotal for automating the pricing calculations within our pricing system and also provide a transparency for customers to better understand our pricing logic.

The proprietary nature of certain parts enables Philips to construct a compelling value proposition. These parts typically command higher price points and margins due to their enhanced value proposition (having high criticality and relevance), offering customers highly differentiated benefits. Conversely, generic parts accessible from numerous suppliers, such as PCs or displays, are priced competitively to match the offerings of direct competitors, generally resulting in lower price premiums and profit margins.

By coupling customer segments with value attributes (type) and assessing the strategic importance of parts to customers, Philips can formulate a powerful strategy that delivers the appropriate value-to-price ratio. This combined algorithm integrates customer segments and the intrinsic nature of each part to optimize pricing.

In the realm of automation, Philips Healthcare embarked on the development and implementation of the Price Simulation Tool, designed to automate parts pricing based on specific part typologies and attributes (see Figure 15.6). While initially providing substantial advancements in optimizing pricing structures, the expansion to over 300 part types and the emergence of diverse sales channels necessitated further refinement. The application of divergent pricing strategies across multiple channels introduced inconsistencies and fragmented the cohesiveness of the overall pricing framework.

Recognizing these enduring discrepancies, Philips has initiated an ambitious transformative project aimed at harmonizing the global pricing strategy across all sales channels. Commencing in early 2024, this endeavor seeks to ensure uniformity, reduce the proliferation of part types, and enhance operational efficiency, thereby significantly improving customer satisfaction and reaffirming Philips' commitment to innovation and excellence in health technology.

Figure 15.6
Elements for the parts price simulation (Source: Philips)

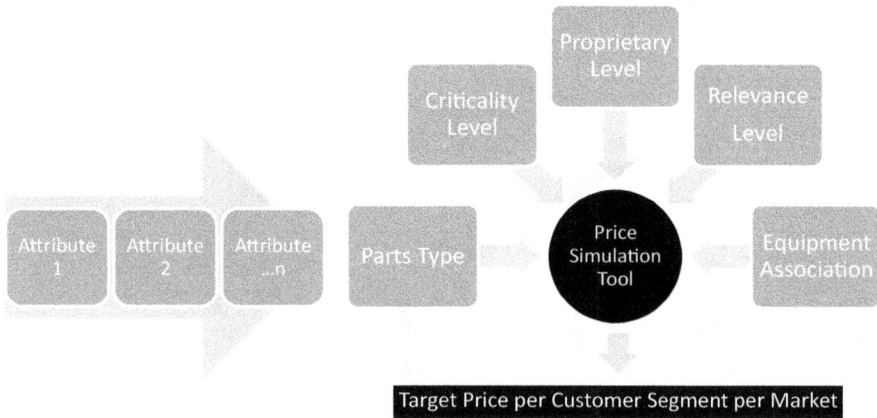

Looking toward the future, with the advancement of generative AI technologies from 2025 onwards, Philips foresees further possibilities for AI-driven automation to eliminate complexities and minimize human errors. Leveraging AI and the capability to create micro-segments, Philips can move beyond artificial grouping of parts, enabling tailored pricing strategies for all parts based on similar value propositions and customers' willingness to pay.

Philips Healthcare has developed a unified commercial policy that standardizes discount offerings based on strategic needs across all business lines and customer segments. This policy enhancement allows Philips' quotation tool (CPQ) to more effectively manage cross-business offers, ensuring a consistent customer experience across diverse markets and channels. By employing a unified discount policy, Philips achieves greater coherence in discount management, enabling precise measurement of discount controls and pricing executions across all sales channels and business units, facilitated by a consolidated dashboard and standardized key performance indicators (KPIs).

Moreover, Philips has established an advanced and comprehensive suite of analytics tools designed to deliver integral insights into pricing and profitability at granular levels. These tools meticulously analyze data for each customer, product, market, equipment, and part, facilitating a detailed understanding of performance metrics (see Figure 15.7). The analytics are versatile, allowing data to be aggregated into various dimensions such as markets, modality, channel types, and parts groups, depending on the specific requirements. The integral nature of these insights encompasses the total price and profitability over the lifespan of installations, encompassing hardware, software, services, contracts, and parts.

Figure 15.7

Advanced analytics display (Source: Philips)

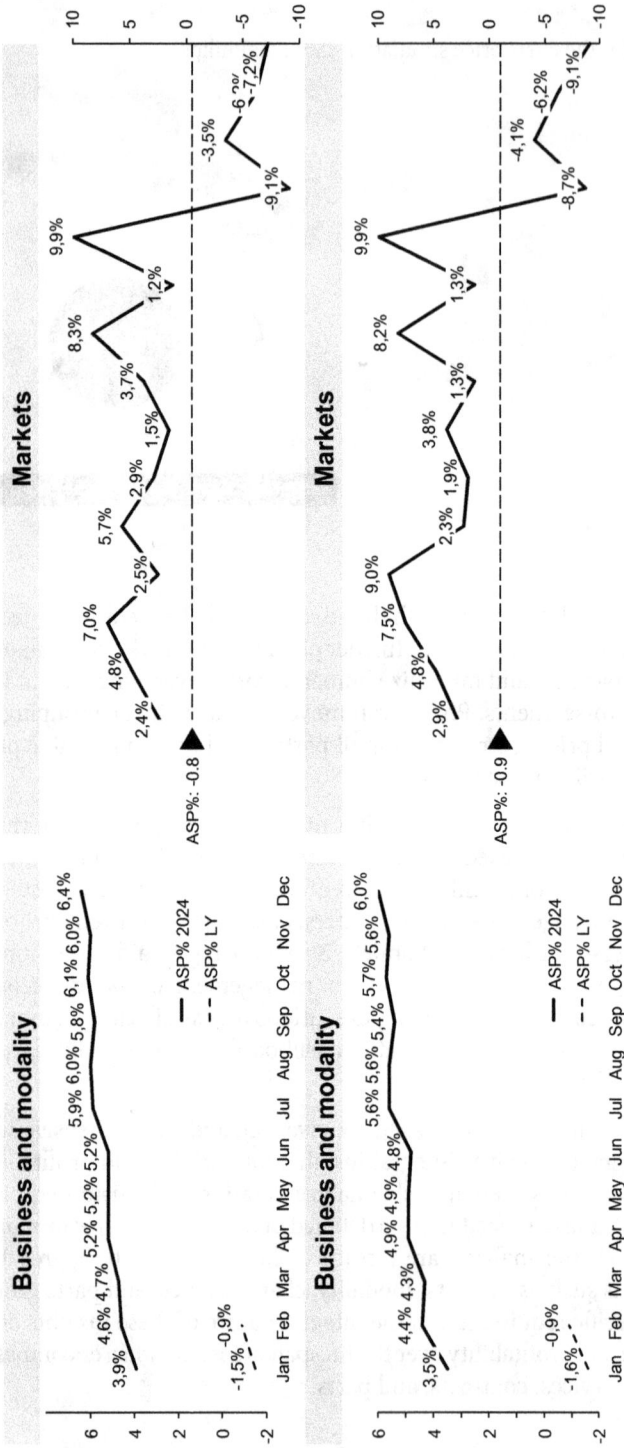

This approach ensures that Philips maintains sustainable business performance across the lifetime of any equipment utilized by its customers. The ability to comprehensively assess and track financial outcomes over the lifecycle delivers substantial benefits, including improved decision-making, enhanced strategic planning, and optimized resource allocation. These analytics tools enable Philips to proactively identify trends, address potential issues, and capitalize on opportunities to drive growth and profitability.

In summary, Philips Healthcare's strategic overhaul of its pricing strategy, processes, systems, and policies—supported by advanced analytics and AI technologies—is poised to deliver substantial improvements in customer satisfaction, operational efficiency, and financial performance. This comprehensive approach ensures that Philips continues to lead in the dynamic field of healthcare technology while maintaining a strong focus on customer-centric innovation.

Philips Spare Parts Costing Approach

Philips Healthcare is actively addressing the challenges associated with centralized manufacturing that result in elevated transportation costs. To circumvent these financial burdens, the company is strategically implementing local repair facilities. This innovative approach enables previously repaired parts to efficiently reenter the marketplace, thus eliminating the necessity for extensive global transportation. These repair facilities are designed to serve multiple countries, provided there are no prohibitive import duties, thereby optimizing operational efficiency across geographical boundaries.

The process of continually improving parts has an inherent consequence: older parts become redundant more swiftly. This dynamic necessitates a paradigm shift in how Philips classifies and manages its spare parts inventory. In conjunction with the introduction of repair facilities, Philips has started differentiating parts based on new criteria, such as being categorized as "latest," "new," and "repaired." This classification enables the company to maintain clarity while managing a vast array of components without further complicating the parts pricing structure. These categorical distinctions have been uniformly applied across the entire parts catalog, ensuring coherence in the pricing model.

Currently, Philips is developing new pricing rules to ensure a consistent and automated pricing logic without necessitating manual intervention. This strategic initiative is pivotal in maintaining an efficient and responsive pricing mechanism that adapts to market demands while preserving operational simplicity.

Inventory management has also garnered significant attention to avoid the unnecessary scrapping of parts, thus optimizing resource utilization. With the introduction of classification criteria, markets now possess the capability to offer increased discounts on parts that are anticipated to be scrapped within a few years, specifically those not classified as "latest." These classifications are meticulously reviewed and updated annually by each business unit, ensuring that inventory decisions are informed and strategically sound.

Looking toward the future, Philips Healthcare is preparing to implement AI-driven solutions to further enhance its pricing strategy. These advanced technologies will automatically monitor the pricing landscape and provide strategic price suggestions as needed. The incorporation of AI will facilitate a dynamic and responsive pricing approach, paving the way for a more intelligent, data-driven strategy that aligns with Philips Healthcare's commitment to innovation and customer-centric excellence.

RESULTS

The introduction of a customer-centric parts pricing strategy ushered in a remarkable transformation for Philips Healthcare. This strategic shift, characterized by transparent and explainable pricing logic, significantly enhanced customers' comprehension of the intrinsic value offered by Philips parts. As a consequence, trust and satisfaction among Philips' clientele experienced a substantial uplift.

Consistency in pricing for analogous and counterpart parts played a pivotal role in reducing customer confusion, thereby streamlining the purchasing experience. Furthermore, the simplification of pricing for grouped parts notably diminished operational complexities and facilitated swifter price updates. This operational agility allowed Philips to respond promptly to market changes, ensuring the pricing strategy remained both relevant and competitive.

Strategic segmentation of parts ensured the continuous availability of critical components, thus minimizing machine downtime and bolstering customer operations. This approach enabled healthcare providers to maintain uninterrupted service delivery, reinforcing the dependability of Philips as a supplier of essential healthcare technology.

By intricately aligning pricing strategies with customer value and prevailing market dynamics, Philips Healthcare succeeded in optimizing both revenue and profitability. This alignment not only enhanced financial outcomes but also underscored the company's commitment to delivering value-driven solutions tailored to the needs of its diverse customer base.

Additionally, the emphasis on the superior quality and reliability of Philips parts further solidified the company's reputation as a trusted partner in the realm of healthcare technology. The consistent delivery of high-quality parts and transparent pricing has ensured that Philips Healthcare remains a sought-after choice among hospitals, clinics, and healthcare providers worldwide.

The adoption of a customer-centric parts pricing strategy has yielded multifaceted benefits for Philips Healthcare, including increased customer trust and satisfaction, streamlined operations, optimized revenue and profitability, and a reinforced reputation for excellence in healthcare technology. These outcomes underscore the pivotal role of strategic pricing in driving business success and maintaining leadership in a competitive market.

SUMMARY

Philips Healthcare's adoption of a customer-centric approach to parts pricing represents a paradigm shift from a traditional cost-plus model to a strategy that rigorously prioritizes customer needs, operational efficiency, and market dynamics. This transformative journey has enabled the company to refine its pricing framework, ensuring it is both responsive and attuned to the demands of its diverse clientele.

The strategic segmentation of parts plays a crucial role in this new approach, allowing Philips to categorize components based on their criticality and relevance, thereby ensuring consistent availability and minimizing machine downtime. Transparent pricing logic has been pivotal in enhancing customer understanding and trust, demonstrating the value inherent in every Philips part. Such clarity in pricing has significantly improved the purchasing experience and fostered stronger, more enduring customer relationships.

Philips Healthcare's unwavering emphasis on the superior quality and reliability of its parts has reinforced its reputation as a trustworthy partner in healthcare technology. This commitment to excellence has driven sustainable growth, optimized profitability, and secured long-term success in an increasingly competitive market. The holistic approach to parts pricing underscores the company's dedication to delivering value-driven solutions that resonate with customer expectations and market dynamics.

This case study is a testament to how a strategic, customer-focused pricing approach can effectively transform challenges into opportunities. By prioritizing customer-centric principles, Philips Healthcare has successfully elevated pricing to a pivotal role—one that drives significant value for both the company and its customers. The evolution of Philips' parts pricing strategy serves as a compelling model for other organizations seeking to enhance their operational efficiency, customer satisfaction, and financial performance through thoughtful and strategic pricing.

In essence, the adoption of a customer-centric parts pricing strategy has not only optimized operational processes for Philips Healthcare but has also fortified its position as a leader in healthcare technology. This approach has opened new avenues for growth, underscoring the importance of strategic pricing as a core driver of business success and customer value, ensuring continued excellence and innovation in the dynamic field of healthcare.

16

Terex

Parts Pricing Excellence with RGM, Data, and Technology

This case study was made possible thanks to the contribution of Kai Ostendorf, Director, Parts, Sales & Pricing at Terex Corporation. Kai has around 15 years of experience in pricing, aftermarket, and sales, with focus on digitalization and implementation of advanced pricing models to enhance customer experience and sustainable growth.

TEREX'S PROFILE AND PARTS PRICING CHALLENGES

Terex Corporation, a global manufacturer of lifting and material-handling solutions, has been a cornerstone of the construction, infrastructure, and industrial sectors for decades. Headquartered in Norwalk, Connecticut, Terex operates in over 80 countries, offering a diverse portfolio of products, including aerial work platforms, cranes, material handlers, and crushing and screening equipment. With a strong focus on innovation and customer satisfaction, Terex generates annual revenues of approximately 5 billion USD.

Terex has today three main business units. The first, called Aerial Work Platforms acts with one brand, namely Genie, selling products are used to lift personnel and material safely to height. These are leading global brands known for quality, purposeful innovation, and customer support. The second is called Material Processing and is a substantial portfolio of businesses that serves five key verticals: Aggregates, Environmental, Concrete, Handling, and Lifting. Sold through a specialized distribution network or directly to end customers and rental companies. Terex also created in 2024 a third business unit via the acquisition of the Environmental Solutions Group, serving the solid waste and recycling industry together with the Terex Utility products.

Terex Materials Processing's (MP) commitment to excellence extends beyond its machines to its aftermarket services, which include spare parts, maintenance, and support. However, managing the pricing of spare parts across a global network presented significant challenges. With customers in diverse regions and local competitors influencing market dynamics, Terex MP needed to align its pricing strategies with customer expectations, regional conditions, and product-specific factors in complex environment.

DOI: 10.4324/9781003647416-19

The Terex MP segment, which will be the focus of this case, has a particularly complex after-sales business. Here are the key facts and figures: >100 active price lists, >1,500 active dealers in 112 countries, around ~1 m active list prices, >110,000 different SKUs sold in the last three years, > 10 m historical list prices, >10%–20% of the total MP's revenues, >20 brands, >15,000 machines with telemetry (see Figure 16.1).

For years, Terex MP relied on traditional parts pricing methods, which were managed in isolation by the pricing function. With a strongly growing number of brands, spare parts, price lists, and dealers, the historical parts pricing approach became increasingly cumbersome.

The lack of a centralized price coordination, also aligned with sales and product management, represented a source of frictions. The result was a time-consuming process that hindered Terex MP's ability to optimize prices and react to market dynamics.

On top of this, Terex MP relied on manual processes and Excel spreadsheets to manage parts pricing. As the volume of data grew—spanning basic item information, sales figures, cost structures, and price history—inefficiencies became evident. It was difficult to visualize data, incorporate it into pricing logic, and respond quickly to market changes.

SOLUTION

To overcome its pricing challenges, Terex MP first merged pricing, sales, and product management under its newly created Revenue Growth Management function. The link of those functions helped to get the same understanding of defined targets (see Figure 16.2).

While in the past sales were blaming pricing and pricing blaming sales and product management, while pursuing a different strategy, with the new organization all this changed. There is harmony and alignment. The only function left to discuss with is supply chain, if in very seldom cases they don't have the right parts, in the right quantity in the right location/warehouse. But this represents an exception.

To overcome its IT pricing challenges, Terex MP passed from pricing managed in Excel to a pricing software solution designed to streamline processes, enhance visibility, and enable data-driven decision-making. Terex MP thus had a tool needed to analyze pricing data, identify opportunities, and implement optimized pricing strategies across its global operations.

At the core of this transformation there was a key innovation: the inclusion of a large set of data (displayed in Figure 16.3) that once assessed, allowed Terex MP to optimally manage its parts pricing.

While other corporations may use several other data points while setting parts pricing, this set of data indicated in Figure 16.3 turned out to be very relevant at Terex MP in the pricing and sales approach to drive revenue. A few of these data points are obvious like current list price, current costs, and competitor pricing, but some

Figure 16.1

Key facts about Terex's Materials Processing spare parts business

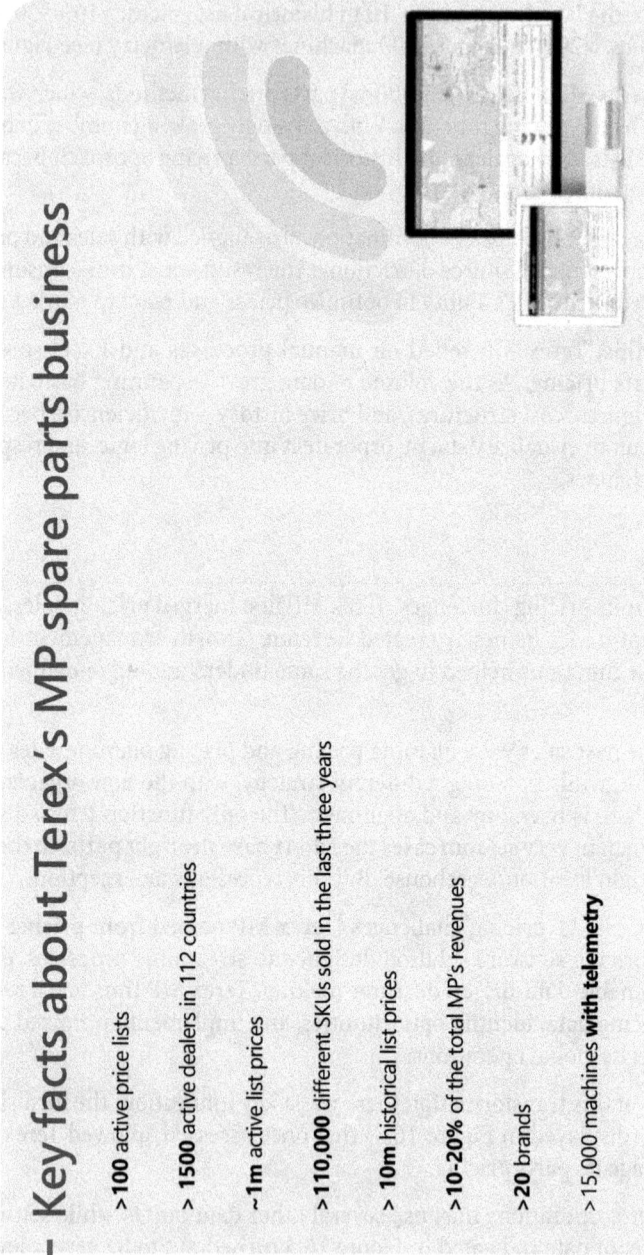

— Key facts about Terex's MP spare parts business

> **100** active price lists

> **1500** active dealers in 112 countries

> **~1m** active list prices

> **110,000** different SKUs sold in the last three years

> **10m** historical list prices

> **10-20%** of the total MP's revenues

> **20** brands

> **15,000** machines **with telemetry**

TEREX

Figure 16.2

The coordinated role of the Revenue Growth Management Department

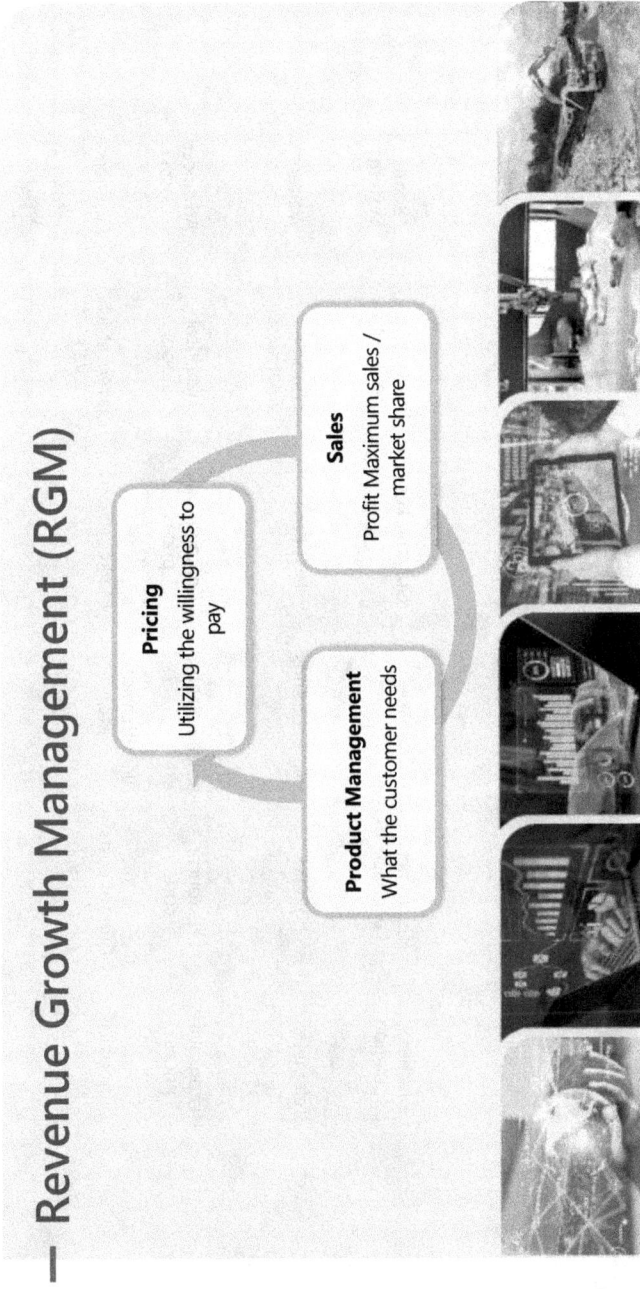

— Revenue Growth Management (RGM)

Pricing
Utilizing the willingness to pay

Sales
Profit Maximum sales / market share

Product Management
What the customer needs

TEREX

Figure 16.3
New Terex MP pricing approach relies on multiple data sources

Data points considered in the new MP pricing approach

Exclusivity	Price Claims	Quality	Logistics	Loyalty	Sales
Machine population	Customer Feedback	Service	Gray market	Purchasing behavior	Bonus Systems
Telemetry	(S)BOM	Market trends	First Pass	Google Analytics	Warranty
Historical list prices	Historical costs	Price Relations	Competition prices	Historical stocks	Advanced Cost+
Current list prices	Current costs	Length, width, etc.	Market shares	Current stock levels	Experience

TEREX

others are very important to consider during the price setting like potential based on (service) Bill of Materials (S)BOM in combination with telemetry data or current and historical stock levels and sales.

Centralized Data Visualization and Integration

Before implementing the new pricing software solution of the leading provider Syncron, Terex MP struggled to consolidate and visualize critical data, such as item details, sales volumes, costs, and price history. Increasing its pricing maturity with a new pricing software solution helped to create a centralized repository for all pricing data, seamlessly integrated with Terex MP's ERP system. This integration ensured that pricing managers always had access to the most up-to-date information, enabling faster and more informed decision-making.

Kai Ostendorf, Director Global Parts Strategic Pricing at Terex MP, states:

> The biggest challenges prior to the parts pricing software implementation was the visualization of data—from basic item information over sales, cost, and price history—and to include that in our pricing logic was quite complicated and also not very effective. The integration into the Syncron pricing software tool of competitive data delivered by Markt-Pilot generated valuable insights, generating transparency on market dynamics which were missing in the past and therefore led to suboptimal price setting efforts.

Dynamic Pricing Logic and Automation

The new parts pricing solution enabled Terex MP to implement dynamic pricing logic, replacing manual processes with automated workflows. This allowed Terex MP to adjust prices quickly and efficiently, improving responsiveness to market changes. The system also supported detailed price logic calculations, ensuring that pricing decisions were fair, realistic, and customer-focused.

Kumar Nandlal, Parts Analyst & Administrator of Franna, a Terex brand, indicates:

> Thanks to the interface between the parts pricing solution and the ERP system, price updates can be implemented very quickly. Additional changes can be made in the list price calculation through detailed price logic, leading to better customer experiences

Improved Customer Experience

By aligning pricing strategies with customer expectations, Terex MP enhanced the overall customer experience. For example, the system enables Terex MP to align pricing for related parts, such as left-hand and right-hand counterparts, ensuring logical and consistent pricing.

Bronagh McConnell, Price Analyst at Terex MP, concludes:

> Within Terex MP, we have a lot of parts where you have the left-hand and right-hand counterpart. We can join those parts together so that they remain aligned throughout the pricing journey, improving the customer experience.

RESULTS

The introduction of a Revenue Growth Management organization to manage parts pricing, combined with a data point leverage, marked a turning point for Terex MP, transforming its pricing strategy from an uncoordinated, manual, and reactive process into an aligned, proactive, data-driven approach.

Taking as much data as possible into account also helped improve Terex MP's customer experience by generating a better understanding of customers' needs in terms of which parts are needed when and where.

The results were significant:

- Faster and Better Pricing Decisions: Price updates and adjustments could be implemented quickly, reducing lead times, and improving market responsiveness.

- Increased Profitability: By identifying and capitalizing on pricing opportunities, Terex MP maximized revenue and service profitability.

- Inventory Management: Terex MP can manage inventory proactively, particularly during the early lifecycle phases of new machines.

"There's a significant relationship between pricing and inventory. That's typically driven by the common sharing of the data, which drives both key functions," highlights Marco Piovano, Vice President, Parts & Solutions, Terex MP. "At Terex MP, the new software solution is really helping us to improve our aftermarket mission. We are not only selling machines—we also need to ensure that our machines are up and running 24/7," summarizes Kai Ostendorf, Director Global Parts Strategic Pricing at Terex MP.

During this parts pricing maturity journey, Terex MP identified several success factors of RGM Excellence, summarized in Figure 16.4: a team with strong commercial, data, and number-driven mindset; short decision-making processes, understanding from top management, ownership, provision of necessary resources; know the score, KPIs to measure success, recognize trends early on, and react to them as quickly as possible; the right tools, technologies and skills to secure and process the previously mentioned amount of data—"single source of truth" —comes with a data strategy; continuous review and systematic improvement of all processes and strategies based

Figure 16.4

Success factors for RGM excellence

What is needed for RGM excellence

- **A team** with a strong commercial, data and number-driven mind-set
- **Short decision-making processes**, understanding from top management, ownership, provision of necessary resources
- **Know the score**, KPIs to measure success, recognize trends early on and react to them as quickly as possible
- The **right tools, technologies and skills** to secure and process the previously mentioned amount of data - "single source of truth" – comes with a data strategy
- **Continuous review and systematic improvement** of all processes and strategies based on a clear vision
- **Development plans** for and training of employees to meet the constantly growing requirements

TEREX

on a clear vision; and development plans for and training of employees to meet the constantly growing requirements.

SUMMARY

By introducing a Revenue Growth Management approach in parts pricing and leveraging data and technology, Terex MP revolutionized its spare parts pricing, achieving greater efficiency, market transparency, profitability, and customer satisfaction.

The Revenue Growth Management approach brought a better alignment between sales, pricing, and product management. The leverage of data, including competitive insights, increased at the end customer experience. And a new pricing software solution of Syncron, one of the leading parts pricing solution providers, helped streamline processes and improve decision-making.

Innovating its parts pricing, Terex MP has turned pricing into a strategic asset, driving growth, efficiency, and long-term success in the competitive world of aggregates, environmental, concrete, lifting, and material-handling equipment.

17

Ariston Group
Automation in Parts Pricing

This case study was made possible thanks to the contributions of Andrea Capello, Group Head of Parts Business Unit at Ariston Group and Lorenzo Caravati responsible for Business Development & Product Management Parts at Ariston Group.

ARISTON'S PROFILE AND PARTS PRICING CHALLENGES

Ariston Group is a global leader in sustainable solutions for hot water and space heating, components, and burners. In 2023 the group reported almost 3.1 billion euros in sales. Worldwide, Ariston Group has more than 10,000 employees, representative offices in 40 countries, 29 production sites, and 29 R&D centers in 5 continents.

Ariston is strongly committed to sustainability through the development of renewable and high-efficiency solutions, such as heat pumps, water heating heat pumps, hybrids, domestic ventilation, air handling, and solar thermal systems. The Group also stands out for the continuous investment in technological innovation, digitalization, and advanced connectivity systems. Ariston operates under global strategic brands Ariston, Elco, and Wolf, and brands such as Calorex, NTI, HTP, Chaffoteaux, Atag, Brink, Chromagen, Racold, as well as Thermowatt and Ecoflam in the components and burners business.

Ariston's vision is to provide everyone, in every corner of the world, with high-quality heating and hot water solutions, while protecting the environment. Therefore, the Group set up its own mission: to be the world's preferred partner in delivering energy efficient and renewable solutions for heating and hot water. It's fundamental to be able to understand the consumers' needs and to satisfy them worldwide, with leading brands and an extensive offer of products and services in the thermal comfort, burners, and components sectors.

Ariston is also strongly committed to support his customer base with an outstanding after-sales service, offering timely parts availability and technical information and documentation.

Referring to parts pricing, over the last decades, Ariston relied on a cost-plus pricing approach, locally managed in several markets, without a central governance and coordination. However, the complexity of the parts business made of more than 150,000 different SKUs sold in more than 50 markets, forced the Group to foster the

DOI: 10.4324/9781003647416-20

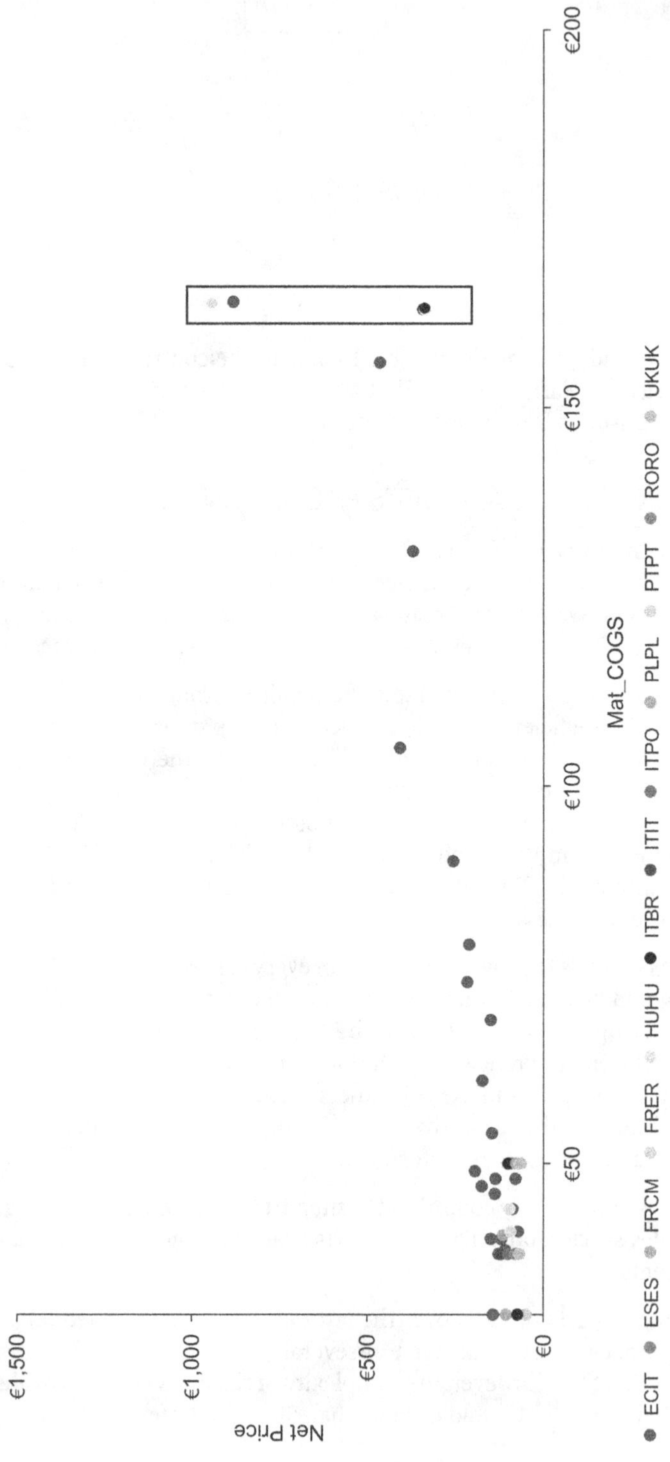

Figure 17.1

(a) Geographical spare parts price misalignments. (b) Product spare parts price misalignments

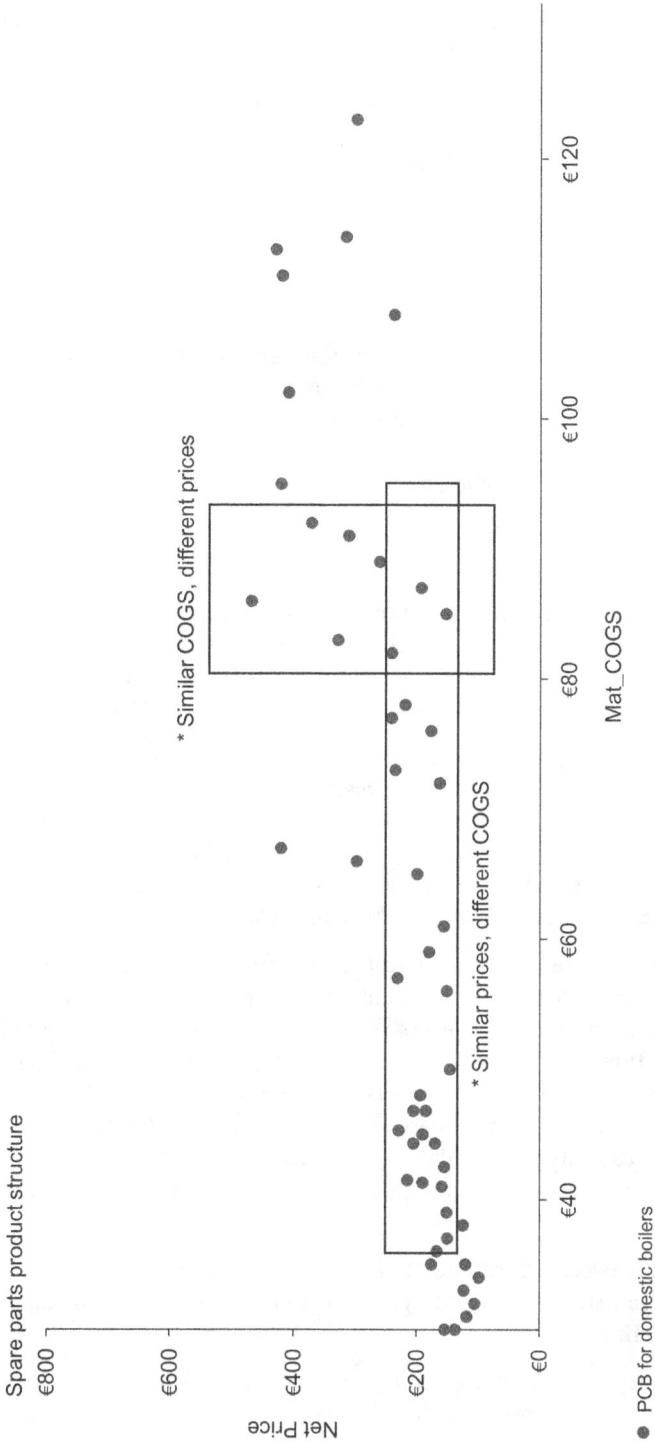

Spare parts product structure

Net Price

€800
€600
€400
€200
€0

€0 €40 €60 €80 €100 €120

Mat_COGS

* Similar COGS, different prices

* Similar prices, different COGS

● PCB for domestic boilers

initiative to develop a structured process to harmonize, optimize, and automize the spare parts pricing management.

Main pain points to be addressed were related to misalignment in pricing both geographically (see Figure 17.1a) and among product families (see Figure 17.1b) that could potentially impact negatively on profitability and sales opportunities, and for sure it was increasing operation costs and complexity, but moreover it could generate customer dissatisfaction and disaffection.

SOLUTION

To address those challenges, Ariston established a centralized process to manage and control the price lists for all the parts globally, focusing on four key pillars: relay on robust datamart management, move from cost-plus to a value-based approach, exploit business intelligence to collect market inputs and strengthen benchmarking, and develop deep data analytics.

Datamart Management

Ariston Thermo ensured the evolution of its spare parts pricing approach through rigorous master data and lifecycle management, meticulous tracking of supersession history, and careful maintenance of links between finished products and spare parts—supported by historical sales volumes and financial data.

The starting point of the analyses was based on clusters of product families linked to the official Harmonized Commodity Description (HS codes, used from the custom authorities for product classification, selected for its granularity and being sure it must be maintained) that have been further enriched by adding functional and product-related characteristics, to better evaluate the real value of each product family, but also among spare parts belonging to the same product family.

This activity supported by the technical team responsible for managing the datamart and the spare parts' technical documentation was executed in collaboration with the R&D departments for each range of finished goods. For each spare part family key technical features have been identified in order to collect additional parameters to determine how complex a spare part is compared with other parts belonging to the same product family. Examples are the number of plates for heat exchangers and the flow rate capacity for circulators. According to the material composition such as plastics and copper, other enrichments were related to additional insight such as "critical to function."

The balance between information richness and simplicity was ensured by introducing only parameters that added significant value in the pricing calculation and are long-term maintainable.

The basic purpose of this important task was to increase our capacity to assign different values to spares according to their technological complexity, and other relevant parameters, that could be straightforward linked to the customer's willingness to pay.

This is the reason why not only technical parameters were taken into account but also considerations related to patents and exclusivity were linked to a specific spare part master data.

From Cost-Plus to Value-Based Approach

This full set of information allowed Ariston Thermo to set up the algorithms and to develop a value-based pricing tool, internally developed, by assigning a multiplicator index to each single parameter used to enrich the spare parts datamart and information, which indicator would be used to adjust the initial price level defined according to the cost of the product.

The algorithms calculate the prices based on the features of the spare part (technical and commercial) and the relation between spare parts and finished products to ensure the price is increased or decreased based on the value of the products that are mounting it and the average age of the installed base.

The approach aims to set an adequate price level for each spare part, which is not just related to the cost of the product, but also taking into consideration the impact on our customers: for instance, we want to make sure that the customer will find it convenient to repair their appliances despite they could be already quite old, keeping a reasonable lower price for the needed SP, instead of being obliged to change the whole product. Also, in case of cheap finish product we set the price level for the related SP in a way that the weight of a repair cost will not be that relevant compared with the cost of a new appliance.

The new pricing tool also allowed Ariston to mitigate or even eliminate the inconsistencies and incoherencies present in the previous set of price lists, not just referring to the product features, but also among market, thanks to the definition of a master price list from which every country price list is retrieved, through the application of country factor index, which has been defined in collaboration with the markets, by considering commercial discount policies and different purchasing power. This implementation allowed Ariston Group to set up spare parts price lists at country level, which have dramatically reduced the risks of cross-market business opportunities (grey market), supported the identification of risks related to loss of sales volumes, creating opportunities related to additional volumes in case of uncompetitive prices, and, obviously, maximize profits in some cases.

Business Intelligence and Benchmarking

An important element, which contributes to provide coherence and consistency to the new pricing model, has been the introduction of a new process to periodically monitor the market feedback and tendency in a structured way.

Ariston introduced a monthly process to collect all feedback, claims, and suggestions related to price comparisons coming from the markets through a dedicated platform. This allows the pricing team to rapidly intervene with a harmonized approach in reviewing the parameters of the pricing tool. Moreover, this process allowed to dramatically improve the communication effectiveness, reducing the e-mail traffic and therefore addressing the issue of an heavy effort dedicated to a low-value activity (collecting and processing emails). The second and important element fostered by the team has been the introduction of a constant and structured comparison process between Ariston spare parts prices and the ones publicly published online from distributors and reseller for common products: this allows Ariston to increase its own competitiveness and to propose favorable prices to its customers (Figure 17.2).

Dedicated tables to manage pricing exceptions (unavoidable in the pricing journey due to price modifications for claims or benchmarking purposes, spare part to be sold at a fixed price in certain sales channels) are linked to the model so that it considers the instruction in the tables when setting or recalculating the prices. Exceptions are to be periodically reviewed to individuate and develop in the pricing tool, when possible, rules that can include the pricing calculation logic to avoid it is to be considered as an exception and enriching the pricing calculation model.

Data Analytics

The last and extremely important pillar of Ariston approach to SP pricing has been the development of dedicated data analytics cockpit (Figure 17.3a and 17.3b) to be able to intercept risks and opportunities linked to the correlations between the prices and the business evolutions in each single market for every spare parts. The variance analysis performed at every level of detail allows to better appreciate the way in which the price adjustment performed (at SKU and market level) could reflect on business growth and trends over time.

The internally developed pricing tool also allows Ariston to perform simulation about the potential business impacts driven by pricing adjustments, considering sales volumes and mix assumptions at each level of detail. These capabilities allow Ariston to increase flexibility and agility by accelerating the possibility of implementing pricing adjustments along the year in a dynamic and smart manner, instead of being obliged to adjust the pricing list once a year after performing weeks of excel calculations.

RESULTS

The adoption of a centralized approach in pricing management for spare parts (Figure 17.4) allowed Ariston to overcome difficulties and misalignment and brought significant advantages both in short and long term:

Figure 17.2

Benchmarking dashboard

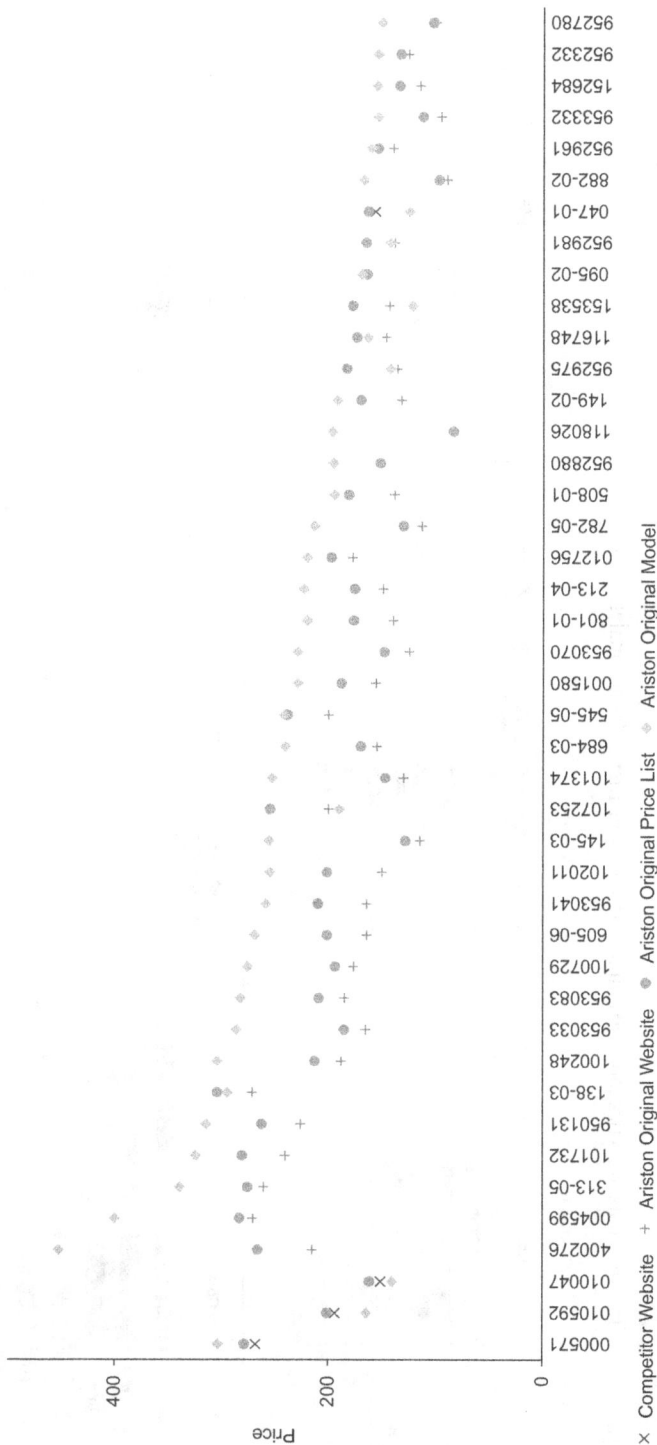

Figure 17.3

(a) Ariston Thermo's data analytics tool—Example 1. (b) Ariston Thermo's data analytics tool —Example 2

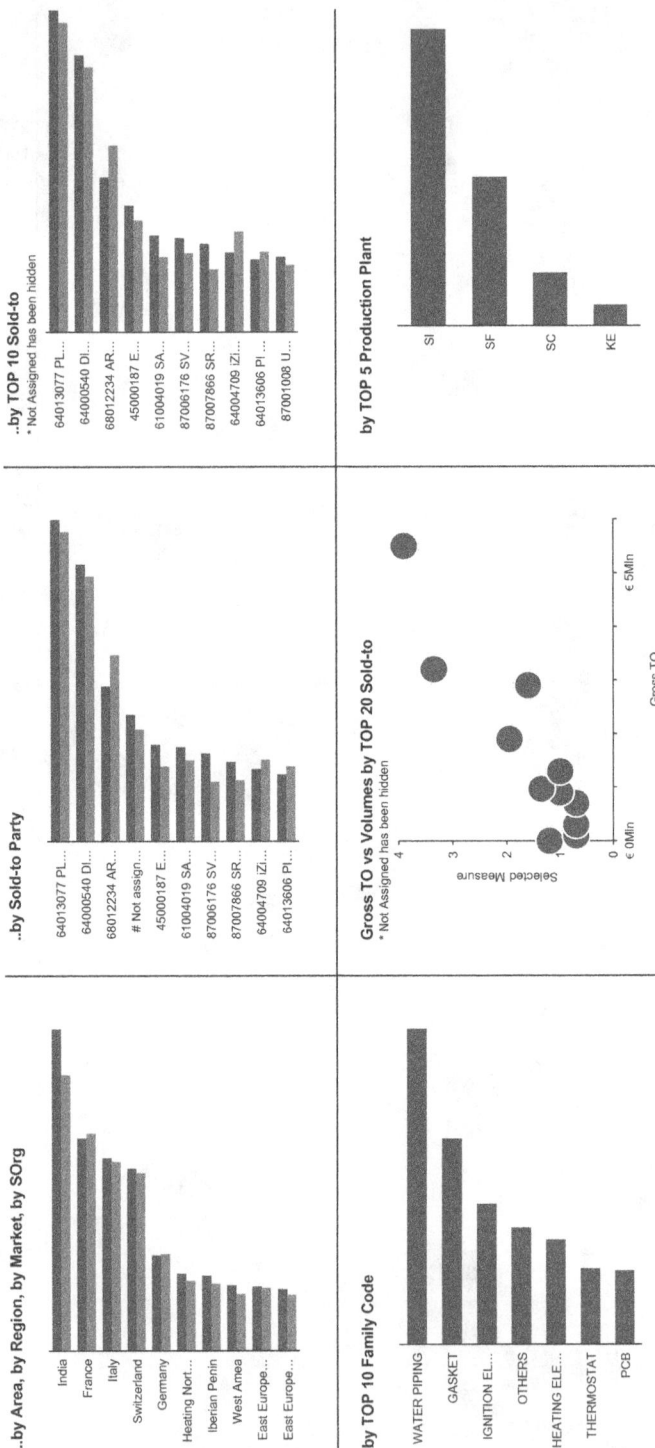

...by Area, by Region, by Market, by SOrg

India
France
Italy
Switzerland
Germany
Heating Nort...
Iberian Penin
West Area
East Europe...
East Europe...

by TOP 10 Family Code

WATER PIPING
GASKET
IGNITION EL...
OTHERS
HEATING ELE...
THERMOSTAT
PCB

...by Sold-to Party

64013077 PL...
64000540 DI...
68012234 AR...
Not assign...
45000187 E...
61004019 SA...
87006176 SV...
87007866 SR...
64004709 iZi...
64013606 PI...

Gross TO vs Volumes by TOP 20 Sold-to
* Not Assigned has been hidden

Selected Measure
€ 0Min   Gross TO   € 5Min

...by TOP 10 Sold-to
* Not Assigned has been hidden

64013077 PL...
64000540 DI...
68012234 AR...
45000187 E...
61004019 SA...
87006176 SV...
87007866 SR...
64004709 iZi...
64013606 PI...
87001008 U...

by TOP 5 Production Plant

SI
SF
SC
KE

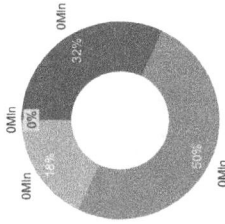

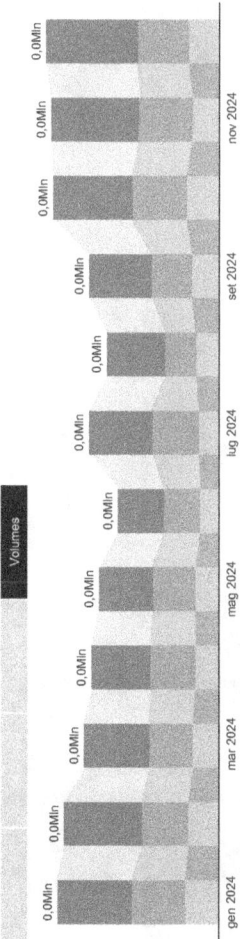

Actual Volumes is higher than Previous Year(0.1 M | 5% ▲).

* Values displayed in k€

Family code 1	PY	ACT	△	△%
WATER PIPING	**415,1**	**541,4**	**126,3**	**30,4%**
COMPETITIVE	380,1	510,2	130,2	34,2%
CAPTIVE	19,5	20,7	1,2	6,3%
Not assigned	15,6	10,5	-5,1	-32,4%
GASKET	**337,1**	**348,2**	**11,1**	**3,3%**
COMPETITIVE	160,6	165,8	5,2	3,3%
CAPTIVE	135,4	138,7	3,3	2,5%
Not assigned	41,1	43,7	2,6	6,2%
IGNITION ELECTRODE	**233,7**	**241,5**	**7,8**	**3,3%**
COMPETITIVE	110,2	105,5	-4,6	-4,2%
CAPTIVE	87,9	96,2	8,4	9,5%
Not assigned	35,6	39,7	4,1	11,5%
OTHERS	**214,1**	**195,2**	**-19,0**	**-8,9%**
CAPTIVE	80,8	79,4	-1,4	-1,8%
Not assigned	76,3	63,3	-13,0	-17,0%
COMPETITIVE	56,9	52,4	-4,5	-7,9%
THREMOREGULATION	0,0	0,0	0,0	-50,0%
Totale	**3.019,1**	**3.162,6**	**143,4**	**4,7%**

Volumes

■ Thermoregulation ■ Not assigned Competitive Captive

Sold-to Party

Figure 17.4

Centralized approach in pricing management

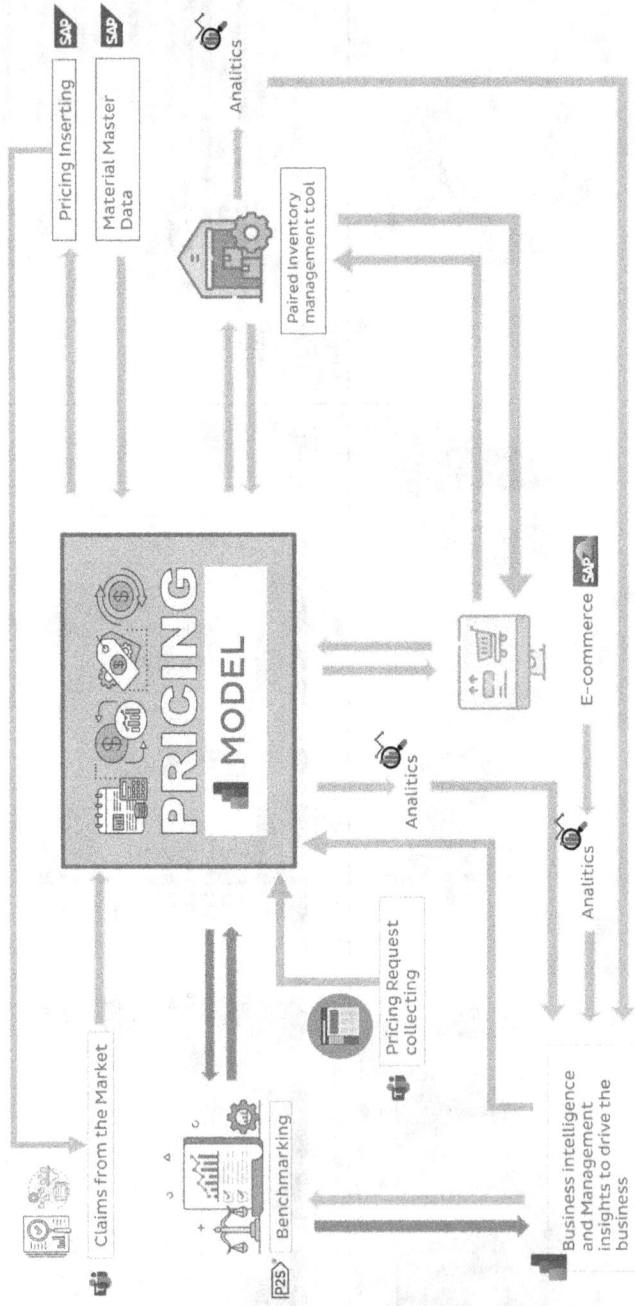

- Workload reduction in price list definition for all markets thanks to a robust and automatized tool internally developed

- Coherence and consistency among price list among markets and among product families

- Business control through detailed data analysis

- Possibility to be faster in assigning prices to new items or to product to be extended to additional markets

- Simplicity to perform simulation about expected impacts on spare parts business driven by price adjustments and assumptions on volumes and mix impacts

- Put the basis for more frequent pricing variations also considering sales forecast and inventory level

The implemented pricing process could also allow in the future to integrate in different streams (such as product classification and clusterization among Ariston products but also vs competitors' products or in the phase of data analysis, etc.) and in some AI simple application in order to further accelerate and refine the pricing definition.

SUMMARY

Thanks to a structured and organized approach Ariston Group is currently capable of managing the spare parts pricing worldwide in a consistent manner, reducing the internal workload and supporting the spare parts business considering the real value of each single product, according to its own features.

A structured process that combines a robust data mart management, an automated and internally developed pricing tool, supported by advanced business intelligence, benchmarking, and data analytics are the key factors for the successful journey of the spare parts pricing management at Ariston Group.

18

Tenneco

Adapting Value Communication to Evolving Parts Purchase Decision-Makers

TENNECO'S PROFILE AND PARTS PRICING CHALLENGES

Tenneco is a leading American automotive components manufacturer with global operations. The company produces both original equipment and aftermarket solutions, specializing in ride control and emissions systems. With approximately 16 billion USD in annual revenues and a workforce of over 60,000 employees, Tenneco serves a wide network of distributors, workshops, and end users.

The central challenge in Tenneco's spare parts pricing strategy was not the parts themselves, but the changing identity of the decision-maker. In the past, car owners played a central role in parts selection, bringing their vehicles to workshops and often requesting specific brands or types. Tenneco's marketing and pricing logic aligned with this structure, focusing on end-user needs and preferences.

However, this changed as vehicle ownership shifted toward models such as leasing, rentals, and car subscriptions. Car use became detached from car ownership, and with it, end users became less involved in maintenance decisions. As a result, workshops and later distributors became the primary decision-makers. This shift required Tenneco to rethink how it communicated value across its aftermarket business.

SOLUTION: EVOLVING THE VALUE PROPOSITION ALONG THE CHAIN

The first step in this transition was to make the company's offerings more attractive to workshops. Tenneco introduced solutions designed to simplify installation and reduce the time required for repairs. After-sales fitting instructions were created and shared to make installers' work easier and more efficient.

New spare part bundles were developed, for example, bringing together all relevant shock absorber components into complete kits. Preassembled kits combining shock absorbers and springs were also introduced, targeting key use cases and significantly saving time during repairs. These more complete repair solutions were offered at higher price points as more SKUs were offered, which however were sustainable because the costs were typically charged back to clients or insurance providers.

As vehicles grew more complex and technologically advanced, the need for professional repairs increased. Installers began to request additional support such as regular training, detailed documentation, and easier installation tools. At the same time,

DOI: 10.4324/9781003647416-21

the parts distribution landscape was consolidating. Distributors expanded through acquisitions and took on a more central role in parts selection. These distributors launched workshop concepts that influenced what installers recommended to end users.

This development marked a new turning point for Tenneco. The company refocused its value communication strategy to align with the needs and priorities of distributors (see Figure 18.1). To meet distributor expectations, Tenneco expanded its product offering significantly. It added product lines such as turbochargers, sensors, commercial vehicles spare parts to support the distributors' goal of becoming one-stop shops.

Distributors prefer to work with fewer but broader suppliers. In response, Tenneco consolidated 30 separately sold brands under a single unified brand, DRiV (See Figure 18.2.). This move allowed the company to simplify operations and present a unified commercial offering. Today, DRiV parts coverage exceed 90% for all spare parts categories offered.

Standardized contracts and incentive programs were introduced to make the distributor relationship easier to manage and more efficient. These included single agreements that allowed performance-based rebates to apply across the entire product portfolio, rather than treating each product group separately.

Although Tenneco continued selling the same types of spare parts—such as brake pads and shock absorbers—the way it communicated value had changed significantly. Initially targeted at end users, then at workshops, and now at distributors, the evolution reflected the company's ongoing effort to stay aligned with the actual decision-makers in the market.

RESULTS AND VALUE COMMUNICATION TODAY

Tenneco's evolution in value communication highlights a crucial principle: the chooser is not always the one who pays. As marketing and communication to end consumers became obsolete, traditional B2C advertising—such as brake pad promotions in newspapers or on TV—disappeared. In its place emerged a B2B strategy centered around the needs of distributors.

For distributors, the value lays in data accuracy, product coverage, and commercial simplicity. They needed highly accurate catalog data to ensure correct part selection.

They valued OEM fitment information, even though it was largely irrelevant to end consumers. They required easy-to-navigate contracts that covered multiple product categories under a single agreement. This approach allowed them to meet revenue targets across the board without needing to negotiate separate terms for each product line.

Tenneco's value argumentation also included technical training and installation videos, ensuring that installers had what they needed to fit parts efficiently and

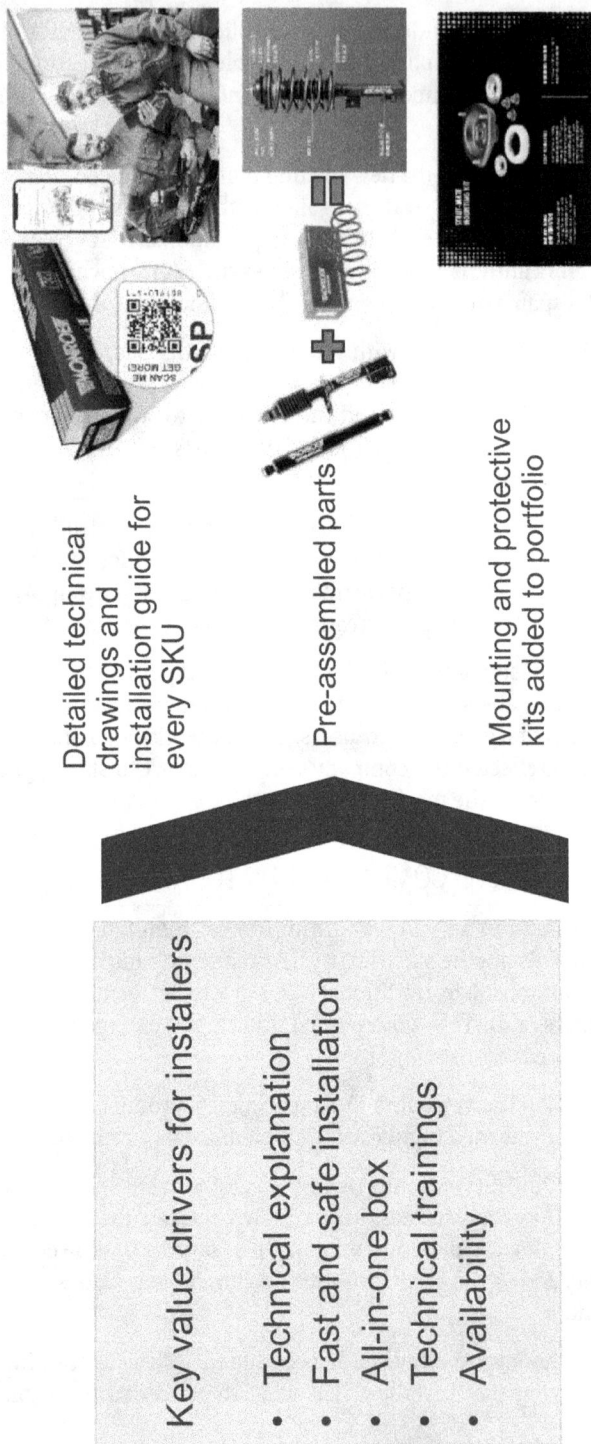

Figure 18.1

Examples of value delivery and communication targeted toward independent workshops

Figure 18.2

DriV as a "hub" for multiple aftermarket brands

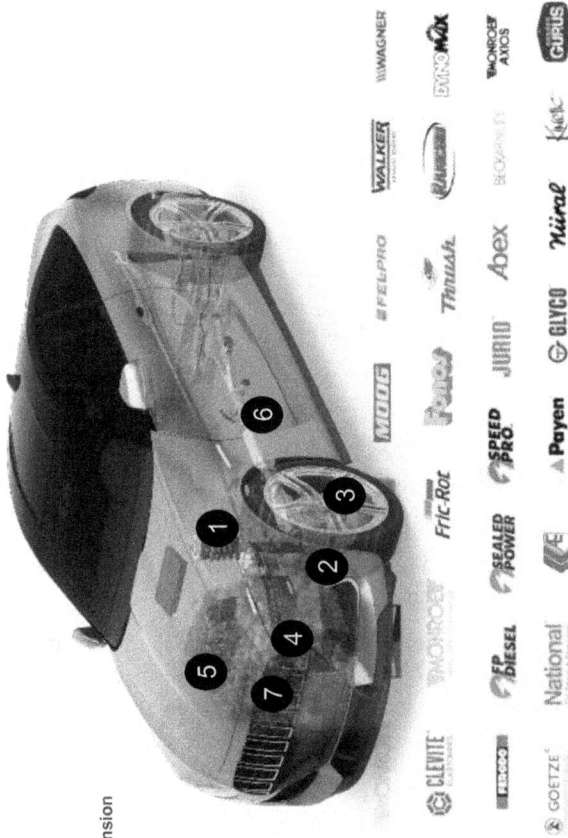

1 Shocks and Struts

2 Steering and Suspension

3 Braking

4 Sealing

5 Engine

6 Emissions

7 Maintenance

GLOBAL
BRAND
PORTFOLIO

correctly. Fitting instructions became a key selling point, supporting distributors in delivering professional services to their downstream customers.

In this evolved setup, Tenneco tracked value not only through pricing structures but through its understanding of who was making the decision and what mattered most to them. Distributors had clear preferences for fewer, more comprehensive suppliers, streamlined commercial terms, and deep coverage of parts. Tenneco's response to this preference—a broader portfolio, a unified brand, and centralized contracting—allowed it to maintain relevance and competitiveness in an increasingly consolidated market.

SUMMARY

Tenneco's journey illustrates a key lesson in aftermarket strategy: value must be defined and communicated according to the chooser, not the payer. Over time, the chooser changed from the car owner to the workshop, and then to the distributor.

At each stage, Tenneco adjusted its offering, its messaging, and its pricing approach to remain aligned with the real decision-makers.

Today, value communication focuses on parts coverage, catalog data accuracy, ease of installation, and unified contracts—all elements that are essential to distributors but irrelevant to end consumers.

Marketing to end users has disappeared. Instead, Tenneco has developed a comprehensive, distributor-oriented strategy that supports its partners with tools, training, and incentives. This shift allowed the company to maintain its market position and turn value communication into a dynamic, adaptable capability—one that evolves alongside the structure of the aftermarket itself.

ACKNOWLEDGMENT

This case study was made possible thanks to the contribution of Rafal Janaczek, EMEA Strategic Pricing Leader at Tenneco.

OPTIMA

Market Intelligence for Proactive Parts Distribution

OPTIMA'S PROFILE AND PARTS PRICING CHALLENGES

OPTIMA packaging group is a globally recognized leader in the design and manufacturing of advanced packaging machinery. Founded in Germany, the company has built a reputation for delivering high-precision, high-performance packaging solutions across multiple industries. With a presence in over 20 locations worldwide and a workforce exceeding 3,150 employees, OPTIMA serves a diverse range of sectors, including energy, food, chemicals, diagnostics, hygiene, and filtration. The company generates more than 620 million euros in annual revenue, reflecting its strong market position and commitment to continuous growth.

Renowned for its engineering excellence and commitment to innovation, OPTIMA integrates cutting-edge technology into its packaging systems, ensuring efficiency, sustainability, and adaptability to evolving market demands. By investing in research and development, the company remains at the forefront of automation and digitalization, offering smart packaging solutions that enhance productivity and reduce operational costs.

Beyond its core business in packaging machinery, OPTIMA also places a strong emphasis on customer service, particularly in its aftermarket operations. Recognizing the critical role of spare parts availability in maintaining machinery performance and minimizing downtime, OPTIMA has developed a centralized aftermarket strategy that supports all its business units.

However, operating in the global spare parts market comes with significant challenges. The competitive landscape demands a strategic approach to pricing and availability, while limited transparency on market prices and delivery times complicates decision-making. Additionally, balancing speed and quality is essential for meeting customer expectations and sustaining a competitive advantage.

By addressing these challenges, OPTIMA aims to optimize its spare parts pricing strategy, ensuring both profitability and customer satisfaction while reinforcing its position as an industry leader.

DOI: 10.4324/9781003647416-22

SOLUTION

To enhance its pricing and sales strategy, OPTIMA adopted MARKT-PILOT's market intelligence solutions, integrating advanced data analytics to refine its spare parts pricing model. Recognizing the need for a more transparent, flexible, and competitive approach, OPTIMA leveraged market insights to align its pricing strategy with industry benchmarks while ensuring optimal customer value. By focusing on key regions—DACH, the United States, and South America—the company identified critical pricing inefficiencies and areas for improvement, allowing it to make more informed decisions in a highly competitive aftermarket environment.

Parts pricing insights like the ones sanitized in Figure 19.1 provide parts data information on, for example, part numbers, product groups, purchase and sales prices within a dashboard. Figure 19.1 is an example dashboard, not related to OPTIMA.

A major advantage of the new system was its ability to provide updated pricing and lead time data twice a year, offering OPTIMA a clearer view of shifting market dynamics across multiple geographies. Previously, a lack of visibility into competitor pricing and delivery timelines made it difficult to adjust strategies proactively. With access to market data, OPTIMA could now track pricing trends, benchmark spare parts costs against competitors, and implement dynamic adjustments in response to market fluctuations.

With this new market transparency it was easily possible to detect pricing opportunities, for example, when spare parts were underpriced (see Figure 19.2—example not related to OPTIMA).

The solution enabled OPTIMA to identify parts with pricing discrepancies, ensuring that its pricing remained both competitive and profitable. By leveraging data-driven insights, OPTIMA was able to minimize risk and improve margin control—key factors in maintaining a sustainable and scalable aftermarket business.

With a more transparent and responsive pricing strategy, OPTIMA successfully strengthened its market position and improved pricing flexibility across its global operations. The adoption of MARKT-PILOT's solution transformed pricing from a static function into a strategic lever for growth, enabling OPTIMA to anticipate market shifts, respond to competitive pressures, and deliver greater value to customers.

RESULTS

By leveraging market data and intelligence-driven insights, OPTIMA successfully transformed its spare parts pricing strategy, leading to greater competitiveness, enhanced operational efficiency, and stronger customer relationships. The implementation of MARKT-PILOT's market intelligence solution allowed the company to optimize pricing structures, ensuring that spare parts were competitively priced while maximizing profitability. This shift not only boosted overall sales performance but

Figure 19.1

Market data dashboard with part numbers, product groups, purchase, and sales prices as an example, not related to OPTIMA

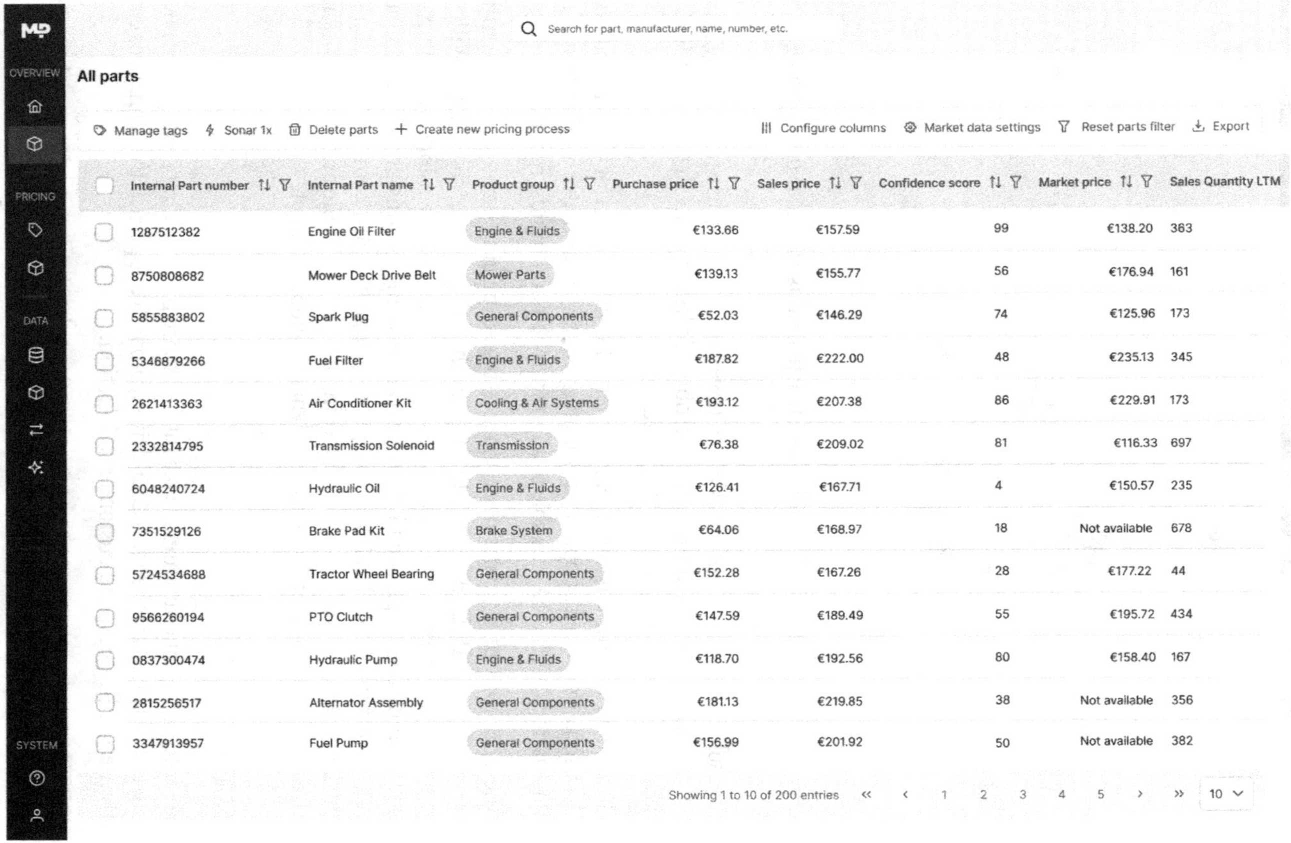

Internal Part number	Internal Part name	Product group	Purchase price	Sales price	Confidence score	Market price	Sales Quantity LTM
1287512382	Engine Oil Filter	Engine & Fluids	€133.66	€157.59	99	€138.20	363
8750808682	Mower Deck Drive Belt	Mower Parts	€139.13	€155.77	56	€176.94	161
5855883802	Spark Plug	General Components	€52.03	€146.29	74	€125.96	173
5346879266	Fuel Filter	Engine & Fluids	€187.82	€222.00	48	€235.13	345
2621413363	Air Conditioner Kit	Cooling & Air Systems	€193.12	€207.38	86	€229.91	173
2332814795	Transmission Solenoid	Transmission	€76.38	€209.02	81	€116.33	697
6048240724	Hydraulic Oil	Engine & Fluids	€126.41	€167.71	4	€150.57	235
7351529126	Brake Pad Kit	Brake System	€64.06	€168.97	18	Not available	678
5724534688	Tractor Wheel Bearing	General Components	€152.28	€167.26	28	€177.22	44
9566260194	PTO Clutch	General Components	€147.59	€189.49	55	€195.72	434
0837300474	Hydraulic Pump	Engine & Fluids	€118.70	€192.56	80	€158.40	167
2815256517	Alternator Assembly	General Components	€181.13	€219.85	38	Not available	356
3347913957	Fuel Pump	General Components	€156.99	€201.92	50	Not available	382

Showing 1 to 10 of 200 entries

Search for part, manufacturer, name, number, etc.

Manage tags   Sonar 1x   Delete parts   + Create new pricing process   Configure columns   Market data settings   Reset parts filter   Export

All parts

OVERVIEW
PRICING
DATA
SYSTEM

Figure 19.2

Detecting pricing opportunities—underpriced parts as an example, not related to OPTIMA

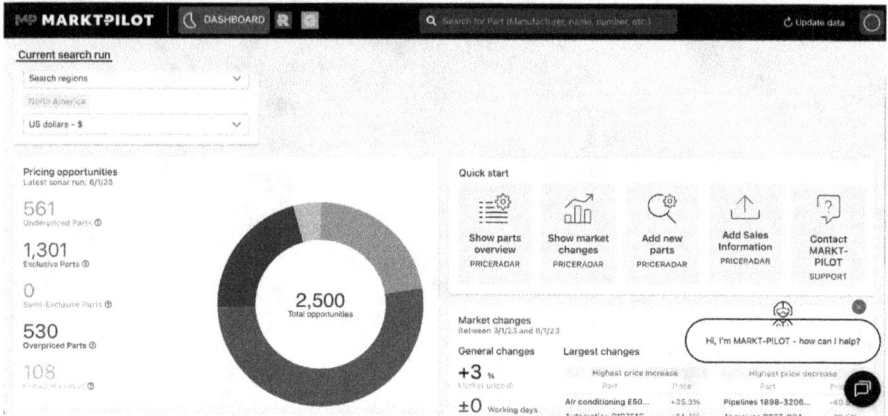

also reinforced OPTIMA's position as a trusted industry leader in the global packaging machinery market.

The solution in use at OPTIMA also allowed to create a consistent pricing process in an efficient manner with intuitive dashboards like the one displayed in Figure 19.3 as an example, not related to OPTIMA.

Beyond sales and customer experience, the integration of data-based sourcing decisions improved supply chain management. With better visibility into market fluctuations, OPTIMA was able to align with demand trends, reducing inefficiencies.

The adoption of a structured, market-based pricing strategy has significantly strengthened OPTIMA's ability to adapt to changing market conditions. With greater transparency, responsiveness, and efficiency in pricing decisions, the company has successfully future-proofed its aftermarket operations. This proactive approach has not only reinforced OPTIMA's competitive edge but also contributed to long-term business stability, ensuring that the company remains agile and well-positioned for sustained growth in an increasingly dynamic global market.

SUMMARY

By integrating market intelligence into its spare parts pricing strategy, OPTIMA has successfully transitioned to a data-driven, proactive approach that enhances competitiveness, efficiency, and customer satisfaction.

OPTIMA gained access to pricing benchmarks, lead time data, and competitor insights, enabling more strategic and informed decision-making.

Figure 19.3

Managing the pricing process with an intuitive dashboard, as an example, not related to OPTIMA

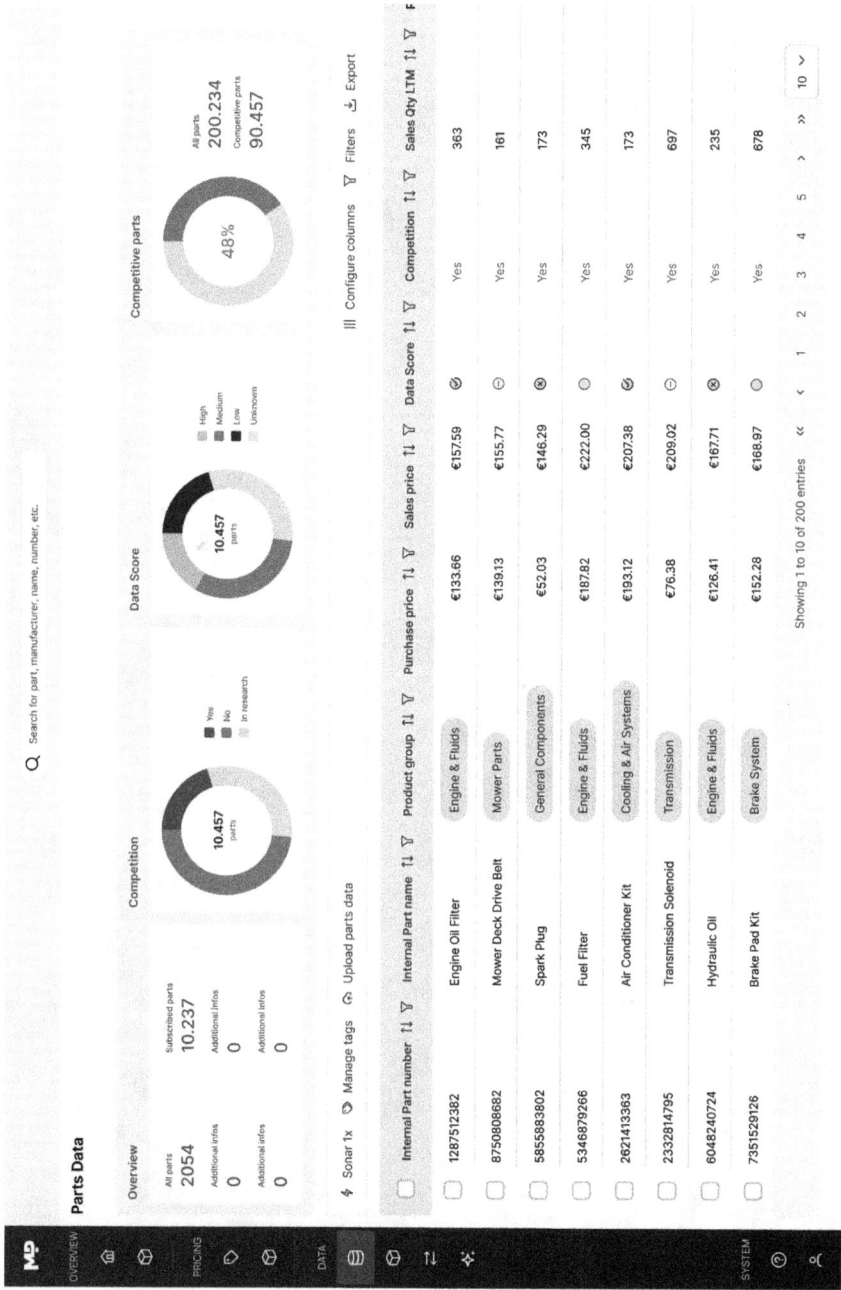

Parts Data

Overview
- All parts: 2054
- Subscribed parts: 10.237
- Additional infos: 0
- Additional infos: 0
- Additional infos: 0
- Additional infos: 0

Competition — 10.457 parts
- Yes
- No
- In research

Data Score — 10.457 parts
- High
- Medium
- Low
- Unknown

Competitive parts
- All parts: 200.234
- Competitive parts: 90.457
- 48%

Internal Part number	Internal Part name	Product group	Purchase price	Sales price	Data Score	Competition	Sales Qty LTM
1287512382	Engine Oil Filter	Engine & Fluids	€133.66	€15.759		Yes	363
8750808682	Mower Deck Drive Belt	Mower Parts	€139.13	€155.77		Yes	161
5855883802	Spark Plug	General Components	€52.03	€146.29		Yes	173
5346879266	Fuel Filter	Engine & Fluids	€187.82	€222.00		Yes	345
2621413363	Air Conditioner Kit	Cooling & Air Systems	€193.12	€207.38		Yes	173
2332814795	Transmission Solenoid	Transmission	€76.38	€209.02		Yes	697
6048240724	Hydraulic Oil	Engine & Fluids	€126.41	€16.71		Yes	235
7351529126	Brake Pad Kit	Brake System	€152.28	€168.97		Yes	678

Showing 1 to 10 of 200 entries   « ‹ 1 2 3 4 5 › »   10

Sonar 1x   Manage tags   Upload parts data   Configure columns   Filters   Export

The transformation brought significant improvements to OPTIMA's operations. OPTIMA can now respond quickly to market shifts, ensuring long-term stability in an evolving industry.

ACKNOWLEDGMENT

This case study was made possible thanks to the contribution of Jonas Kiene, Team Leader Service Parts Management at OPTIMA Packaging Group.

20

Nokia Hardware Services

Shift to a Value-Centric Commercial Strategy

This case study was made possible thanks to the contributions of Saeed Qadri, Head of Portfolio Commercial Management at Nokia, and Chandra P. Singh, Commercial and Product Manager at Nokia.

NOKIA'S PROFILE AND PARTS PRICING CHALLENGES

Nokia delivers maintenance and support services for its products and solutions; this represents around 10% Nokia's mobile revenue. For its hardware products, Nokia provides wide range of hardware services focusing on comprehensive hardware support and maintenance.

Nokia hardware services (HWS) delivers a comprehensive suite of hardware-focused offerings, including spare parts sales, preventive maintenance, troubleshooting, repairs, and replacements (see Figure 20.1).

The core mission of HWS is to minimize network downtime and maintain seamless operations for telecom operators worldwide. This is achieved through a blend of on-site support, remote diagnostics, and a highly efficient spare parts management system.

Nokia's spare parts sales (SPS) plays a pivotal role in supporting customers' ongoing network maintenance needs. Each year, HWS manages 439K hardware service transactions (including repair, advanced exchange and SPS transactions), refurbishes 30,000 hardware units, and contributes to sustainability by avoiding 6,000 tons of CO_2 emissions through its circular services. Altogether, it supports over 2.2 million contracted network elements across a customer base of more than 420 telecom operators globally.

Nokia HWS aimed to radically rethink its after-sales commercial approach by putting value—not cost—at the center of its hardware services. In a telecom industry where every minute of downtime can affect millions of end users, Nokia's hardware services play a mission-critical role, but have long been treated internally and externally as a transactional, cost-plus support function, pressured to lower prices rather than recognized for the value they deliver.

This perception is now changing. Nokia HWS is evolving from a reactive, price-driven service provider into a proactive, value-driven business with a clear commercial

DOI: 10.4324/9781003647416-23

strategy focused on creating measurable customer outcomes, capturing a fair share of that value, and implementing value-based pricing models that reflect its true impact.

SOLUTION

Nokia HWS recognized the urgent need to redefine its commercial strategy in response to the shifting priorities of its telecom operator customers. These operators are navigating a landscape of growing complexity, characterized by multi-generation, multi-vendor networks, intense pressure to reduce operational expenditures without compromising service quality, increasing demands for sustainability from both regulators and end users, and the rise of new business models that depend on faster, more dependable hardware support.

The feedback from the market was unequivocal: customers no longer seek just low-cost services or efficient spare parts delivery—they expect solutions that create clear and measurable business value. In response, Nokia HWS developed a new commercial strategy centered on value creation, value capture, and equitable value sharing, all structured around three key strategic lenses (see Figure 20.2).

The first lens, *Portfolio Enrichment*, focuses on creating value through relevant and competitive offerings. Nokia HWS has redesigned its service portfolio to ensure it delivers tangible business benefits to telecom operators.

The portfolio is now tailored according to each operator's installed base, network criticality, and business objectives, ensuring that spare parts coverage and availability are aligned with operational needs.

New services powered by next-generation technologies, such as AI-driven diagnostics, automated repairs, and proactive fault prediction, shift the approach from reactive repairs to predictive, outcome-based interventions. Additionally, Nokia has integrated sustainability principles into its service design, embedding circularity through asset reuse, component recycling, and repairability—supporting operators in achieving their Environmental, Social, and Governance goals without sacrificing performance.

These enhancements allow Nokia to deliver differentiated offerings priced according to the real value they generate: improved uptime, risk reduction, and lower environmental impact.

The second lens, *Lean Operational Cost*, is about capturing value through efficiency and transparency. Nokia HWS has restructured its operations to be lean and highly efficient.

By streamlining logistics, planning, and repair processes, it has significantly reduced turnaround times, ensuring that spare parts are delivered precisely when and where needed. Digital platforms support this efficiency by optimizing inventory, eliminating unnecessary stock, and reducing operational costs.

Figure 20.1

Nokia hardware service's portfolio

Spare Part Sales	Return for Repair	Spare Part Management	Third Party Support	Circular Products & Services	AI / ML New Services
• New spares • Multi-Vendor Spares • Pre-owned spares	• Identical Repair • Repair or Replacement in days • Life Extender	• Advanced exchange in days / hours • Instant Spare Availability (SPM O) • Multi-Vendor Supply Chain Management	• MN 3P support • NM/SON 3rd Party HW services	• Asset Recovery • Circular Products & Parts • Refurbishment • Recycling	• Predictive Hardware Analytics

NOKIA

Advanced digital control towers and planning engines offer full real-time visibility, both to Nokia and its customers, enabling predictable and high-quality service delivery. As a result, operators benefit from a lower total cost of ownership and consistent service levels.

Nokia HWS reflects these operational gains in its pricing, ensuring that cost inefficiencies are not passed along and that the benefits of improved efficiency are shared.

The third lens, *Commercial Value Addition*, ensures value-based pricing and long-term, sustainable partnerships. Nokia HWS has implemented robust mechanisms to protect commercial integrity and prevent value leakage.

The AI-driven Service Availability Matrix (SAM 2.0) identifies risks in contractual execution, ensuring services remain within agreed scope and safeguarding against revenue loss. Enhanced contractual governance avoids uncontrolled free-of-charge repairs and clarifies service terms.

Most significantly, Nokia HWS is moving away from traditional "pay per incident" billing toward outcome-based commercial models. Pricing is now tied to measurable business outcomes such as network uptime, fault resolution speed, and Service level agreement performance. This approach ensures that operators pay for results, not inputs—allowing Nokia to capture a fair share of the value it delivers while customers benefit from reduced operational risk and improved service outcomes. The result is a sustainable, win-win partnership based on shared success.

RESULTS

The new commercial strategy at Nokia HWS is no longer focused on simply selling hardware services and spare parts—it is centered on delivering business outcomes.

These outcomes include improved network uptime, faster fault resolution, reduced OPEX and total cost of ownership, more sustainable lifecycle management, and greater commercial predictability.

With this shift, Nokia HWS is moving away from transactional, commoditized service models and embracing value-based partnerships with telecom operators. Clients now receive differentiated and competitive service offers, benefit financially from Nokia's operational efficiencies, and pay based on the actual value delivered rather than inflated service costs.

Central to this approach is the principle that value must be created before it can be captured. As a result, commercial models now include outcome-based contracts, shared value agreements, transparent commercial governance, and optional AI or automation add-ons priced according to their business impact. In a rapidly evolving telecom landscape, Nokia HWS's strategy supports customer growth, protects margins, and aligns service offerings with real business needs. It represents a definitive move from cost-plus to value-plus—a partnership model built on measurable impact and mutual benefit.

Figure 20.2

The three lenses of the new Nokia HWS after-sales commercial strategy

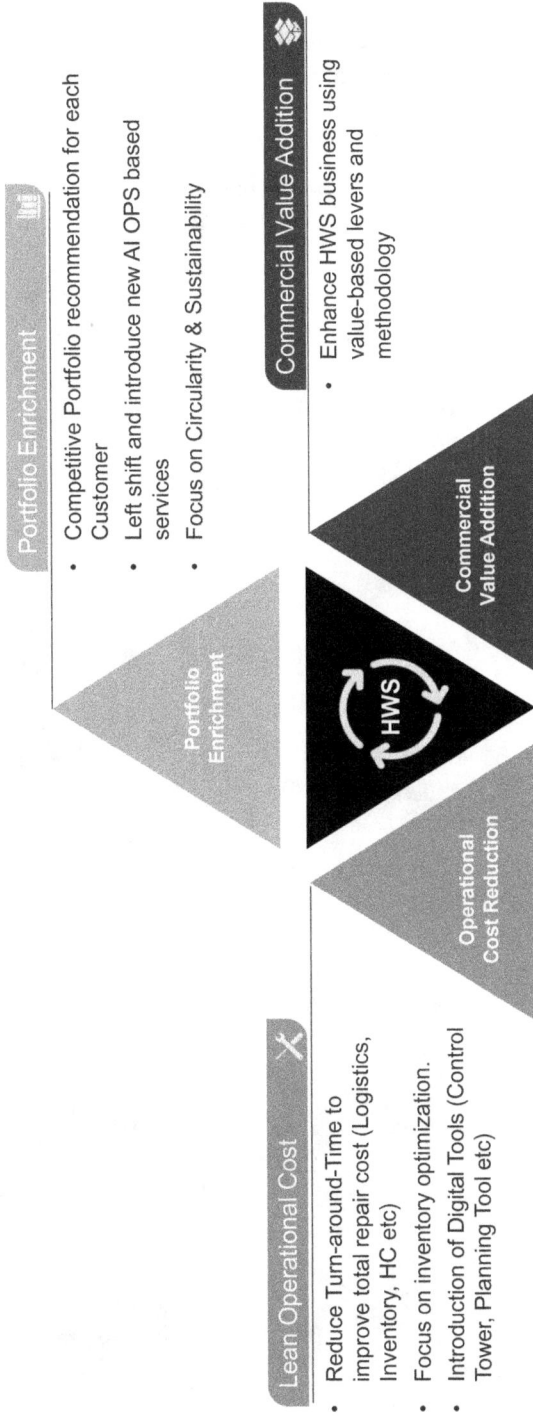

Portfolio Enrichment

- Competitive Portfolio recommendation for each Customer
- Left shift and introduce new AI OPS based services
- Focus on Circularity & Sustainability

Commercial Value Addition

- Enhance HWS business using value-based levers and methodology

Lean Operational Cost

- Reduce Turn-around-Time to improve total repair cost (Logistics, Inventory, HC etc)
- Focus on inventory optimization.
- Introduction of Digital Tools (Control Tower, Planning Tool etc)

SUMMARY

Nokia HWS transformed its after-sales strategy from transactional, cost-plus support to a value-driven model centered on business outcomes. By enriching its portfolio, optimizing operations, and enforcing commercial discipline, it now delivers measurable value in uptime, cost-efficiency, and sustainability.

Outcome-based pricing ensures customers pay for results, not incidents, fostering win-win partnerships. This marks a shift from cost-plus service to value-plus collaboration.

ACKNOWLEDGMENT

This case study was made possible thanks to the contributions of Saeed Qadri, Head of Portfolio Commercial Management at Nokia, and Chandra P. Singh, Commercial and Product Manager at Nokia.

21

Mercedes-Benz

Advancing Parts Pricing Maturity via a Unified EU Spares Strategy

MERCEDES-BENZ PROFILE AND PARTS PRICING CHALLENGES

Mercedes-Benz is globally recognized as a leader in premium automotive engineering, luxury vehicles, and top-tier after-sales services. Headquartered in Stuttgart, Germany, the brand operates in markets worldwide, selling around 2 million vehicles with revenues of 146 billion euros in 2024. Spare parts pricing represents a critical lever for profitability and customer loyalty across the brand's extensive network of authorized dealerships and workshops.

Historically, the company relied on a Central German Price model, exporting all spare parts from Germany and using transfer price logic to establish the market pricing. Price alignment between Germany and the rest of the world typically took place once a year to reflect macroeconomic factors such as inflation. Local marketing teams had the flexibility to adapt gross and net prices based on customer segmentation, local competition, and market-specific exploitation strategies.

However, the landscape began to shift dramatically. Mercedes-Benz faced increasing pressure to protect its aftermarket margins in the face of intensified competition. The number of price-sensitive customers in segments II and III—that is, customers who are diving a car that is from 4 to 12 years old—grew steadily, while overdiscounting in some markets started to erode margins and jeopardize customer penetration efforts.

The scope of the challenge was significant. With a spare parts catalog encompassing over 500,000 part numbers, traditional pricing tools and approaches began to fall short. While the company had access to a wealth of data—including competitor gross prices, internal sales data by channel, online prices, historical trends, and price indices—most of the pricing work required extensive manual effort.

A further complication lay in organizational silos. Pricing expertise was distributed across European markets without effective exchange or alignment between local teams. Much of the market knowledge remained concentrated in the hands of a few individuals. In some markets, constrained full-time equivalent resources further limited the ability to make timely and strategic pricing decisions.

DOI: 10.4324/9781003647416-24

SOLUTION

To address these challenges, Mercedes-Benz launched a Europe-wide pricing strategy transformation initiative anchored in three core pillars: collaboration, data-driven decision-making, and tool-based automation.

The first step was to establish a pricing community group, composed of representatives from both headquarters and local EU markets. This community was designed to foster knowledge exchange, encourage standardization, and collaboratively develop a common pricing framework. Early commitment from executive leadership created a strong sense of urgency and alignment, enabling the community to deliver tangible results in a short timeframe.

The team quickly identified three primary use cases as priorities: yearly price alignment across regions, in-year price management in response to shifting conditions, and campaign-based pricing actions to support growth and retention strategies. By focusing on these targeted objectives, the pricing community was able to create clarity, scope, and momentum for broader change.

Centralized Data Visualization and Integration

One of the cornerstone achievements of the program was the development of the Region Europe (ReEU) Pricing Analytics Tool. Designed collaboratively with pricing experts from the EU markets and headquarters, this tool provided a flexible, Excel-based environment tailored to each market's needs. Despite its spreadsheet foundation, the ReEU Pricing Tool was fully integrated with headquarters systems via a central data lake (see Figure 21.1).

This central integration made it possible to consolidate key data points—including sell-in and sell-out data, pricing history, and competition insights—into one accessible platform. The tool was built around a comparison logic that used the German base price as a reference point, enabling local markets to assess their pricing decisions in relation to the central benchmark.

More importantly, the tool incorporated a scoring logic that translated pricing strategies into clear, data-driven actions. Each market could define its pricing strategy based on local conditions while aligning with common rules and KPIs established by the broader pricing community. Monthly sales and competitor monitoring dashboards provided up-to-date insights, ensuring decisions were made in real time and supported by consistent intelligence.

Dynamic Pricing Logic and Automation

The ReEU Pricing Analytics Tool allowed Mercedes-Benz to move away from manually intensive pricing processes toward a model based on automation and standardized pricing logic. Previously, local experts needed to consolidate data across multiple systems and manually decide on pricing adjustments. Now, embedded scoring logic and rules-based pricing enabled much faster and more consistent decision-making (see Figure 21.2).

Pricing strategies became quantifiable through KPIs that assessed competitive pressure, sales development in relation to Germany, and price alignment status. These inputs formed the basis of automated scoring models that guided pricing actions in each market. The reduction in manual workload helped local teams respond faster to changing conditions, even in regions with limited pricing personnel.

At the same time, the approach preserved local flexibility. Each market retained the ability to customize its pricing logic within the tool to reflect market-specific priorities, customer segments, and strategic objectives—ensuring that global alignment did not come at the cost of local responsiveness.

Improved Customer Experience

Alongside the pricing tool, the team developed a central campaign basket identification tool. Based on best practices from one of the leading EU markets, this solution enabled local teams to proactively identify parts where pricing adjustments or promotional activities were likely to generate impact.

The campaign tool required only minimal input from local markets—specifically, vehicle models and marketing codes (i.e. groups of similar parts like oil filters)—and used this data to generate a prioritized list of parts. A simple scoring logic, based on KPIs such as common parts share, net turnover per part, and over the counter share versus turnover year-over-year development, enabled teams to rapidly identify opportunities for campaigns, discounts, or retention measures.

The result was a more targeted, responsive pricing model that directly supported market needs. Campaigns could be rolled out faster and with greater impact, reinforcing Mercedes-Benz's ability to offer compelling value to its customers across segments and markets.

RESULTS

The pricing transformation led by Mercedes-Benz yielded significant benefits. The new pricing solution enhanced pricing consistency, sped up decision-making, and allowed for more strategic pricing actions across Europe's most important markets.

By reducing reliance on manual processes, the company was able to make faster pricing updates and respond to market dynamics more effectively. Transparency across markets improved, particularly in regions where pricing had previously been ad hoc or undocumented. The campaign tool supported proactive commercial activities, while centralized KPIs enabled consistent tracking of pricing effectiveness.

Figure 21.1

View of process and systems to gain efficiency and quality

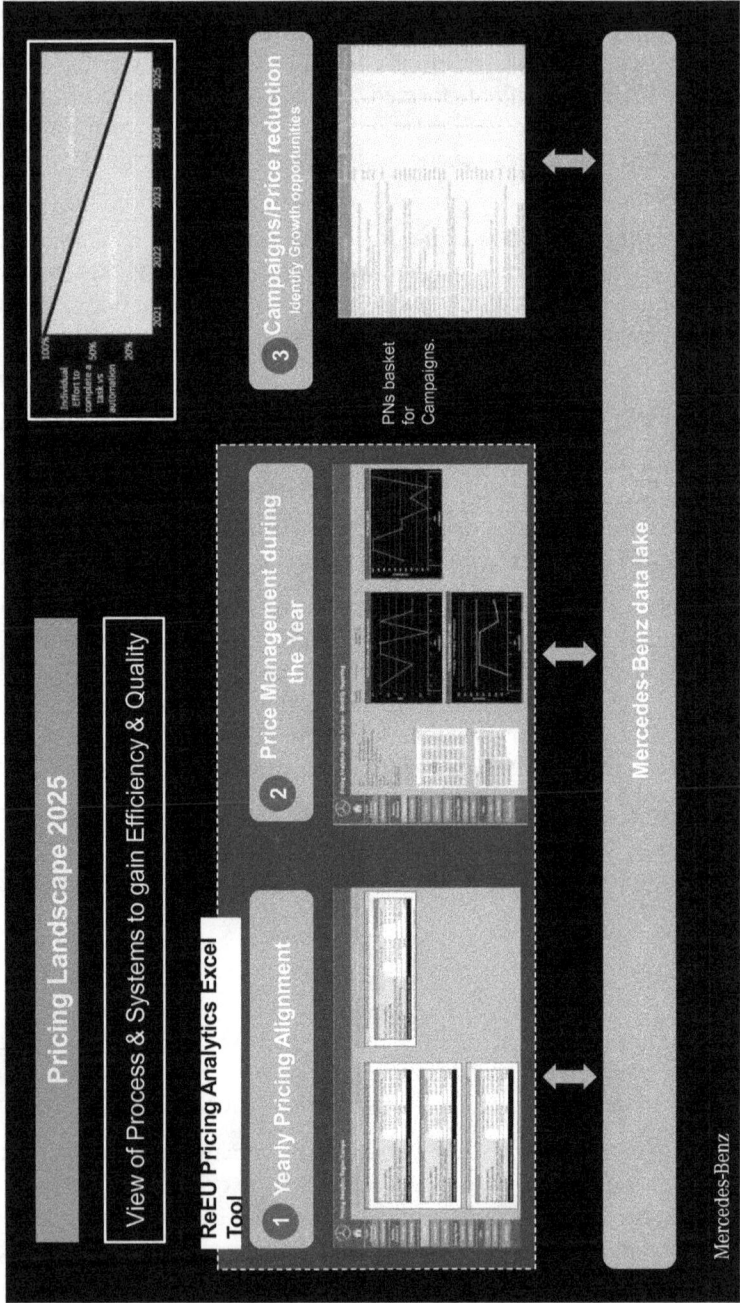

Perhaps most importantly, the transformation laid the groundwork for further digitization. With structured pricing logic, a centralized data lake, and clear pricing workflows in place, Mercedes-Benz is now well-positioned to explore artificial intelligence applications and expand the program to all EU markets.

Success Factors for Pricing Excellence

Several success factors emerged from Mercedes-Benz's journey toward pricing excellence.

First, the establishment of a cross-market pricing community enabled knowledge sharing, standardization, and collaborative problem-solving across the region.

Second, strong executive sponsorship ensured that the transformation had the necessary visibility and resources to move quickly.

Third, a shared set of KPIs and transparent scoring models created alignment across markets while preserving local autonomy. The integration of data into a central platform allowed for real-time visibility and faster, more accurate decisions.

Finally, the decision to design tools with flexibility and customization in mind ensured high adoption and relevance in each individual market.

With a foundation of collaborative structures, data discipline, and tool-driven automation, the pricing function at Mercedes-Benz is now seen as a strategic driver of revenue, margin, and customer loyalty.

SUMMARY

By introducing a coordinated pricing strategy across Europe and investing in data-driven tools and processes, Mercedes-Benz has elevated its spare parts pricing to a new level of maturity. What was once a fragmented, manual, and locally siloed operation is now a connected, transparent, and performance-oriented function.

The creation of the pricing community, the deployment of the ReEU Pricing Tool, and the campaign basket solution together represent a powerful toolkit that empowers local teams while enabling regional alignment. As the company continues its journey, future steps include expanding the initiative to all EU markets and exploring artificial intelligence to automate even more aspects of the pricing process.

Through this transformation, Mercedes-Benz has shown that even in highly complex, decentralized organizations, pricing can be transformed into a strategic asset—supporting profitability, agility, and customer satisfaction across every market it serves.

Figure 21.2

Pricing analytics tool overview of Mercedes-Benz

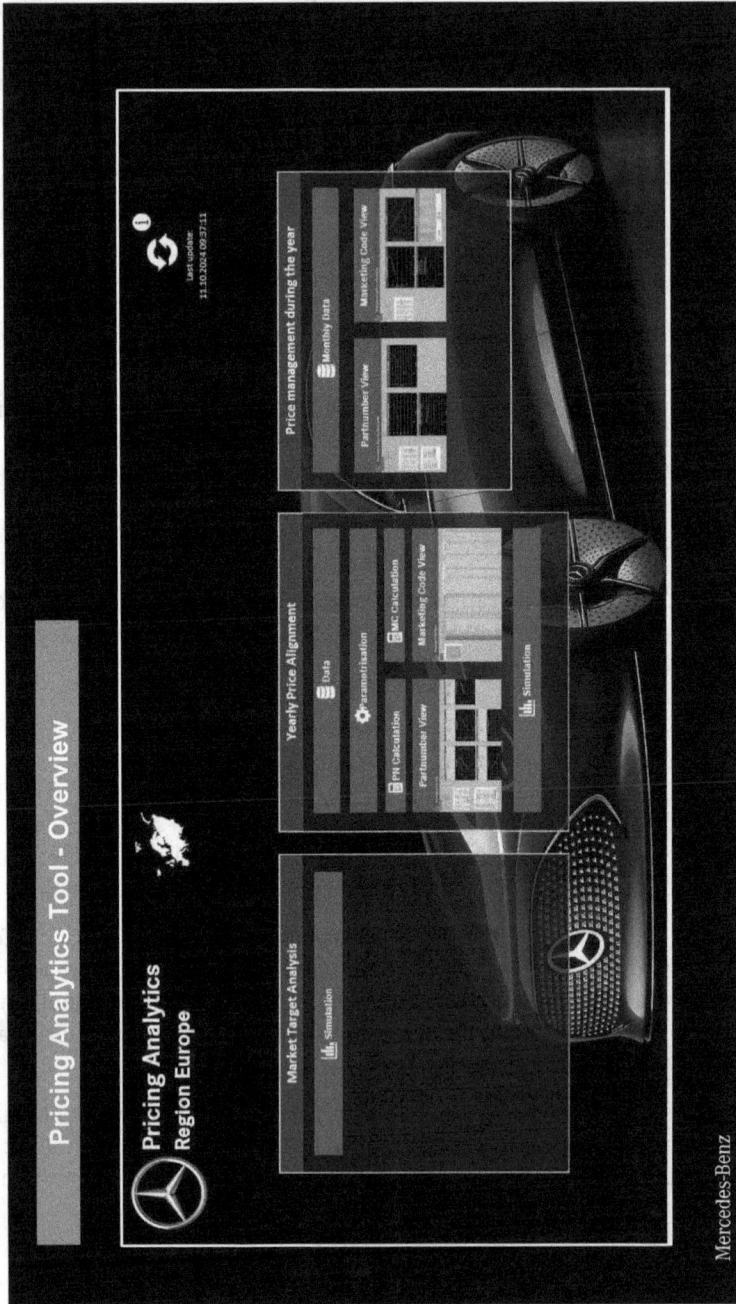

ACKNOWLEDGMENTS

This case study was developed based on internal insights and the contributions of Paolo Pascarella, a key stakeholder in the Mercedes-Benz parts pricing transformation program across the European market. With years of experience in pricing, regional coordination, and aftermarket strategies, Paolo has played a vital role in reshaping how Mercedes-Benz approaches pricing in an increasingly competitive and complex environment.

22

Maserati

From Cost Plus to Value Pricing

MASERATI'S PROFILE AND PARTS PRICING CHALLENGES

The Maserati story begins in 1914, in the heart of Italy—Bologna—where the Maserati brothers set out not to build just cars, but icons of speed and beauty. From the very start, Maserati was driven by motorsport, with its early race cars dominating circuits and earning victories that would cement its reputation as a force to be reckoned with.

Through triumph and turmoil, the trident emblem—inspired by Neptune's trident in Bologna's Fountain of Neptune—became a symbol of power, performance, and prestige. Now headquartered in Modena, Italy, the birthplace of some of the world's finest automobiles, Maserati continues to blend racing DNA with luxury craftsmanship.

Today, Maserati is part of Stellantis, a global automotive powerhouse, yet it maintains its unique identity. With over 1,800 employees dedicated to creating handcrafted machines, Maserati generates an estimated annual revenue of $2.5 billion USD, selling its masterpieces across the world to those who demand more than just transportation—they demand an experience.

In 2017, based on ambitious plans and product launches, Maserati sold a record of over 50,000 vehicle. Seven year earlier sales were just at one tenth of this level.

A Maserati is more than a car. It's a statement, a whisper of Italian artistry wrapped in thunderous performance. Every model carries the soul of the racetrack, infused with bespoke luxury and unmistakable style.

GranTurismo: A modern-day legend, this grand tourer is a fusion of power and elegance, offering a thrilling V6 Nettuno engine and an all-electric Folgore version, proving that speed and sustainability can coexist.

MC20: The brand's supercar rebirth, powered by the revolutionary 3.0L twin-turbo V6 Nettuno engine delivering 621 horsepower, engineered for those who crave adrenaline.

Grecale: Maserati's newest luxury SUV, offering a balance of sophistication and sportiness, with a choice of hybrid or high-performance Trofeo editions.

Levante: The "Maserati of SUVs," blending all-terrain capability with Italian flair, featuring a Ferrari-built twin-turbo V8 in its most powerful versions.

DOI: 10.4324/9781003647416-25

Quattroporte and Ghibli: Timeless sedans that redefine executive luxury, offering raw performance, fine Italian leather interiors, and precision engineering.

Maserati also embraces the future, introducing its Folgore (Italian for "lightning") electric lineup, proving that performance and sustainability can go hand in hand.

Unlike mass-produced luxury, every Maserati is hand-assembled in Modena, where artisans meticulously shape leather, stitch interiors, and tune every exhaust note to perfection. No two Maseratis are alike, thanks to the Fuoriserie customization program, which allows clients to create their dream car, from exclusive color palettes to one-of-a-kind details.

Maserati is not just about speed—it's about emotion. The purr of the engine, the feel of the Alcantara-wrapped steering wheel, the unmistakable growl of a Trident-badged machine taking flight on the open road.

With a growing presence in markets around the world, Maserati continues to captivate those who seek more than just luxury—they seek an experience. An experience where speed meets art, where history meets the future, where every journey is a masterpiece.

Turn the ignition. The road is waiting. This is Maserati.

Maserati executives were forward-thinking and understood that increasing production capacity and entering new segments will require an advanced parts pricing strategy to master the increasing complexity for more and more spare parts linked to the growing car model lineup.

COST-PLUS PRICING AS A STARTING POINT

Maserati's after-sales division aimed to position the prices of spare parts for vehicles in new segments while maintaining profitability and preserving the brand's price image in the market. To address these and other challenges, Maserati embarked on a multiyear excellence program for after-sales pricing transforming its pricing from a cost-plus pricing approach toward value-based pricing.

Although already profitable, Maserati's after-sales division was not fully leveraging its potential. Previously, Maserati determined spare parts prices using the cost-plus method, a traditional and straightforward approach that factored in material costs and a few other indicators necessary for price optimization. However, this system was inadequate to manage the complexity of an offering that included tens of thousands of diverse spare parts.

There were several problems generated by the cost-plus approach: similar parts, like the right rear mirror and the left rear mirror were priced inconsistently because of different volumes and thus different costs that automatically generated distorted prices. Dealers and customers were complaining about prices, which seemed to lack any kind of logic. These cost-plus issues were very common among automakers using cost-plus pricing.

Another issue with cost-plus pricing was its inability to capture the higher willingness-to-pay linked to vehicles positioned at higher prices. If customers of the MC20 have a higher willingness-to-pay for this car compared to the GranTurismo than this is also true for the spare parts of the MC20 vs the one of the GranTurismo. With cost-plus pricing it is however not possible to capture this higher willingness-to-pay: there is a misalignment (see Figure 22.1).

Additionally, Maserati subsidiaries purchased spare parts directly from central warehouses with a fluctuating exchange rate against the euro. They then created their price lists using a similar logic. If they initially benefited from a favorable exchange rate, new spare parts would be cheaper and thus priced lower than the official Maserati reference list. The opposite would occur if the exchange rate was unfavorable.

These discrepancies between price lists encouraged parallel imports across markets— importers could source parts at lower prices in favorable markets—hindering Maserati's ability to implement a globally consistent pricing strategy.

IMPLEMENTING VALUE PRICING FOR SPARE PARTS

Maserati gradually replaced the cost-plus approach with value pricing, which incorporates multiple indicators to address the complexities of after-sales pricing effectively. Unlike fixed markups, value pricing determines market-driven prices based on the following elements (Figure 22.2):

- *the internal perspective:* profitability targets and parts segmentation;
- *the market perspective*: competitive intensity and competitors' pricing positions;
- *the customer perspective*: understanding customers' willingness to pay for each spare part.

The customer perspective was ignored by the cost-plus pricing approach. Adding this perspective was a novelty and a key element to succeed in introducing value-based pricing.

Maserati now prices spare parts by considering, among many factors, like price positioning of the car model they refer to. This enables the company to capitalize on the willingness to pay of high-end segment customers without alienating price-sensitive customers in lower segments. Maserati is also selective with annual price increases, being cautious with highly competitive parts while strategically adjusting prices for captive parts.

Once the central price list was created using these new principles, Maserati standardized international pricing for subsidiaries, revolutionizing its pricing

Figure 22.1

Misalignments between Car Prices and Spare Parts Prices

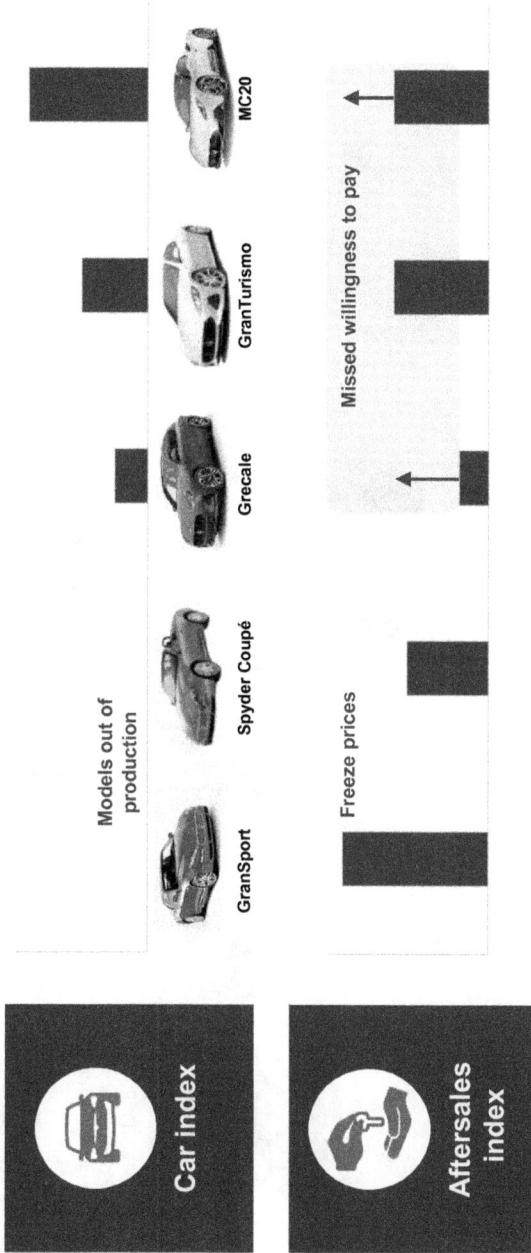

Figure 22.2

The Three Elements Used for Value-Based Pricing

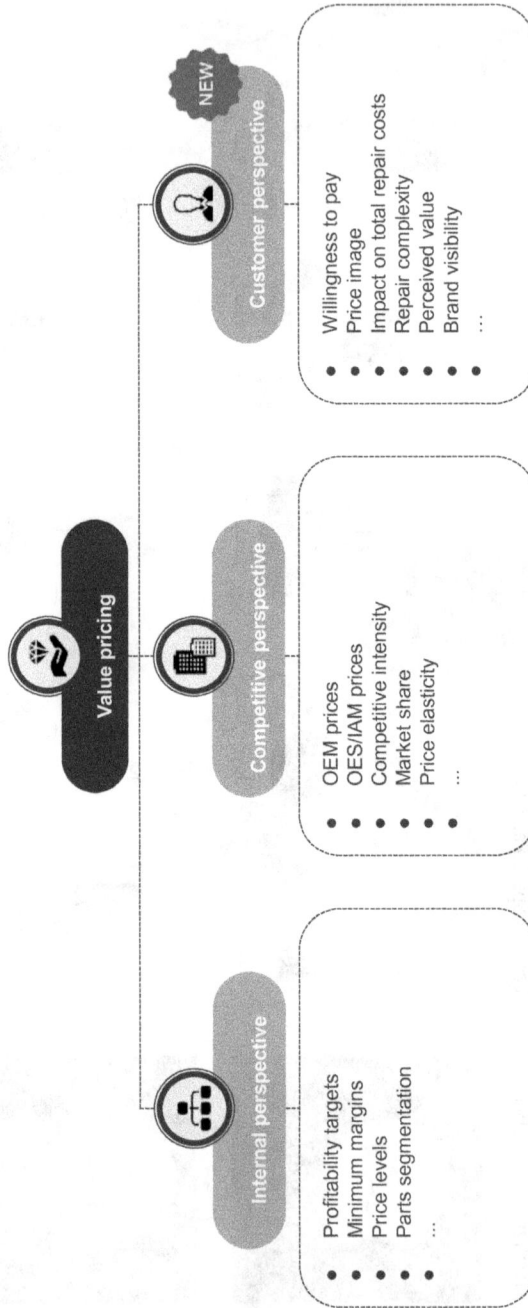

Value pricing

Internal perspective
- Profitability targets
- Minimum margins
- Price levels
- Parts segmentation
- ...

Competitive perspective
- OEM prices
- OES/IAM prices
- Competitive intensity
- Market share
- Price elasticity
- ...

Customer perspective   NEW
- Willingness to pay
- Price image
- Impact on total repair costs
- Repair complexity
- Perceived value
- Brand visibility
- ...

Figure 22.3

List Price Optimization via Value-Based Pricing: Extra-European List Price Example

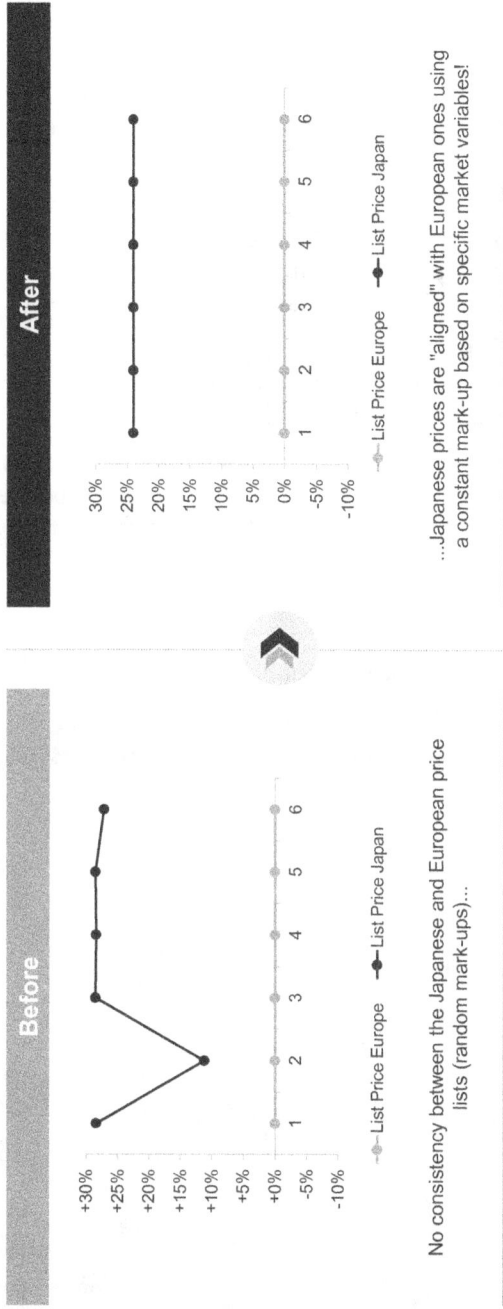

Before

No consistency between the Japanese and European price lists (random mark-ups)...

After

...Japanese prices are "aligned" with European ones using a constant mark-up based on specific market variables!

algorithms. Instead of basing subsidiary pricing on purchase costs, the new approach applies market-specific multipliers to the central price list.

These multipliers allow Maserati to tailor price lists to the needs of each individual market while maintaining the central pricing structure. They are updated annually based on new exchange rates and market-specific price adjustments. With this system, Maserati always knows the relative cost of each spare part across different international markets and can reposition its offerings to virtually eliminate parallel imports (see Figure 22.3).

Managing international pricing effectively is crucial for Maserati, as well as for many other top-tier European brands, since domestic markets account for a limited share compared to the American and Asian markets.

Once the price of, for example, a battery is defined in the European headquarters a retail factor multiplies the entire price architecture to reposition it to a local level to, for example, obtain the price for Japan (see Figure 22.4).

The advantage of this approach is that the list price architecture is optimized only once at HQ level and then multiplied for all regions with their respective multipliers. Value-based pricing lead to a significant profit uplift without volume losses.

Figure 22.4

Optimization of list Prices between Subsidiaries

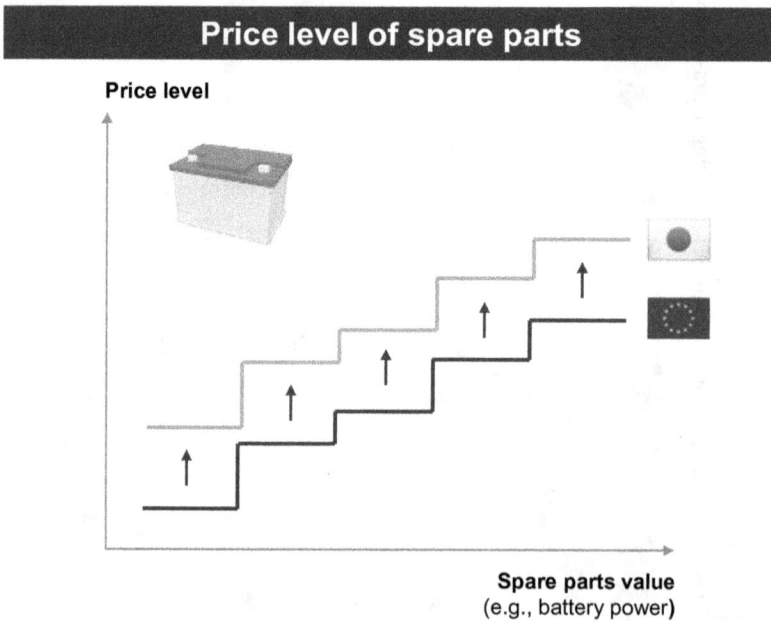

Price level of spare parts

Price level

Spare parts value
(e.g., battery power)

SUMMARY: BENEFITS OF VALUE PRICING

Thanks to its after-sales pricing excellence program, Maserati can now set parts prices based on value with ease. The pricing logic has been embedded into a suite of tools that enable Maserati to calculate and update spare parts prices automatically in every market.

Passing from cost-plus pricing to value-based pricing helps reaching a number of advantages like:

- profit boost without volume loss

- price consistency that eliminated customer and dealer complaints

- ease of price adjustments driven at HQ level and replicated with retail factors internationally

This case also shows that the benefit generated through value pricing in after-sales is significant, typically in the range of 3% to 9% in terms of higher RoS. Companies with low pricing maturities that have previously invested less in pricing and relied on cost-plus approaches can achieve particularly significant RoS increases.

ACKNOWLEDGMENTS

This case study was made possible thanks to the contribution of Armando Bigliocchi, Worldwide After Sales Marketing Manager at Maserati. We also take this opportunity to thank George Mauro, Aftersales Director at Maserati, and Marco Zaccarelli, marketing expert within Maserati's after-sales team, for their vision and commitment to implementing value pricing at Maserati.[1]

NOTE

[1] Source of the case: Zatta el al., 'Price Management Vol. II', *Franco Angeli*, Milan 2013

Part IV

How to Win in Parts Pricing

Victory is a word that is often wrapped in grand gestures. It evokes imagery of battles won, final moments of triumph, and the roar of a crowd. We have come to associate victory with the loudest of celebrations, with conquering obstacles in a blaze of glory. But when we look closer, especially in the nuanced world of spare parts pricing, true victory is something much subtler.

It is not a forceful domination of the landscape, nor a fleeting burst of celebration. True victory in parts pricing is a quiet, thoughtful triumph—a matter of strategic vision, disciplined execution, and the profound wisdom to choose the right hill to climb. It is about understanding that the real win lies not in conquering all, but in conquering with purpose and precision.

To win in parts pricing is not about overpowering your competition or blindly following a prescribed path. It is about orchestrating a harmonious, deliberate pricing process. It's about recognizing the complexity of the challenge before you and transforming that complexity into simplicity. Like a conductor guiding a symphony, a leader in pricing does not need to play every instrument. But they must understand each part, know when to direct, and feel the rhythm of the entire performance. It is about finding the balance between data and intuition, volumes and profits, logic and human emotion, strategy and adaptability.

In this journey, we will move from the realm of tactical survival to one of strategic mastery. We will talk about the methods and frameworks that guide us, but we will also speak of mindset. We will also explore the artistry of pricing, how to create something meaningful, something that resonates deeply with both the market and the customers. Because when pricing is done well, it is far more than just a transactional act. It becomes a creative expression. A craft that requires skill, attention to detail, and an understanding of the subtle forces that shape consumer behavior.

Those who win in parts pricing are not necessarily the loudest voices in the room. In fact, they are often the ones who speak the least. They are the ones who have learned to listen—to the market, to their customers, to their team, and even to the whispers in the noise that so often go unnoticed. They are masters of discernment, able to sift through the chaos and hear the underlying signals. These individuals are like the Renaissance thinkers of their time—blending the precision of mathematics with the beauty of aesthetics, the rigor of structure with the spontaneity of inspiration. They

DOI: 10.4324/9781003647416-26

understand that parts pricing is not just about numbers; it's about people, emotions, and stories.

This part of the journey is your compass. It is not a path to follow blindly, nor is it a trail someone else has already blazed. It is about charting your own course—creating your own vision and building your own strategy. It is not about imitation, but about imagination. The real work of winning in parts pricing is about finding your own purpose and aligning everything you do with that purpose. Just as value cannot be imposed from the outside, neither can purpose. Purpose must be discovered, nurtured, and earned. And when you win with purpose, you don't just succeed in pricing; you succeed in building something lasting, something that resonates far beyond the numbers on a spreadsheet.

To win in parts pricing is to win with integrity, with intentionality, and with a deep sense of understanding. It is not a destination, but an ongoing journey—one that requires patience, creativity, and a willingness to embrace both the art and the science of pricing. And in the end, when you win with purpose, your victory will be quiet, but it will be profound. Because you won't have just achieved a goal; you will have transformed the way your organization thinks, works, and values its place in the marketplace.

```
┌─────┐
│ 23  │
└─────┘
```

Getting Started

The spare parts and aftermarket business has historically been underprioritized—often treated as a stable, low-volatility segment that simply "ticks along" in the background. Yet this perception is rapidly shifting. Spare parts pricing is no longer a back-office activity; it's becoming a frontline battleground, shaped by new entrants, rising customer expectations, and fast-evolving technologies. From afterthought it became a strategic advantage.

Several powerful trends are accelerating this transformation (see Figure 23.1).

First, digital transformation is enabling both newcomers and incumbents to engage customers directly through online channels. Parts buyers can now browse, compare, and purchase from the convenience of a screen—eroding the traditional dealer stronghold.

Second, cross-industry competition is intensifying. Companies are no longer just defending their own service networks—they are actively targeting the installed base of competitors, seeing aftermarket services as an open playing field with lucrative margins.

Third, high historical margins have attracted new challengers. These outsiders—from e-commerce giants to specialized service firms—recognize that spare parts are often among the most profitable segments in capital goods industries.

Finally, customer expectations are changing. Industrial buyers now expect a seamless, consumer-like purchasing experience—complete with transparent pricing, fast fulfillment, and personalized offers.

In response, many OEMs are launching digital platforms that provide instant quotes, simplified ordering, and dynamic pricing. But to make these platforms effective, pricing capabilities must evolve in parallel. The digital channel demands pricing that is data-driven, automated, coherent, and responsive.

FACING THE EVOLUTION: GETTING STARTED

Getting started with spare parts pricing can feel daunting—especially in environments with fragmented data, legacy systems, and organizational complexity. But waiting for ideal conditions before taking action is a costly mistake. The most

DOI: 10.4324/9781003647416-27

Figure 23.1

The evolution of spare parts pricing

Digital transformation: New entrants and established players are leveraging online channels to reach customers directly, reshaping the competitive landscape.

Cross-industry competition: Competitors are increasingly targeting each other's service businesses, recognising the lucrative opportunity of servicing machines they don't manufacture.

High margins attract outsiders: Historically high margins in spare parts make this business an attractive target for new challengers.

Evolving customer expectations: Customers now demand a seamless, consumer-like purchasing experience, even for industrial spare parts.

In response, companies are launching online platforms with instant quotes and streamlined purchasing. To support these platforms, pricing capabilities must evolve to meet the demands of this dynamic market.

successful pricing organizations know that progress begins before perfection. They start with what they have, structure their thinking around proven principles, and improve incrementally from there.

This chapter provides a blueprint to launch or accelerate your parts pricing transformation by following ten pragmatic principles that balance ambition with reality (see Figure 23.2). These are not theoretical ideals—they are the lived experience of companies that have succeeded in turning pricing into a strategic advantage. Get started, then improve continuously.

Perfect data doesn't exist. And waiting for it is a trap. Pricing excellence doesn't require flawless foundations. What it does require is momentum. Begin optimizing pricing decisions based on your current information, while setting up parallel workstreams to clean and enhance your data over time. A "test-and-learn" approach builds capability and confidence while delivering early wins. You don't need a perfect launch pad—just a willingness to evolve.

Getting started creates visibility into what's broken and what's already working better than you thought.

Tailor Your Approach by Part Type

Not all spare parts are created equal. And they shouldn't be priced with a one-size-fits-all method. Captive parts, where the customer has limited alternatives, offer greater pricing freedom. Competitive parts require careful market alignment. Accessories, consumables, and core components each follow distinct customer expectations and usage patterns. Understanding these dynamics is essential. Tailor your pricing strategy to the nature of the part, the degree of competition, and the customer's perceived value. This segmentation allows pricing teams to prioritize effort and avoid overengineering low-impact areas.

Use Competitive Proxies Where Market Data Is Limited

For a small set of high-impact parts, invest in direct market research. But for the long tail—where granular competitor data is scarce—leverage indirect indicators. Look at how revenue or discount trends evolve over time. Analyze customer segments and behavioral patterns. Use these proxies to estimate pricing relevance and identify outliers. Even when external data is limited, smart assumptions can fill the gaps.

Often, internal transaction data can serve as the most reliable mirror of external pricing pressure.

Be Pragmatic with Value Pricing

Value-based pricing is the gold standard—but it's resource-intensive. Don't try to apply it to everything. Instead, apply detailed value pricing logic to strategic parts—those

Figure 23.2

How to start off: Eight principles for effective spare parts pricing

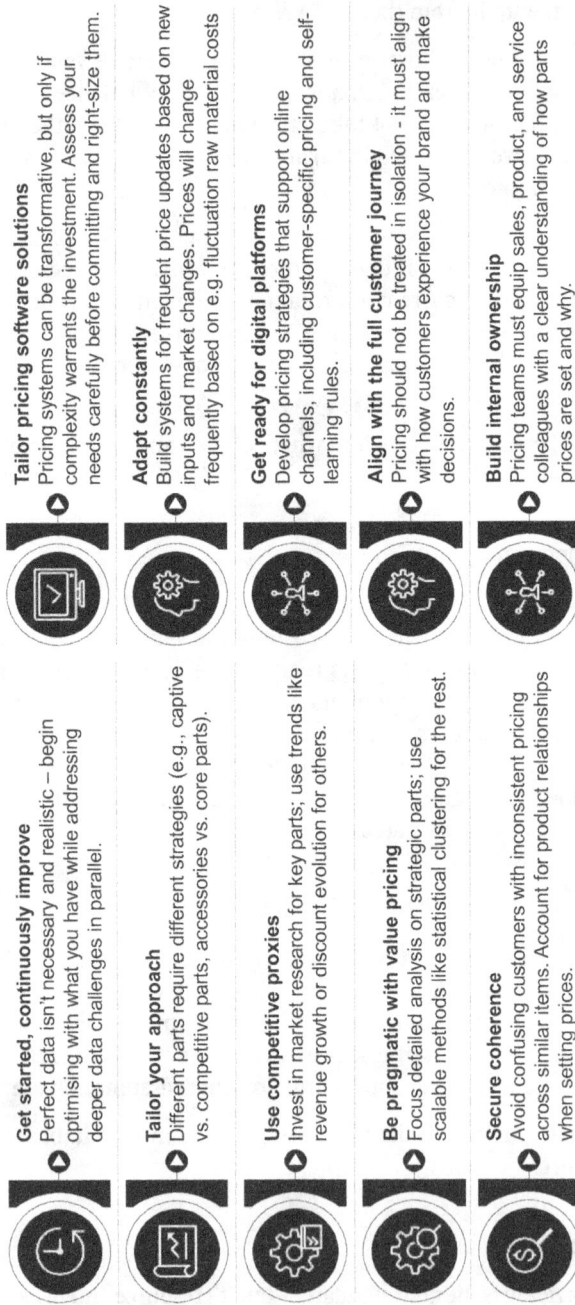

Get started, continuously improve
Perfect data isn't necessary and realistic – begin optimising with what you have while addressing deeper data challenges in parallel.

Tailor your approach
Different parts require different strategies (e.g., captive vs. competitive parts, accessories vs. core parts).

Use competitive proxies
Invest in market research for key parts; use trends like revenue growth or discount evolution for others.

Be pragmatic with value pricing
Focus detailed analysis on strategic parts; use scalable methods like statistical clustering for the rest.

Secure coherence
Avoid confusing customers with inconsistent pricing across similar items. Account for product relationships when setting prices.

Tailor pricing software solutions
Pricing systems can be transformative, but only if complexity warrants the investment. Assess your needs carefully before committing and right-size them.

Adapt constantly
Build systems for frequent price updates based on new inputs and market changes. Prices will change frequently based on e.g. fluctuation raw material costs

Get ready for digital platforms
Develop pricing strategies that support online channels, including customer-specific pricing and self-learning rules.

Align with the full customer journey
Pricing should not be treated in isolation - it must align with how customers experience your brand and make decisions.

Build internal ownership
Pricing teams must equip sales, product, and service colleagues with a clear understanding of how parts prices are set and why.

with high volume, high margin, or strong brand significance. For the rest, use scalable techniques like statistical clustering, pricing corridors, or elasticity modeling to set prices more efficiently. A hybrid approach balances rigor and scale.

Applying value pricing where it matters most drives disproportionate profit impact with manageable effort.

Secure Pricing Coherence Across the Catalog

One of the fastest ways to lose credibility with customers is through incoherent pricing. If two similar items are priced vastly differently without justification, customers—and dealers—will notice. Ensure that related parts (e.g. left-hand and right-hand versions, or different sizes of a similar product) follow a logical pricing relationship. Structure your catalog to reflect value—not randomness. This principle becomes even more important in the digital era, where prices are increasingly visible and comparable. Coherent pricing strengthens trust and simplifies both sales conversations and purchasing decisions.

Be Strategic with Pricing Software

Pricing tools can be transformative. But only when used appropriately. Not every company needs a full enterprise solution on day one. Before committing, assess whether your pricing complexity truly justifies automation. The most successful implementations are those that match capability to context. Start simple if needed but choose systems that can grow with your needs. Focus on usability, transparency, and integration with existing processes.

Great tools amplify great strategies. But they can't compensate for a lack of structure or ownership.

Build for Agility, Not Just Accuracy

Price stability is no longer the norm. Raw material costs, competitive intensity, and global supply disruptions are all triggering faster price changes. Your pricing infrastructure must be built to update frequently and respond quickly. That means designing systems with flexible rules, reliable update cycles, and minimal manual intervention. Agility doesn't replace accuracy. But it enables your pricing to stay relevant in a fast-moving market.

When speed becomes a source of value, pricing must keep up with the business—not hold it back.

Prepare for Digital Distribution

Online sales are no longer optional. They are becoming the standard. Pricing must be ready to support e-commerce and digital dealer portals with consistency and logic.

This means ensuring customer-specific pricing rules, regional pricing differentiation, and automated pricing adjustments are integrated into your digital strategy. As platforms evolve, pricing must adapt ideally through self-learning mechanisms that refine logic based on performance data.

Digital platforms don't forgive inconsistency. A flawed logic is instantly visible and easily compared.

Align with the Full Customer Journey

Pricing should not be treated in isolation. It must align with how customers experience your brand and make decisions. From online configuration tools to after-sales service visits, pricing influences perception at every touchpoint. Ensure spare parts prices are consistent with your broader brand positioning, customer promises, and sales messaging. A well-priced part can reinforce loyalty; a poorly explained price can erode trust.

Do not optimize parts pricing in isolation: it could affect the total cost of ownership of a machine or car, leading to lost main product sales. Bring pricing into the conversation early—across marketing, sales, and service—and let it support the full lifecycle of customer interaction.

The right price at the right moment builds trust, reinforces brand value, and drives long-term loyalty.

Build Internal Pricing Ownership

Even the best pricing strategy will fail without cross-functional support. Pricing teams must equip sales, product, and service colleagues with a clear understanding of how prices are set and why. Training sessions, internal playbooks, and transparency around pricing logic help build trust and reduce resistance. Empower regional and commercial teams with tools to understand and defend pricing decisions. When everyone understands the "why" behind the price, they're more likely to protect margin and reinforce consistency in the market.

When pricing becomes a shared language across teams, it turns from a risk into a core capability.

SUMMARY

Getting started in spare parts pricing doesn't require a perfect setup. It requires clarity, structure, and momentum. These ten principles provide a practical framework for OEMs and aftermarket teams to begin transforming pricing from a static function into a dynamic driver of profitability and customer value.

Each point emphasizes action over perfection. From leveraging imperfect data and customizing strategies by part type, to aligning with digital platforms and customer journeys, the real progress happens when teams take initiative regardless of constraints.

When pricing is coherent, data-driven, and strategically supported, it becomes a growth engine, not just a control mechanism. And when everyone in the organization takes ownership—from pricing to product to sales—it turns into a competitive advantage that others can't easily replicate.

Every successful journey in parts pricing starts with a decision: not to wait, but to act. And then improve continuously. The principle is start smart, scale fast.

24

From Excel to State-of-the-Art Pricing Software

For years, Excel has served as the primary tool for managing spare parts pricing in many organizations. It offers familiarity, flexibility, and immediate access, making it the default platform for pricing analysts and aftermarket managers alike. In its early use, Excel provides more than enough functionality to manage simple pricing calculations, simulate margin scenarios, and control lists across a limited set of products.

However, as pricing complexity increases—driven by the growth of product portfolios, regional markets, customer-specific discounts, and competitive pressure—Excel becomes less of a solution and more of a liability. Manual updates, version confusion, formula errors, and siloed files begin to slow down processes and introduce inconsistencies. More critically, Excel lacks the scalability, governance, and automation capabilities needed to support modern pricing organizations. It simply wasn't designed to manage dynamic pricing logic across tens or hundreds of thousands of SKUs in real time.

Excel may be a powerful tool to get started, but in the context of advanced pricing, it becomes a bottleneck. Today's parts pricing requires speed, consistency, and adaptability: capabilities that only a dedicated pricing software solution can deliver. The imperative is to break free from spreadsheets if state-of-the-art parts pricing is the ambition.

WHY PRICING SOFTWARE IS NO LONGER OPTIONAL

The evolution of spare parts pricing into a strategic lever—one that must respond to competition, cost volatility, digital channels, and customer behavior—demands a modern infrastructure. Pricing must now reflect real-time market dynamics, account for product relationships, support multichannel logic, and be regularly updated. Doing this across thousands or even millions of SKUs is not feasible without technology.

State-of-the-art pricing software allows organizations to manage complexity through intelligent algorithms, centralized governance, and configurable logic. It enables businesses to set optimized prices across their entire catalog, incorporating cost trends, competitor insights, customer segmentation, and usage data: all in a coherent and efficient way.

DOI: 10.4324/9781003647416-28

And yet, even the most advanced system cannot replace human intelligence. The introduction of software does not make pricing teams obsolete. Rather, it elevates their role: from operators of spreadsheets to strategic stewards of value. A successful transition requires pricing professionals who understand the context behind the numbers, guide the system's configuration, and retain ownership of key pricing decisions. The system can recommend, but only humans can decide. Therefore, any organization looking to implement pricing software must ensure it has a strong, centralized pricing team ready to oversee its deployment and use.

HOW TO SELECT THE RIGHT PARTS PRICING SOFTWARE

Selecting and implementing the right pricing software is a transformation in itself. It must be approached methodically, with clarity around business needs, internal readiness, and expected outcomes. This journey can be broken down into three key stages.

The first stage *is defining requirements and prioritizing use cases.* Before looking at tools or vendors, a business must assess its own internal processes and clarify its goals. This means identifying current pricing pain points, understanding what the future state should look like, and specifying the strategic, functional, technical, and economic requirements for a new solution (see Figure 24.1). These requirements should be clustered into categories of importance, distinguishing what is essential from what is merely desirable. They must then be translated into practical use cases that reflect real-world pricing needs.

This could include processes such as setting list prices for new parts, revising prices based on cost changes, aligning price relationships between similar items, or calculating discounts for specific markets. Each use case should reflect a concrete pricing lever. Prioritization is critical. Not everything has to be solved immediately. Instead, focus on the use cases with the highest value impact, typically those affecting high-margin or high-volume parts.

Once the requirements are clear, the second stage is to *select vendors and prepare for proof-of-concept* (PoC) workshops. This begins by creating a longlist of potential software providers, based on market research and benchmarks from similar organizations. This list should then be narrowed to a small group of vendors whose solutions best align with the company's specific needs and priorities. At this point, the evaluation criteria must be clearly defined.

These criteria often include usability, configurability, integration capabilities, reporting depth, vendor experience, and cost structure. Vendors are then invited to participate in PoC workshops, where they are asked to demonstrate their ability to support the company's actual use cases. These workshops are not generic demos— they must simulate real pricing scenarios based on real data, allowing the business to evaluate how each solution handles complexity and collaboration. Timelines, expectations, and goals for these workshops must be clearly communicated and adhered to. The PoC stage provides critical insights into both the software and the vendor's ability to support a transformation.

The final stage is *business-case-driven tool selection*. This phase involves quantifying the expected return on investment. A business case should be developed to estimate the potential financial benefits from improved pricing accuracy, faster updates, increased margin, and reduced error rates—alongside the costs of implementation, integration, and training.

Following the PoC workshops, the evaluation team must document its findings, compare each solution based on predefined criteria, and prepare a clear recommendation. This includes not only the preferred vendor, but also a high-level roadmap for the transformation—outlining timelines, phases, and resource needs.

The recommendation is then presented to top management or the steering committee, who ultimately approve the decision and launch vendor negotiations. Once the vendor is selected, implementation planning begins.

STAKEHOLDER INVOLVEMENT: BALANCE INCLUSION WITH FOCUS

Because pricing software impacts multiple departments—such as sales, product, IT, service, and finance—it is important to involve the right stakeholders early in the process. Their input ensures that the system meets both strategic and operational needs. However, the selection process must remain efficient. Keeping the core project team small and empowered is essential to maintaining momentum.

Broader stakeholders can be consulted during structured checkpoints, but decision-making should rest with a focused cross-functional group that understands both the business logic and the technical implications of pricing.

LEADING VENDORS IN THE MARKET

There are several pricing software vendors. Some of the more well-established ones with strong capabilities in the parts pricing space that stand out are in alphabetical order:

- Pricefx is a cloud-native platform known for speed and flexibility, making it a strong choice for organizations looking for rapid deployment.

- PROS stands out for dynamic pricing capabilities and integration into, for example, larger CPQ environments and CRM systems.

- Syncron is particularly prominent in industrial and OEM settings, offering integration with service and inventory data. It has a long history and track record in parts pricing.

- Vendavo provides robust segmentation and business rule configuration, supporting complex discount logic and customer-specific pricing.

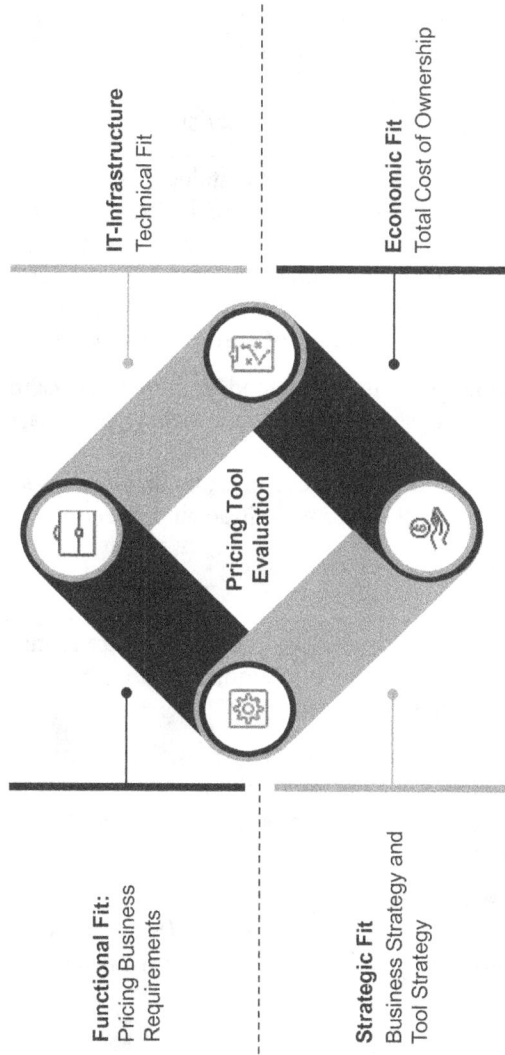

Figure 24.1
Four key software selection requirements

IT-Infrastructure
Technical Fit

Economic Fit
Total Cost of Ownership

Pricing Tool Evaluation

Functional Fit:
Pricing Business Requirements

Strategic Fit
Business Strategy and Tool Strategy

- Vistex offers solutions designed to help businesses optimize their pricing strategies for spare parts and components integrating them with ERP systems like SAP.

- Zilliant focuses on B2B pricing with strong AI-powered analytics and elasticity models enabling data-driven decisions.

Each of these platforms has unique strengths, and the right choice will depend on your specific industry, pricing model, and technical ecosystem.

WHEN ALGORITHMS MEET HUMAN STRATEGY

Setting optimal prices for an entire parts catalog—especially across diverse markets, product types, and cost structures—is virtually impossible without the help of data science and automation. AI-driven algorithms bring structure to chaotic datasets, reveal patterns invisible to the human eye, and generate price suggestions that are both consistent and commercially relevant. Yet no algorithm can fully understand brand strategy, product positioning, or customer sentiment.

This is why a pricing system is only as good as the team managing it. Before launching a tool, organizations must ensure they have the people in place to govern it. Pricing managers must act as interpreters of the algorithm, guiding how data is structured, how logic is applied, and where exceptions are justified. The system may offer scale, but only human judgment can provide strategic coherence.

SUMMARY

The shift from Excel to professional pricing software is more than a technology upgrade: it's an organizational evolution. It is the point where pricing becomes embedded, scalable, and intelligent.

The advantages are profound: faster decisions, deeper insights, better governance, and more consistent pricing outcomes. But no system works in isolation. Its success depends on a thoughtful selection process, a clear business case, the involvement of the right people, and the continuous input of a capable pricing team.

In the world of spare parts, complexity is the norm. And without the right tools, complexity becomes chaos. But with the right software—guided by the right people—pricing transforms from an operational chore into a strategic advantage.

25

From Intransparency to Market Visibility

For many years, spare parts pricing remained in the shadows. Hidden beneath legacy systems, opaque cost structures, and fragmented spreadsheets, prices were often set without a clear understanding of their position in the competitive landscape. Pricing teams operated in silos, and decisions were driven more by internal habit than external logic. Customers were left puzzled, dealers frustrated, and companies missed out on significant margin opportunities. The result was an inefficient and sometimes incoherent aftermarket strategy.

But the industry is shifting. Fast. Today, spare parts pricing must move from intransparency to market visibility. This transformation is not just a technological change. It is a strategic pivot.

The companies that lead in pricing maturity are those that see their prices not as static numbers on a list, but as active levers of competitive positioning, customer trust, and revenue growth. And to make this leap, benchmarking against the market becomes an essential activity.

THE IMPERATIVE OF MARKET VISIBILITY

Market visibility means having a clear, ongoing understanding of how your parts are priced relative to others in the market. This includes direct original equipment suppliers (OEM) competitors, OES that sell parts under their own brands, and the independent aftermarket (IAM), where parts of varying quality and origin flood the digital shelves of global e-commerce platforms. Benchmarking enables companies to see how they compare in this complex, dynamic ecosystem—and to use that knowledge to improve.

Without such visibility, companies are essentially flying blind. Spare parts may be overvalued, leading to lost sales and eroded customer loyalty, or they may be undervalued, leaving margin on the table that will never be recovered. Worse still, similar parts may be priced inconsistently, causing confusion and complaints from dealers and end users alike. And in a world where online comparison tools are just a click away, customers will notice.

DOI: 10.4324/9781003647416-29

CHALLENGES OF TRADITIONAL PRICING MODELS

In many traditional pricing models, particularly those still rooted in cost-plus logic, such distortions are common. These models fail to account for the customer's perception of value, the availability of alternatives, or the nuances of competitive pressure. A recent Valcon study in the industrial sector found examples of parts priced at multiple times the going market rate simply because of legacy markups that had never been reviewed. Not only did this harm sales, it undermined the trust that customers had in the brand.

Benchmarking corrects this. It brings context to pricing decisions and helps companies detect when their internal logic diverges from external expectations. Traditional systems may be simple to administer, but they are ill-equipped to deal with a dynamic and transparent marketplace. They treat pricing as an internal exercise, when in fact it is a public message. And one that customers evaluate constantly.

EMBRACING MARKET-BASED PRICING STRATEGIES

When a company begins adopting market-based pricing strategies, it shifts from relying on internal costs to using external signals. This transformation involves the systematic gathering of competitive prices across product lines, channels, and regions. It also involves analysis—understanding which parts are outliers, which are aligned with market norms, and which have room to move.

Once the data is collected and interpreted, it must be integrated into the organization's pricing logic. This doesn't mean blindly matching competitor prices. It means using those prices as a compass—setting competitive corridors, determining acceptable pricing thresholds, and aligning price points with customer expectations and willingness to pay.

This is where providers like Eucon in the automotive industry and MARKT-PILOT come into play. These platforms automate market price research, provide real-time competitor intelligence, and enable pricing managers to make informed decisions without spending weeks collecting fragmented data. When integrated with ERP systems and pricing engines, they make benchmarking not just a research task, but a continuous capability.

BENEFITS OF MARKET VISIBILITY

The advantages of achieving market visibility are considerable.

First, it enhances competitiveness. By knowing where your prices stand relative to others, you can ensure that your parts remain attractive and defensible—especially in price-sensitive segments.

Second, it increases profitability. When you identify parts that are priced below market levels, you can correct them to capture more value with minimal risk.

Figure 25.1

Parts segmentation: A centrally defined part segmentation for spare parts is critical

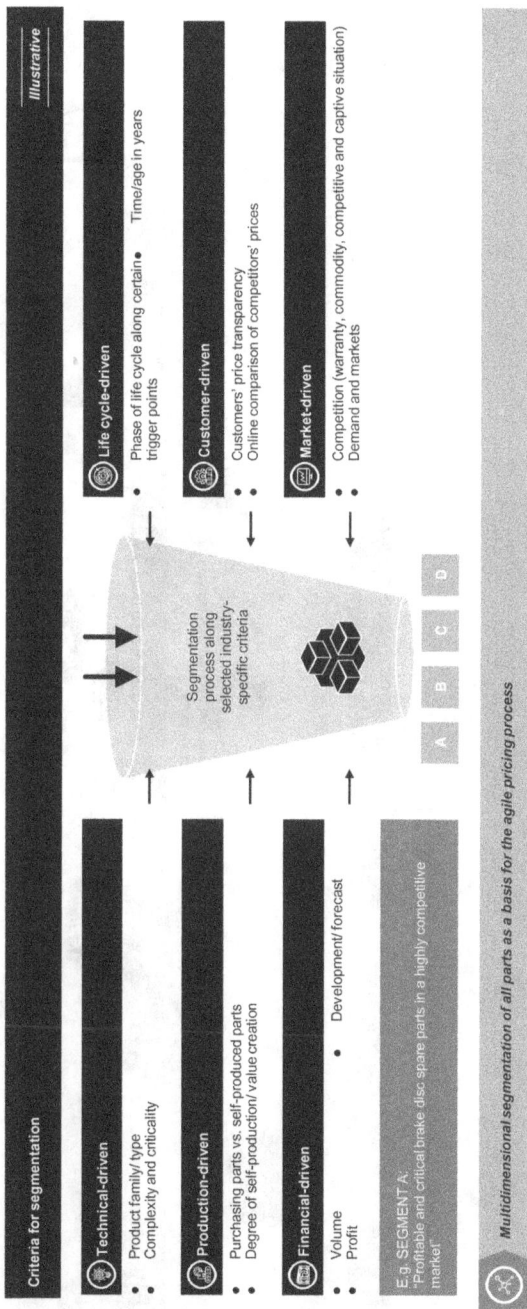

Illustrative

Criteria for segmentation

Technical-driven
- Product family/ type
- Complexity and criticality

Production-driven
- Purchasing parts vs. self-produced parts
- Degree of self-production/ value creation

Financial-driven
- Volume
- Profit
- Development/ forecast

E.g. SEGMENT A:
"Profitable and critical brake disc spare parts in a highly competitive market"

Segmentation process along selected industry-specific criteria

A B C D

Life cycle-driven
- Phase of life cycle along certain Time/age in years trigger points

Customer-driven
- Customers' price transparency
- Online comparison of competitors' prices

Market-driven
- Competition (warranty, commodity, competitive and captive situation)
- Demand and markets

Multidimensional segmentation of all parts as a basis for the agile pricing process

Figure 25.2

Segmenting spare parts to differentiate price setting

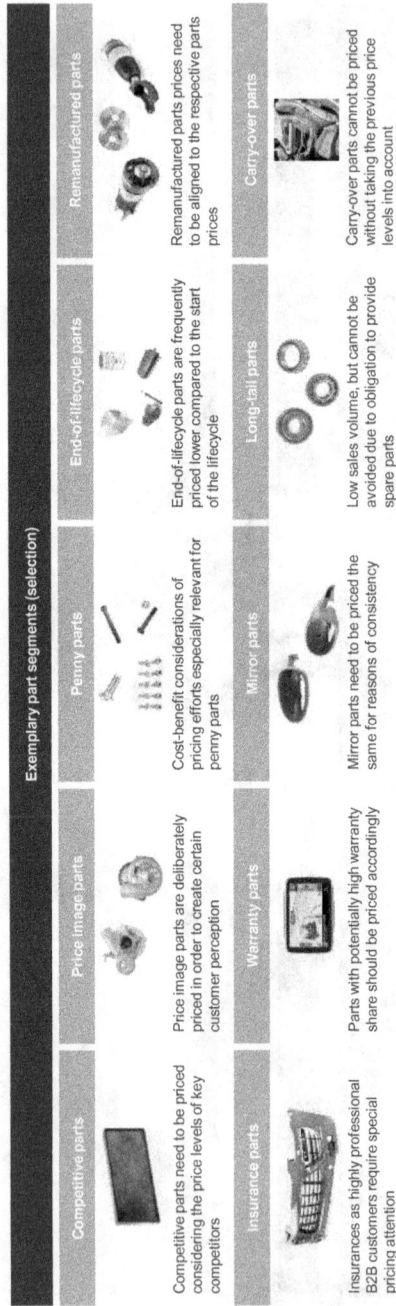

Exemplary part segments (selection)

Competitive parts
Competitive parts need to be priced considering the price levels of key competitors

Price image parts
Price image parts are deliberately priced in order to create certain customer perception

Penny parts
Cost-benefit considerations of pricing efforts especially relevant for penny parts

End-of-lifecycle parts
End-of-lifecycle parts are frequently priced lower compared to the start of the lifecycle

Remanufactured parts
Remanufactured parts prices need to be aligned to the respective parts prices

Insurance parts
Insurances as highly professional B2B customers require special pricing attention

Warranty parts
Parts with potentially high warranty share should be priced accordingly

Mirror parts
Mirror parts need to be priced the same for reasons of consistency

Long-tail parts
Low sales volume, but cannot be avoided due to obligation to provide spare parts

Carry-over parts
Carry-over parts cannot be priced without taking the previous price levels into account

Third, customer trust improves. Transparent, logical pricing earns credibility, while erratic or unexplained pricing undermines confidence.

Fourth, operational efficiency rises. Pricing teams no longer need to spend time debating or justifying decisions based on limited or outdated information. Instead, they can act swiftly, backed by reliable market data.

And finally, market benchmarking provides insights that go beyond pricing— shedding light on product positioning, substitution risks, and competitor behavior.

IMPLEMENTING MARKET-BASED PRICING: A STRATEGIC APPROACH

Putting this strategy into practice requires several deliberate steps. The first is to segment parts in a meaningful way. Segmentation can be driven by technical, lifecycle, customer, market, production, or financial criteria as indicated in Figure 25.1. Ideally the segmentation methodology combines a variety of different criteria to ensure optimal product group formation. The selection of criteria depends on the product characteristics, the customer's individual market situation, and the availability of data. A customer and market perspective should never be missing as the predefined segments serve as the basis for base price determination.

Not all parts should be treated equally. Captive parts with low visibility and no competitive alternatives might allow for more pricing freedom. Competitive parts, on the other hand, need tight alignment with market benchmarks (see Figure 25.2). Accessories and consumables may follow seasonal patterns, while safety-critical parts may have higher perceived value. Understanding these differences helps companies apply benchmarking where it matters most.

Next, companies must monitor market trends continuously. Competitive prices are not static. They shift based on seasonality, demand surges, product lifecycles, and macroeconomic forces. Keeping tabs on these movements allows pricing teams to stay ahead of the curve.

Another important dimension is organizational alignment. Benchmarking will only succeed if the entire pricing ecosystem—sales, marketing, regional offices, and dealer networks—understand and support the logic behind the new price setting. Internal communication is critical to prevent resistance and build consensus.

Technology investment also plays a central role. Market visibility at scale is not possible through manual means. Companies must equip their teams with tools that gather, structure, and visualize data, and that can push updates across large catalogs efficiently.

SUMMARY

The shift from intransparency to visibility is not just a digital transformation. It is a mindset shift.

It marks the difference between reactive pricing and strategic pricing. Companies that embrace parts benchmarking gain clarity, agility, and control.

They know which prices to defend, which to adjust, and where they can lead the market rather than follow.

This clarity strengthens relationships with dealers and end customers. It supports profitability, not through shortcuts or discounts, but through precision and confidence. It enables pricing teams to focus not just on updating numbers, but on managing value. And it protects the brand from price erosion and margin leakage.

In spare parts pricing, what you don't know can hurt you. But what you do know—if you act on it—can become your competitive edge. The journey from intransparency to market visibility starts by looking outward, understanding the landscape, and then turning those insights inward to create a pricing engine that is fair, fast, and future-proof.

Every successful transformation begins with one choice: to stop guessing—and to start knowing.

26

The Future of Spare Parts Pricing

The future does not arrive all at once.

It lands like dust—quietly, imperceptibly, until a thin layer covers everything we thought we knew. What once seemed far-fetched becomes mundane.

The fax becomes the email. The map becomes the GPS. The mechanic becomes the algorithm. And in this slow revolution, even something as grounded and granular as spare parts pricing undergoes transformation.

But not just any transformation—a paradigm shift.

We are entering a world where the traditional principles of pricing—cost, competition, value—are being joined, and sometimes displaced, by new logics: sustainability, circularity, predictive intelligence, personalization, ecosystem dynamics, and above all, adaptability.

THE END OF LINEAR THINKING

"Nothing is created, nothing is destroyed, everything is transformed" were the word of Antoine Lavoisier. Lavoisier spoke of chemical reactions, but the same law could soon apply to products and their parts. The classical supply chain—source, build, sell, discard—is crumbling under the weight of its own obsolescence.

In its place?

Circularity!

Tomorrow's pricing will not only account for the cost of manufacturing but for the cost of recovery. That means evaluating how easy a part is to refurbish, what its expected reuse value might be, and whether it can be 3D printed locally instead of shipped globally. These are no longer questions for R&D alone. They are pricing factors.

In this new logic, price becomes not just a number, but a signal—of repairability, longevity, and environmental responsibility. A filter through which the customer evaluates not just cost, but conscience.

DOI: 10.4324/9781003647416-30

WHEN CARBON HAS A PRICE

There was a time when the biggest constraint in pricing was material cost. In the near future, the constraint may be carbon.

With carbon taxes, emissions reporting, and pressure from ESG-driven capital, companies will increasingly need to factor environmental costs into their pricing architecture.

A steel bolt made in a low-emission, solar-powered facility in Italy may command a premium over a nearly identical one forged in a coal-fired plant in another country.

The future buyer—institutional or individual—will not simply ask: "What's the price?" They will ask: "What's the footprint?"

The price tag may soon include a second line:

€11.20 — 0.9 kg CO_2-eq

Like calories on a food label, or country of origin on a wine bottle, environmental impact will become a visible—and monetizable—part of value.

DIGITAL TWINS AND THE ALGORITHMIC EYE

We are pricing into a mirror that remembers.

Imagine a world where every part has a digital twin. A real-time virtual model that tracks usage, wear, and stress. These digital twins can predict when a part will fail, and therefore, when it will be needed. This is not science fiction. It is Siemens. GE. Rolls-Royce. Pirelli.

Pricing, in this context, becomes temporal.

It is not only about what part and which customer—but also when.

At the moment of greatest need, what is the value of certainty? Of immediacy? Of uptime?

We will move from static price lists to dynamic, context-aware pricing. From Excel sheets to neural networks. From retrospective to predictive.

Just as the weather forecast now runs on supercomputers, so too will pricing models in complex after-sales environments.

THE 3D FRONTIER

"He who controls the parts, controls the power" is a saying.

But what happens when you can print the part?

3D printing, or additive manufacturing, is not just a threat to logistics—it is a transformation of pricing authority.

Imagine a world where customers download parts instead of ordering them. In that world, the file becomes the product, the license becomes the currency, and the printer becomes the channel.

The price of the future may no longer be set on the production floor, but on the server.

This shift brings opportunities—and challenges. Will OEMs protect their IP through subscriptions? Will they offer "per print" pricing like songs on iTunes once were? Will decentralized production challenge brand control—or extend it?

GREEN IS GOLD

In this new landscape, sustainability becomes a differentiator—and pricing is the language through which it speaks.

The brands that succeed will not just offer the cheapest spare parts, but the wisest: parts that last, parts that return, parts that pollute less. Parts that tell a story—not just of performance, but of purpose.

And purpose, as we are learning, is the new profit.

FINAL THOUGHTS: THE PRICING PHILOSOPHER

The future will demand not just data scientists and pricing analysts, but pricing philosophers.

These will be people who ask the right questions before feeding the model. People who understand that value is both numeric and narrative. People who see pricing not just as science, but as ethics.

In the end, the smartest part of parts pricing won't be the algorithm. It will be the human who taught it what to care about.

"The future belongs to those who give the next generation reason for hope," as stated by Pierre Teilhard de Chardin.
Now it is time to draw conclusions for your company and start your own spare parts pricing journey.

Please let me know how you liked this book and feel free to reach out to me to share your thoughts. I also would love to hear your opinion on the parts pricing quick wins as well as your own experiences. You can reach out via the email below or connect with me and approach me on LinkedIn.

I wish you a successful parts pricing transformation!
Keep in touch,

Dan
zatta.danilo@gmail.com
www.linkedin.com/in/danilo-zatta

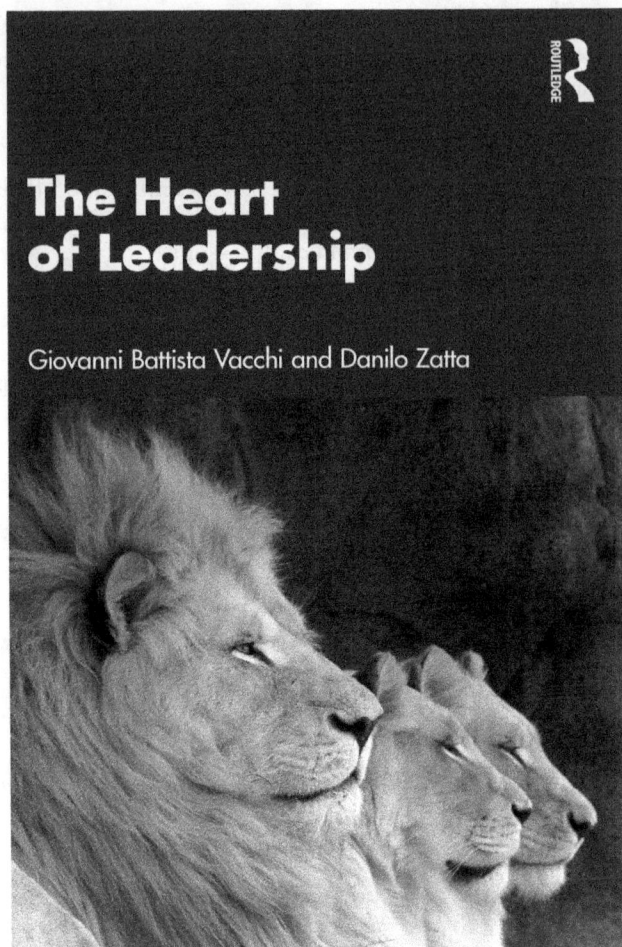

Squarely aimed at leaders and aspiring leaders, *The Heart of Leadership*, written by two renowned management experts, presents practical examples and engaging insights to answer the key question of how to be a successful leader.

This book reveals the key characteristics of a great leader and shows you how to develop the skills needed to motivate your team and overcome challenges. Leadership means successfully taking your place at the head of an enterprise and is both a shared journey and an adventure over the course of a career. Using an engaging and accessible style throughout, the book maps out how to achieve tangible results. It presents portrayals of some of history's greatest leaders, from Gandhi to Steve Jobs, from Angela Merkel to Lisa Su, in order to inspire and help develop your own top leadership skills.

This book is essential reading for CEOs, CFOs, HR managers, entrepreneurs, trainers, and those who are seeking a leadership position in an organization and want to understand how to succeed within it.

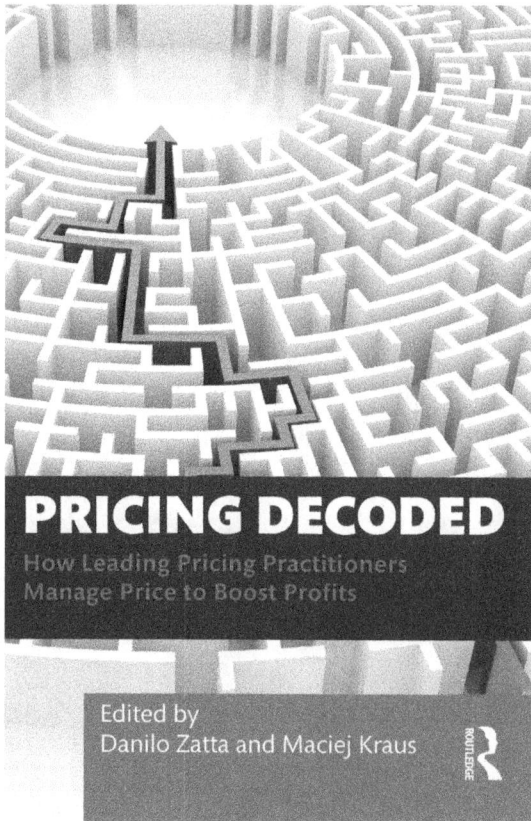

Pricing is a key priority of every company globally, as both customers and businesses grapple with ever more challenging economic conditions. *Pricing Decoded* is an authoritative but easy-to-read guide to support the transition to robust pricing to drive profitability.

Renowned pricing experts Danilo Zatta and Maciej Kraus show organizations how to boost profitability and build a competitive advantage, transforming the way to set and manage prices. Case studies from the world's leading pricing practitioners in both B2C and B2B organizations, such as Alcatel-Lucent, Asashi, Google, BP-Castrol, Unilever, Microsoft, Borealis, Hilton, Nike, MediaWorld, Philips Healthcare, Schneider Electric, DHL, Zalando, Zuora, Workday, Assa Abbloy, and Coor, are presented throughout. This book makes smart and innovative pricing more accessible and understandable for all. It provides a strong foundation in the concepts as well as the application in business, empowering you to judge monetization opportunities in a more effective way and ultimately make better decisions.

The book is relevant to C-levels, managers, entrepreneurs, investors, as well as sales, marketing, and pricing managers, who want to learn more about topline potentials and monetization through pricing and achieve sustainable growth.

For Product Safety Concerns and Information please contact our EU
representative GPSR@taylorandfrancis.com
Taylor & Francis Verlag GmbH, Kaufingerstraße 24, 80331 München, Germany